Three Theories of Child Development

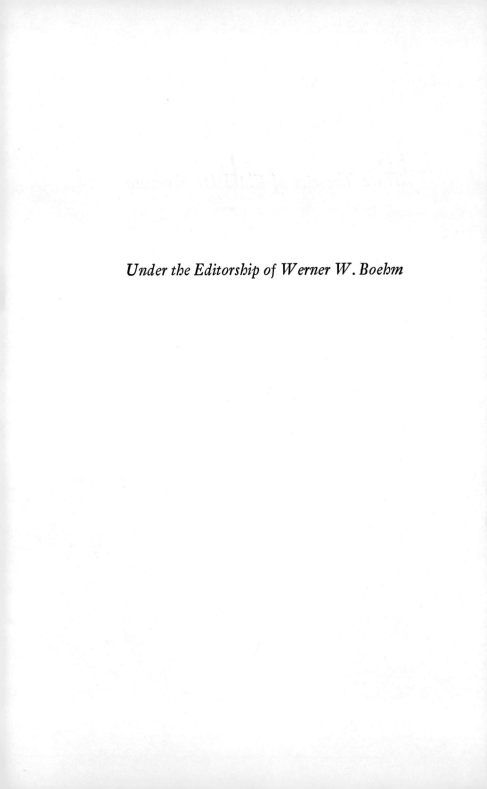

Under the Editorship of Werner W. Boehm

Three Theories of
CHILD DEVELOPMENT

*The Contributions of Erik H. Erikson, Jean Piaget,
and Robert R. Sears, and Their Applications*

Henry W. Maier

University of Washington

Harper & Row, Publishers
New York

Contents

Editor's Introduction

THE DEVELOPMENT OF KNOWLEDGE and new possibilities for the application of theory to practical problems have their mainspring in two approaches: research into problems of interest to the scientist and the creation of new theoretical frameworks which bring together heretofore separate strands of knowledge. Too often, however, the second approach, instead of being a synthesis, is limited to a review of literature. When that is the case, the approach tends to have disparate pieces of theory unrelated, rather than placing them into a cohesive whole.

The synthesis of existing theories would seem to be a particularly fruitful approach for the helping professions, because the practitioner of these professions is faced with the problem of tapping knowledge that comes from a variety of sources. For example, the task of a social worker, or of any other "professional helper" concerned with furthering a child's development, typically requires the utilization of a great many theoretical formulations. Through the intermediary of an interdisciplinary framework, concepts that hail from such diverse scientific homes as sociology, social psychology, anthropology, and psychology can be brought to bear on the understanding of practical problems at hand.

This kind of synthesizing approach to theory-building for the practitioner is neither widely recognized nor widely followed.

Nor is it easy to attain such a goal, because the formulations of any one scientific field upon which the practitioner must draw frequently are not sufficiently systematized to make possible their linkage with the formulations of another scientific field. Theories seldom spring full blown from a scientist's head; they tend to grow by spurts and starts and sometimes follow a tortuous route of contradiction and revision. When this has happened, a prior task is necessary—that is, the systematic presentation of the thinking of one theorist in a given field. After this task has been accomplished, it becomes possible to think of the next steps: the synthesis of related theories and their application to problems of practice.

Professor Maier has made giant strides toward the attainment of both goals. He has furthered the development of comprehensive theories of child development by presenting, in systematic form, the major premises of such renowned theorists as Erikson, Piaget, and Sears. Beyond that, his identification of similarities in and differences between these three theories paves the way for the development of a more comprehensive theoretical base in child development. Finally, he has brought us closer to the use of these theories in child-development practice.

In order to attain this second goal, the author has developed a conceptual framework of the helping process. This framework, in itself a noteworthy contribution to practice theory, provides the practitioner of child development and other interested persons with conceptual tools that will enable them to make use of the three theories in the course of their problem-solving activities.

The author lays no claim to having achieved a definitive presentation of the three theories, or to having exhausted their implications for practice, but he has made solid progress toward the attainment of these goals. Beyond that, the book has the merit of providing the student of such cognate fields as Social Work, Psychology, and Child Development with intellectual excitement and a sense of direction which should not fail to bring into being both better theory and better practice.

WERNER W. BOEHM

Graduate School of Social Work
Rutgers–The State University

Foreword

THIS BOOK SEEKS A RATIONALE for the helping professions in the work of three developmental psychologists, one of
them undoubtedly familiar to most social workers, the others less
familiar, but promising in their potential contribution. In this
endeavor the author was greatly helped by his professional background and experience as a social worker with both normal and
severely disturbed children and youth. Sometime associate of Dr.
Fritz Redl, Dr. Earl A. Loomis, and Dr. Benjamin Spock, the author
has been firmly grounded in clinical concepts and practice. As
an academician at the University of Pittsburgh, the University
of Minnesota, and now the University of Washington, and in his
studies in developmental psychology and social work, he has
achieved a thorough understanding of the fact that the process
of development occurs in a social matrix composed of people,
institutions, cultural norms, attitudes, behaviors, and the like.

The general area known as "child development" originated a
generation ago as an interdisciplinary movement, not as a discipline
in itself. Its students, drawn from a number of disciplines, carry on
research and teach in colleges and universities; there is no practic-
ing profession of child development *per se*. Consequently, there
are many and diverse viewpoints and approaches to theory.

Among many available, the author has selected for study three points of view—those of Erik H. Erikson, Jean Piaget, and Robert R. Sears. All three viewpoints are contemporary; all have grown out of research—although the research differs in style—and all have exerted considerable influence upon other scientists and upon practitioners. It seemed worthwhile to discover whether these rather different viewpoints, considering similar phenomena, provide useful theoretical support on which research pertinent to social work and its practice might be based.

Erikson has presented the most organized, systematic viewpoint of the three chosen. He is foremost a clinician, a human and humane observer, insightful and sympathetic. Hardly an experimentalist, he is an astute observer of representative, oft-recurring behavior as well as an investigator of the unusual, or even the bizarre. His material was possibly the easiest to develop. He represents a system, however, rather than a theory; he has not yet formulated his basic propositions and principles in rigorous form, but has permitted them to remain at a more loose, descriptive level. Nevertheless, his general concepts have proved useful as a systematic way of organizing ideas about the growing personality for practitioners dealing with molar behavior.

Erikson's point of view represents a synthesis of developmental phenomena and psychoanalytic constructs, and his schematic approach is rather easily grasped by a nonscientifically trained person who brings to bear on it only his own experience and understanding. He emphasizes the phenomenological point of view —that the world as it exists to the perceptions of the experiencing organism is the reality with which the practitioner must be concerned. As the basic point of view concerning personality development at the White House Conference of 1950, Erikson's work is already familiar to many practical workers. His system thus was a logical choice for inclusion in this book.

Piaget's writing was perhaps the most difficult to develop. There is so much of it; it is abstractly, and even obscurely, stated; and Piaget himself has changed his point of view during a lifetime of work. Strictly speaking. Piaget has not yet presented a systematic theory, though he is approaching it. Most recently, he has attempted to use the device of symbolic logic rather than mathematics to state the principles by which observed phenomena can be interrelated, but he has not yet extended this treatment to all the many phenomena he has considered over the years.

Piaget himself may be said to represent an interdisciplinary position. Trained originally as a biologist, he leans heavily upon observation and demonstration as sources for his ideas and concepts. From this position he develops hypotheses which he then puts to experimental test. His experiments are perhaps among the most ingenious devised by child psychologists. Moreover, Piaget is a cognitive theorist. He is interested in the intellectual life of the child, not just the behavioral—though he uses behavior to make inferences about psychic processes. The selection of his work as a possible source of fruitful theory in an area of interpersonal relations was also, therefore, logical.

Robert Sears, a psychologist, represents a third, quite different, position. He is not a synthesist, but he has attempted to make a consistent approach to molar problems and concepts in the spirit of the analytical, behavioristic point of view in psychology. His method has been primarily that of the experiment or quasi-experiment—though he has not shunned the systematic interview, as those familiar with his studies know. Central to his position are the concepts of prediction and control of behavior as the primary aim of science and of theory as statements of formal propositions concerning relationships among data—particularly the relationships of cause and effect, from which are derived hypotheses subject to crucial test.

Much of his more recent work has been devoted to parent behavior as the antecedent and to child behavior as the consequent. He sees parent training as a complex of specific behavioral acts, including attitudes and feelings, and embodying expectations and aspirations. He has given considerable importance to the concept of the dyad, the simple interactive relationship between two persons. This is an old concept in social psychology, restated and placed in the elegant style of the hypothetico-deductive system by Professor Sears.

The author of the present book, analyzing these three rather different systems, has made a number of contributions of his own.

He has brought an intelligent and perceptive grasp of the semantic problem to the issue of interrelating these three conceptual systems. He first identifies the assumptions of each and attempts to state the "world-view" or philosophical position of each author. This initial step, sometimes overlooked by the behavioral scientist, is fundamental to any theory. For a theory, after all, must embrace definitions, assumptions, and "givens," as well as the empirical phenomena the scientist seeks to interrelate. The author then attempts to identify operationally the referents in each system and to show how common operations and common processes may be described in somewhat different language by each of the systematists.

As his further contribution, the author advances two major ideas, the conceptualization of the helping process as intervention in development and the conceptualization of the helping process as essentially a continuum between two processes, diagnosis and treatment.

Professor Maier also presents a statement of the implications of his selected theories for practice in the helping professions. It is this section of his material that possibly will be read most eagerly by his colleagues in social work, clinical psychology, psychiatry, and counseling. When the helping process is seen as intervention into an on-going developmental process, rather than the substitution of one developmental stage for another, the practical worker finds that he must relate what he knows about developmental processes to the interventions he seeks to make and to the age-related practices adults typically use with children. Here, the identification of common elements in three rather different developmental systems of thought proves useful. The practical worker is reassured when he discovers common ground in seemingly quite different positions. The syntheses and implications spelled out by Professor Maier give him a rationale for his own attack on problems often bewilderingly complicated.

DALE B. HARRIS

Department of Psychology
The Pennsylvania State University

Preface

THIS STUDY WAS UNDERTAKEN in the belief that both research and practice must stem from a foundation of theory. The author concurs with Calvin S. Hall and Gardner Lindzey that to begin with "no theory" in any systematic undertaking is impossible (61). Initial practice and research both proceed from a theoretical formulation—however primitive—to an operational hypothesis which is to be tested by experience or is to be validated through new investigation. In either case, hypothesis is a consequence of theory, and is reached through a deductive chain of thought. Dale B. Harris suggests the existence of a bridge between theoretical and empirical scientific endeavors: "In theory construction the observation and verification of fact are replaced by sets of postulates and theorems from which may be deduced larger sets of empirical laws to be tested in crucial experiments" (61a, 4).

Similarly, it is the purpose of this book to present the theories of Erik H. Erikson, Jean Piaget, and Robert R. Sears, together with some of their implications for current practice, in the hope that they will generate new ideas, enhance our commitments, guide our professional practices, and in one form or another lead to renewed explorations in the realm of child development.

A few comments on the methodology of this study are in order. The presentation of these three theories is based upon research in the primary literature of all three writers. (In the case of Piaget, we used the English or German translations unless the material was available only in its original French. Piaget himself believes the translations of his work have made it more succinct and readable; he states: "... I feel that my original somewhat difficult text has become in English more understandable, thanks to the efforts of my translators" [**100,** v].) Each theory presents a synthesis of all the work of each theorist. We have tried to offer the most recent concepts whenever newer ones have superseded earlier findings. Technical terminology employed by each of the theorists has been retained, and, since all three theorists avoid commitment to chronological age levels, age periods have been cited merely for the sake of orientation.

Following an introductory chapter, Chapters 2, 3, and 4 are devoted, respectively, to the theories of Erikson, Piaget, and Sears. For the sake of easy reference and comparison, a similar outline has been used wherever possible in the discussion of each man's work. Chapter 5 presents a comparative synthesis of the three theories, with a view toward providing a single, utilitarian perspective of child development. Chapters 6 and 7 discuss this perspective's practical applications for those active in the helping professions: Chapter 6 deals with the helping process itself, and the ways in which it alters developmental experiences; Chapter 7 attempts to illustrate the applicability of each of the three theories, and of the trifold whole, to the helping process. This final chapter interrelates *help-giving* with *help-needing* by showing how professional intervention can affect developmental processes.

Certain limitations of this book should be pointed out. A concentration upon psychosocial development seems to deny maturational (that is, physical, physiological, motor, and neurological) development. We regret that our apparent preoccupation with the developmental aspects seems to overlook the impact of these factors, and we can only hope that the reader will supplement this void with his own study in these areas. To repeat, when we speak of development, we are referring to the psychosocial-cognitive variables of personality development; other aspects of equal relevance had to be by-passed. Further, our lack of emphasis upon maturational factors placed us in the position of having to use the term *child* rather indiscriminately. For simplicity's sake, *child* refers to individuals in age groups usually included in childhood and adolescence. We employ the term *youth* whenever we intend to convey that the individual's maturational or developmental status has progressed beyond childhood. A possible drawback also may lie in the fact that—to cite Dr. Edmund A. Smith's observations, made while reviewing this manuscript—these theories all have been developed by *men* on a subject more native to women, that is, the *nurturing* development of the dependent child. Moreover, the synthesis and interpretation of these theories have been pursued by a male author, and he, in turn, depended primarily upon men for his critical audience in reviewing this manscript.

This book could not have been written without the pioneering and insightful contributions of Erik H. Erikson, Jean Piaget, and Robert R. Sears, and the author is particularly indebted to Professors Erikson and Sears for the use of unpublished manuscripts, as well as for permission to quote from their works. Responsibility for this book's factual accuracy, however, rests completely with the present author.

I would like to thank the more than thirty publishers who generously granted permission to use the selected excerpts from their publications that appear throughout the book; they are enumerated in the Bibliography. I am grateful for the critical but most helpful suggestions in the reviews of my manuscript, or of parts of it, by Dr. Dale B. Harris, Dr. Gisela Konopka, Dr. Robert W. MacDonald, Dr. Edmund A. Smith, and Dr. Calvin Y. Takagi. Also of great assistance were the thoughtful editorial work of Miss Faith N. Smith and Roger K. Weaver and the careful typing of various stages of the manuscript by many patient secretaries, especially Mrs. Hal H. Hunt and Miss Faith N. Smith. The needed encouragement and support of my friends and colleagues in long, but productive, discussions about the manuscript are much appreciated. The book could not have been completed without the vital interest of Jeanne, my wife, and Mark, Peter, and Scott, my sons, who shared in its long gestation period.

HENRY W. MAIER

Seattle, Washington
March, 1965

Three Theories of Child Development

I

An Introduction to the

Three Theories

Time and experience . . . alter all perspectives . . .
HENRY ADAMS

"TIME AND EXPERIENCE ALTER ALL PERSPEC-
TIVES" could well have been the title of this book. We have
set out to place parallel to one another three essential congruent
theories of child development—those of Erik H. Erikson, Jean
Piaget, and Robert R. Sears—which, when studied together, may
furnish a single perspective on emotional, intellectual, and social
development. These three parallel and congruent theories of child
development will be presented with their implications for the
helping professions, including an analysis of the helping process
itself.

Each theory deals with a separate aspect of development—
emotional,[1] intellectual, and behavioral. All three theories—each
in itself, and all combined as *an associated frame of reference on
child development*—lend perspective to the parts that time and
experience play in psychosocial development.

Our understanding that child development is a unitary develop-

---

[1] Also called "affective" development throughout this book.

mental process, and that professional intervention involves a multidimensional helping effort, are twentieth century accomplishments. Arnold J. Toynbee commends our contemporary state of knowledge for its capacity to

> . . . begin to see all aspects of human life as so many facets of a unitary human nature, instead of having, like our predecessors, to approach the study of Man departmentally, by breaking it up artificially into a number of separate "disciplines": history, sociology, economics, psychology, theology, and the rest. This new possibility of studying human life as a unity ought to enable us to embark on mental voyages of discovery that have hardly been practicable in the past (68, 174).

Our "mental voyages of discovery" in this case will take us along a child's developmental path, because understanding a child's development is a prerequisite to effective work with children and youth, especially when there is a concern over deviations from normal development.

Each helping discipline relies upon its own specifically selected and circumscribed views of child development, garnished by flashes of insight derived from professional practice. A specialist engaged in one or another of the helping professions stresses those concepts most helpful to him in his own professional activities and which are most akin to his professional mode of thinking and value system. The psychiatrist, psychologist, social worker, teacher, etc. extracts from our common body of knowledge what *he* considers the best knowledge for *his* work with children and youth. Actually, each such compilation of knowledge represents an integrated body of theory which is applicable to a particular professional field. An accumulation of knowledge in one discipline may be differentiated from that of the others, and each reflects the purpose for which it was acquired. Yet, striving for a wider understanding of child development will make the helping professional and his social institutions better equipped to help children more knowledgeably, more effectively. Each new increase of understanding is both a challenge and a conquest, and each demands a scrutiny and reorganization of previous knowledge.

THE MEANING OF DEVELOPMENT

To give order to our study of the complex processes of human development it seems necessary here to explain the term *development* as it will be used in this book. Originally *development* was a biological term having to do with physically observable growth in size or structure in an organism over a period of time. When carried into the sociopsychological sciences and applied to personality formation, that aspect of the definition pertaining to temporal-linked processes is emphasized. The study of development, then, takes into consideration the progressive changes in each individual's adaptive functioning, with their consequent integration of constitutional and learned factors. *Development* in this sense refers to the multiple processes which are instrumental in forging each individual's personality.

Child development, specifically, comprises the sequential phases, steps, levels, or stages through which a child's personality passes in his childhood and youth. It is the psychosocial maturational path toward adulthood. Therefore, the study of child development encompasses the dynamics of personality evolvements and their products by dealing with the quantitative and qualitative factors which help to shape an individual personality during this period.

A book devoted to child development theories, and the implications of these theories for professional helping activities, must deal with developmental questions which emerge from the particular theories chosen. So, for the present, it should be noted that, while the term *maturation* will generally be used to suggest organic growth, *development* is employed to denote sociopsychological development; that is, the nonphysical aspects of growth. *Developmental readiness* herein refers to sociopsychological readiness, which may or may not depend upon maturational (physical) attainments.

Development must be differentiated from change. *Change* implies a transition from one state to another, while development focuses upon the dynamic, one-directional elements of change. Development, therefore, is a process; change is a product. The former takes place within systems which are defined by their structures and by their norms of significant capacities. Two of the developmental theorists to be presented, Piaget and Erikson, deal with both questions, while Sears focuses upon existing capacities with little attention to structural considerations.

Contradictory as it may seem, development is influenced by both change and constancy. Development, by definition, entails change, but, by its very reliance upon predictable change, it counts also on a constancy in change. This constancy—this rhythmic regularity—permits the formulation of a generally ordered group of concepts to be used in studying child development. We should remember that, because development encompasses many processes, differing rates of change among them must be recognized. Some processes involve a rapid rate of change, while in others change may hardly be perceptible, and the rates and patterns of change in these processes may vary from phase to phase in an individual's life cycle. But the generally accepted existence of a rhythmic regularity in the processes of normal development paves the way for our consideration of developmental problems.

Any study of personality development must make certain basic assumptions. Whatever assumptions are pertinent to the content of the following chapters are discussed in each chapter's introduction. But several other assumptions bearing on the study of the three theories in general should be stated here.

Any theory of child development immediately invites a challenge of its author's position on the etiology of behavior. He is expected to answer the question: Where and when does the development of behavior originate? A developmental theory, however tentative and descriptive, always implies, or states, a schematic interpretation of nonvisible processes. Moreover, the question of unity-in-continuity versus unity-in-discontinuity cannot be avoided.[2] All three theories in this book have been selected be-

[2] Unity-in-continuity can be illustrated in the learning process, which proceeds along one continuum, whether it occurs within the formal class-

cause, in our opinion, they meet the criteria of unity-in-continuity. In all three theories, quantitative behavior can repeatedly be reduced to previous levels of behavior while, qualitatively, all behavioral changes unfold as products of preexisting layers of behavior, which modify the ongoing flow of development at qualitatively different levels.

Although most personality theories recognize childhood as the formative period of the personality, each theory dealt with here requires a somewhat different interpretation of the extent to which postchildhood development can modify earlier development acquisitions. Each theory contains its own developmental schedule involving its own series of sequential phases. Understanding each system's view of development depends upon understanding the particular system's order of the developmental pattern within the age span studied. Each theory delineates a beginning, which provides the foundation for all development which follows, and later development can always be traced back to an earlier—and, ultimately, a first—phase. Each sequential phase delineated in each theory is characterized by the emergence of new capacities in the individual—capacities of cognition for Piaget; new developmental crises, for Erikson; and new motivational systems, for Sears. As each new phase becomes evident, it is measurable for its own immediate achievements. When the modes of each phase become established and are integrated with those of previous phases, they serve as foundations for newly developing characteristics.

In formulating a general concept of development, we must stress the importance of timing, readiness, and continuity in *all* levels of behavior. Personality development embraces perspectives of physical maturation, cultural pressures, intellectual achievement, emotional adaptations, and behavioral experiences—and all combinations of these factors. Extremely important to the helping professional is the idea that development is a continuing process,

---

room or outside of it. Unity-in-discontinuity, however, can be illustrated by society's legally imposed criterion for an individual's majority, which is generally arbitrarily set at 21 years of age.

for the professional deals with personalities in the making; the phase of development, rather than chronological age, should serve as his chief criterion for assessing personality.

THE SELECTION OF THE THREE THEORIES

At the outset, the author decided that any theory to be included in this volume had to deal with personality development as a continuous and sequential process, starting with a child's status as an infant and dealing with each subsequent stage of psychological growth: early childhood, childhood, and adolescence. Moreover, theories to be selected had to supplement one another to provide a composite explanation or description of human personality development. Pertinent knowledge of physical, psychological, and neurological processes—though important ingredients of personality development—would purposely be omitted because such information had been covered in other publications.

Surprisingly, even though there was a large store of personality theories available, only a small number of them met the aforementioned criteria. Most personality theories are concerned with man as a virtually completed product; only a few are devoted to a study of personality development from birth to maturity. For example, Kurt Lewin and Harry Stack Sullivan have contributed vastly to an understanding of man's relationships to others (61), but they furnish little information on man as a developing individual who is progressing toward a mature state. The recent studies of Alfred L. Baldwin (6) and Gardner Murphy (82) introduce nearly closed theoretical systems of personality development, but their material is intentionally highly eclectic, and is not applicable to this study. Finally, only the conceptual systems of Erik H. Erikson, Sigmund Freud, O. H. Mowrer, Jean Piaget, and Robert R. Sears lent themselves to further consideration within the confines we had established.

These five theoretical systems hinge upon three basic approaches to the study of personality development: (1) the *psychoanalytic*, with its emphasis upon emotional processes—both conscious and unconscious—as the basic motivational forces; (2) the exploration of *learned behavior*, with its reliance upon behavioral manifestations; and (3) the investigation of *cognitive functioning* and its stress on an individual's intellectual conquest of his life experiences.

From the psychoanalytic realm, Erikson's work was ultimately chosen for inclusion in this book in preference to Freud's. We considered his endeavor an extension of Freud's earlier efforts, and felt that it was more reconcilable with contemporary practice and modern approaches to theory construction (70b, 80, 109). Also, we believe Erikson's inclusion justifies the exclusion of theories developed by Karen Horney, Carl Jung, and Otto Rank. While each of these three built upon Freudian theory, in our estimation, only Erikson's work has progressed sufficiently to warrant recognition as a new and substantially different theory which is distinctly separable from Freudian psychoanalytic theory.

Supporters of cognitive functioning as a primary consideration in the study of personality development, although they have contributed much to our present knowledge, are not great in number. Jean Piaget was the obvious choice for inclusion in this volume because his pioneering and unequaled work in this field still holds unexplored sources of knowledge for today's helping professional.

Among learning theorists, Sears' interpretation of learning as a basic force in personality development has been chosen in preference to the one introduced by O. H. Mowrer, a former colleague of Sears. The work of Sears is less eclectic and has apparently found a wider audience than Mowrer's attempt (79) to "marry" learning theory with psychoanalytic formulations.

THE SIGNIFICANCE OF THE THREE THEORIES

Erik H. Erikson pursues psychoanalytic teachings begun by Freud and expands concepts of adaptation and sociocultural experiences into an ego psychology. Others have likewise attempted to reformulate psychoanalytic theory into an ego psychology

(**62, 73, 80, 109, 111**), but it is Erikson's widely varied work which has attracted particular attention and has beckoned the imagination of helping professionals in circles beyond those of psychoanalytic scholars and practitioners—among them, social work, special education, early-childhood education, nursing, and pastoral counseling. His ideas have found a forum in a wide range of periodicals and books (see pp. 297–300). Especially noteworthy is an epoch-making paper on healthy personality development which was prepared for the Midcentury White House Conference on Children and Youth, in 1950 (**50**). As a body of work, Erikson's research, lectures, and writings have significantly extended psychoanalytic thought through the incorporation of integrated insights from such fields as cultural anthropology, social psychology, child development, Gestalt psychology, and the study of man in history.

Jean Piaget's work, though earlier than Sears' and Erikson's, undoubtedly stands as an unsurpassed milestone in the study of cognitive thought. His early publications have found recognition in the pertinent literature of this country and have stimulated an interest in the notion of phasal development. Recently there has been a resurgence of interest in Piaget in the United States, and a boom in the translation and publication of his later writings has come about. The integration in this book of Piaget's writings, research findings, and lectures into a single developmental framework is an attempt to synthesize his diverse contributions into a meaningful, unified theory.

Robert R. Sears' writing and research, based upon concepts and techniques associated with learning theories, add yet another dimension to an understanding of child development. Much of his work involves a reporting and a summarization of the collaborative research of others. However, it is Sears who had the courage to risk his own reputation by publishing under his own name not only his own findings, but also those of others. We suggest, therefore, that the material submitted as Sears' theory can be identified clearly as his own contribution. Sears has ventured where other American learning theorists have not dared to tread by drawing some of his own inferences from what other learning theorists have researched.[3] Essentially, Sears' work covers the field of child rearing as he finds it on the contemporary American scene, specifically, among intact American middle-class families. Sears highlights the impact of environmental forces upon the developmental processes of the growing child. He introduces observations based upon empirical data, and his work merits inclusion here, not only because of its importance to present and future students of child development, but also because it reflects the prevailing research methods employed in the major child-development study centers in this country.

THE THREE THEORIES AS AN ASSOCIATED FRAME OF REFERENCE

The theories of Erikson, Piaget, and Sears deal with distinctly separate but complementary approaches to personality development. Each contributes one part to an understanding of the individual as an indivisible whole; each interlocks, cogwheel fashion, with the others, and, at the same time, leaves undisturbed the sequential phases of development within its own theoretical framework. Considered longitudinally, each theory might be said to possess its own internal consistency in portraying a continuum of development, while upholding the integrity of the other two theories. Considered laterally, each theory may deal at any given stage with a more or less distinct episode which may be defined in terms of one theory without absolving or refuting principles embodied in the others. In practice, the applicability of each theory is determined by the nature of the activity. For example, if the reason for intervention involves a question of social behavior and habit formation, Sears' particular findings stand out as most pertinent; if the need for help has to do with the child's comprehension of a situation, Piaget's detailed account of intellectual development will be instructive and reliable; if the child's

---

[3] An exception may be the most recent effort of Sidney Bijou and Donald M. Baer, in *Child Development: A Systematic and Empirical Theory* (11).

problem is one of emotional maturity, Erikson's concepts will assist the helping person in introducing himself as a potential mentor. Therefore, in helping a child with his development or in diagnosing and treating a developmental problem, the professional should consider all three areas.

A quick glance at the professional life, research methodology, and findings of the three theorists may make one wonder if this book does not bring together three rather strange bedfellows between two covers. But a closer examination of the work of these three suggests that compatibility among their theories is more significant than divergence. In fact, Sybil Escalona cites Piaget's cognitive theory as supplementary to, and compatible with, psychoanalytic theory (93). Similarly, Charles Odier comments:

> . . . the strongest aspect of the Freudian psychoanalytic doctrine is the weakest of Piaget's doctrine, and vice versa. . . . Comparing the evaluation of the individual to a river, I should say that Freud [with his psychoanalytic approach] and Piaget both ascended it to its source but each on his own bank. By definition, this parallelism condemned them never to meet (84, 32).

Furthermore, Peter H. Wolff adds in his monograph, published in late 1960: "Despite their methodological differences and divergent goals, the two methods [Piagetian analysis and Freudian psychoanalysis] may complement each other in providing a comprehensive picture of the developmental process, each supplying the data in those areas where the other is deficient" (138, 11–12). Sears' own conscious effort to unite basic concepts of psychoanalytic theory with those of his own learning theory lends support to our efforts to interrelate the three theories.

At this time we can merely suggest that each theory covered introduces convincingly a set of core processes, and that together they may provide a convenient "core of core processes." Our focus throughout this book is upon developmental readiness and developmental acquisition, both of which are constantly tied to developmental phases. But, in contrast to such maturational indexes as bone age, physical size, and weight, or to such chronological time intervals as days, months, and years since birth, there are no actual norms for measuring developmental readiness, progress, or phases. We must remember that each individual can be measured or appraised only within the context of his own evolvement, and that, while developmental theory may help to provide a generalized understanding of the processes of child development, any such theory can be used successfully only when it is applied to the individual according to the specifics of his own unique situation.

2

The Psychoanalytic Theory
of Erik H. Erikson

A THUMBNAIL SKETCH OF ERIKSON'S LIFE

ERIK H. ERIKSON—one of the most accomplished analysts and scholars on the contemporary American scene—was born of Danish parents in Frankfurt, Germany, in 1902. His father died soon after his birth; his mother remarried, and his stepfather, Homburger, adopted him. For this reason, his early papers bear the name Homburger, but when he became an American citizen in 1939, he chose to be known by his original name.

Erik Erikson attended grammar school and the "humanistic gymnasium" in Karlsruhe, Germany, before embarking on his *Wanderjahre* in central Europe. In his own words, "I was an artist then, which is European euphemism for a young man with some talent but nowhere to go" (49b, 40). During these years he found his real interest and, unwittingly, his first link with this continent, when he was asked to teach with Dorothy Burlingham and Peter Blos at a small American school in Vienna. At the same time, he acquired his psychoanalytic training, with special emphasis on work with children, at the Vienna Psychoanalytic Institute. This comprised his only formal academic career, aside from obtaining a certificate from the Maria Montessori School as probably one of the few men with a membership in the *Montessori Lehrerinnen Verein.* During these years also, he made the personal acquaintance of Sigmund Freud. He taught and practiced psychoanalysis and wrote his first articles (36, 37), in which he applied psychoanalytic thinking to educational questions.

In 1933, Erikson accepted an invitation to practice and to lecture in this country. He practiced in Boston for two years, and, for one year, he served as Research Fellow in Psychology in the Department of Neuropsychiatry of the Harvard Medical School. From 1936 to 1939, he had an appointment with the Department of Psychiatry in the Institute of Human Relations and the Yale School of Medicine. During these years, he worked on three major questions of ego development. These inquiries dealt with concepts of social modalities, and his research focused upon children's spatial play behavior (24, 39, 42, 56). His early preoccupation with ego development was evidenced in his emphasis upon the psychosocial development of children, which was summed up in his chapter on "Problems of Infancy and Early Childhood" in the *Cyclopedia of Medicine* (35). Simultaneously, Erikson got interested in anthropological inquiries about man in time and space. He undertook field trips to an Indian reservation with H. Scudder Mekeel and tried out the clinical approach to anthropological studies of individuals within their sociocultural group (31).

During the years 1939 to 1944, Erikson participated in the longitudinal "Child Guidance Study" of the University of California. Again, his efforts covered three major areas: (1) sex differences in children's play construction (22, 39, 40,); (2) conflict resolutions in various phases of man's life cycles (26); and (3) continued cultural anthropological inquiries around questions of child development (31, 32).

During the six years that followed, he taught at the San Francisco Psychoanalytic Institute, the University of California, and the Menninger Foundation in Topeka, Kansas. His writings of this period reflect an extension of his previous tenuous concepts on modalities and man's efforts to establish child training in the image of his social-historical destiny. He laid the framework for his evolving theory in his first book, *Childhood and Society* (**20**), the title of which summarizes well his own theoretical preoccupation—the synthesis of developmental and social tasks. The book incorporated into Freudian psychoanalytic theory man's efforts to live effectively within his particular social environment. The publication of the work introduced Erikson as one of the leading proponents of ego psychology in this country, a role his former teacher, Anna Freud, had achieved in England. Erikson's work reflects the concerns of his time: interpersonal relations, normal development, and mental health. It is no wonder that he was chosen to contribute to the Midcentury White House Conference of 1950. His material on the basic conditions for a healthy personality (**50, 76**), and subsequent publications (**33, 65, 136**) clearly introduced a new theory of child development.

In 1951, Erikson again moved East and joined the staff of the Austen Riggs Center at Stockbridge, Massachusetts, while he also maintained part-time teaching appointments at Western Psychiatric Institute, the University of Pittsburgh, and the Massachusetts Institute of Technology. Since then, his research and writings have built upon the theory he developed before and during deliberations for the Midcentury White House Conference (**26, 33, 35, 43, 50**). During the past ten years, Erikson's stimulating and scholarly thinking has been sought far beyond the United States. *Childhood and Society* and several other writings have been translated and reprinted in many parts of the world, and Erikson has participated in many interdisciplinary, scientific roundtable explorations (**27, 33, 49a, 49b, 51a, 51b**). In the summer of 1960— after a year at the Center for Advanced Studies of the Behavioral Sciences, at Palo Alto, California—he accepted an appointment as Professor of Human Development at Harvard University, a well deserved distinction for Erikson, a scholar without a formal academic career, and a man with a genuine sense of humility.

Erikson assumes in his writings that basic psychoanalytic formulations are accepted and understood by his readers. His writings are those of an artist; he paints the backdrops with broad strokes

JON ERIKSON

Erik H. Erikson

and fills in the intimate and minute details of the immediate foreground. Like Freud, most of his material comes from his clinical
cases. Where Freud once relied upon Greek mythological drama,
Erikson illuminates his concepts with references to poetry, folk-
lore, and the wisdom of everyday life. Although Erikson lifted
psychoanalytic thought to a new level, he is one of the foremost
proponents and interpreters of Freudian thought (25, 28). His
insight into Freud's work and his integrity as one of the outstand-
ing contemporary analysts and theorists were fittingly honored

when he was asked to deliver the Goethe Centenary Address in 1956 at Frankfurt, Germany—his own birthplace—in honor of Sigmund Freud's one hundredth birthday. Yet, Erikson deserves recognition as a scholar and scientist in his own right; in a recent stimulating paper, Robert W. White pays tribute to Erikson for his capacity to move beyond Freud.[1]

ERIKSON'S THEORY AND FREUDIAN PSYCHOANALYTIC THEORY

Erikson builds solidly upon Freudian analytic theory. He himself terms Freud's work as the "rock" on which all new exploration and advancement on personality theory is based (44, 8). Erikson never suggests that he is preparing a new theory himself; in fact, he intermittently quotes Freud in order to show that, in essence, his ideas are a mere extension of Freudian psychology in the light of present-day knowledge and circumstances (20). Yet, in spite of his protests to the contrary, Erikson's thinking presents a decisive departure from, and an advance beyond, Freudian psychology.

Erikson's theory diverges from the Freudian model in his emphasis of three major areas. First, Erikson completes a shift in emphasis from the id to the ego which Freud already had accelerated with the publication of the *Problem of Anxiety* (55). In the words of Gardner Lindzey, Erikson (along with other ego psychologists) ". . . places great theoretical emphasis on the ego's synthesizing function in developing stable conceptions—meaning, images, themes—of self, significant other individuals and symbolic entities such as 'boss' and 'Mom' in the contemporary United States" (70, 985). Erikson himself describes *Childhood and Society* as a "psychoanalytic book on the relations of the ego to society" (20, 12). He deals with inborn coordination to an average, predictable environment. Erikson's primary concern with

---

[1] White's new conception of *a sense of competence* deserves attention as well as his thought provoking discussion and critique of Erikson's developmental phases (135, 106–107).

the continuity of experience necessitates a shift to the function of the ego beyond Freud's sexual (libidinal) developmental phases. Erikson rebuilds the Freudian organ phases to the point that they lose many of their biosexual implications; yet, he does not break completely with the Freudian model. For Erikson, unconscious motivation is an accepted fact, and consequently, Erikson feels free to devote his studies primarily to the processes of socialization. David Rapaport aptly calls Erikson's formulation a "theory of reality relationships" (109, 14). Due to Erikson's interest in man's struggle to live, to master, and to succeed, he pays less attention to instincts, including the death wish. Erikson writes that, for him, it is a question which

. . . is essentially a philosophical one, based on Freud's original commitment to a mythology of primeval instincts. In order to determine more correctly what kinds of forces are operative in a given clinical situation, it may be more profitable to ask, what it is that we are called upon to accomplish. Maybe by clarifying our function in the situation we can come to grips with the forces which we are trying to understand (20, 64).

Second, Erikson introduces a new matrix; the individual in his relationship to his parents within the context of the family, and in relation to a wider social setting, within the framework of the family's historical-cultural heritage. This social complex replaces the classical Freudian matrix of the child-mother-father triangle. Helen M. Lynd describes Erikson's approach as unique in psychoanalytic circles because of his stress upon the historical reality in which the child's ego develops (73). Erikson concerns himself with the dynamics between members of the family and their sociocultural reality, whereas Freud limited himself to the dynamics within the individual in relation to the reality of his family life.

Third, Erikson responds to the demands of his time. Whereas Freud's mission was to prove the existence and operation of the unconscious, Erikson's mission is to point out the developmental opportunities in the individual to triumph over the psychological hazards of living. Freud's warning of the social doom of man if he is left to his innate strivings is answered in Erikson's optimistic premise that every personal and social crisis furnishes components that are conducive to growth. While Freud devoted his studies to the etiology of pathological development, Erikson focuses upon the successful solution of developmental crises. In addition, he ventures "to speculate the psychosocial implications of the human evolution" (38, 149).

Erikson, then, gives a new direction to psychoanalytic theory. This approach allows a more optimistic interpretation and a wider application to everyday life. The latter renders it more immediately available to formulation of hypotheses and research than its Freudian predecessor.

ASSUMPTIONS BASIC TO ERIKSON'S THEORY

Any survey of the basic assumptions in Erikson's theory necessarily must include the Freudian formulations which Erikson takes for granted. In the following material, Freudian assumptions will be specified. Assumptions which are not so labelled may be credited to Erikson. The assumptions to be presented can be summarized in the following seven subheadings:

1. Approach to theory formation
2. Order of human life
3. Fundamental human values
4. Etiology of human behaviour
5. Core of human functioning
6. Newborn
7. Physical, social, cultural, and Ideational Environment.

Approach to Theory Formation

Erikson naturally relies upon psychoanalytic methods and techniques for obtaining his data. In his investigations, he gives special attention to the "signals" of unconscious and preconscious material as it is revealed in spoken communication and in play behavior. Psychoanalysis, according to Erikson, depends upon understanding individual habits which are idiosyncratic, and which become the "unofficial ways"—the open delight or secret concern —of the individual in the process of his daily life. Erikson assumes that, since the major processes of human development reveal themselves only by their symptoms of apparent discord, a study of gross personality deviation provides the necessary clues to an understanding of normal development. He expands the psycho-analytic domain from the analytical appraisal of the individual to that of groups of individuals and whole cultures; he applies the knowledge of psychoanalysis to the social sciences. In contrast to Freud, who considered the study of dreams the road to the adult's unconscious, Erikson submits that play provides the best situation for studying the child's ego.

Erikson assumes, also, that no scientific investigation can be undertaken without a guiding theory. Any one aspect of develop-ment must be evaluated within a theoretical understanding of the total context of development. His samples are comprised of clini-cal cases. He observes individuals in their natural surroundings and studies folk biographies. He stresses that each case study is to test as well as to add to the fabric of his total theory. As he writes, "We are more interested here in the overall *configuration* and *integration* of developing approaches to the world than in the *first appearance of specific abilities* which are so well described in the child-development literature" (50, 104). Altogether, Erikson ex-hibits a bold confidence in his own intuitive sense of timing, selec-tion of samples, and choice of techniques. His interest is in quali-tative data more than in quantitative measurements. His theory grows from deductions from data secured through his own insight into highly selected and pertinent problems. His model is a fusion of his own psychoanalytic efforts and his knowledge of allied fields—Freudian psychology, child development, cultural anthro-pology, and history.

Order of Human Life

Erikson concedes that "In naming a series of basic balances on which the psycho-social health of a personality seems to depend, I found myself implying a latent universal value system which is

based on the nature of human growth, the needs of the developing
ego, and certain common elements in child training systems" (65,
185). For him, psychological phenomena have undergone an evolutionary history similar to biological structures; biological and
psychological phenomena are closely interrelated. In man's evolutionary history, there has been a simultaneous development of
physiological structure and of psychological endowment. For
instance, the most primitive living organisms' primary structure
consists almost exclusively of an oral cavity, and their primary
mode of life is to ingest—that is, to incorporate. The more complex organisms possess additional functional structures and more
complex psychological modes, and Erikson sees in each man's
psychogenic life cycle a repetition of his phylogenic evolutionary
history. The infant's first developmental phase, similar to the oral
incorporative strivings, is not much different from the jelly fish's
basic nature. Each developmental phase finds a counterpart in the
phylogenic evolution of man; personality development follows
biological principles.

However, *biological* evolution ceases with birth. "The maturing organism continues to unfold, not by developing new organs,
but by a *prescribed* sequence of locomotive, sensory, and social
capacities" (50, 97). Psychological and social development super-
sede biological development; ego development reciprocally joins
the human organism and his world: "The same acts which help
the baby to survive help the culture to survive in him" (21, 325).
Erikson also reconciles unity-in-continuity with the social demands of unity-in-discontinuity. Unity is the product of continuous pulls in opposite directions throughout the various phases of
development. The developing individual strives for unity with his
trust in, and identity with, a continuous past and future. Yet, most
cultures demand separate patterns of behavior for various age
levels. Erikson assumes that epigenetic laws of time and space
operate wherever growth takes place:

Growing is a differentiation of preplanned parts during a given
sequence of critical periods. In personality growth, it is the task of the
ego (in the psychoanalytic sense) and of the social process together to

maintain that continuity which bridges the inescapable discontinuity between each of these stages (**27, 7**).

In the final analysis, the individual unites biological, psychological, and social forces. To quote Erikson, "A human being, thus, is at all times an organism, an ego, and a member of society and is involved in all three processes of organization" (**20, 32**).

Fundamental Human Values

Erikson stresses the creative and adaptive power of the individual, and respects each individual's unique capacity to forge his way of life, to bring to bear his own faith and his own indignation. He sees human behavior as neither "good" nor "bad"; rather, each human being has the potential to produce both "good" and "bad." Erikson reminds us of Freud's more hope-inspiring axioms: "Men are not only worse, but also better, than they think they are" (**20,** 288). Erikson's faith in man's social creativity is reflected in his own optimistic comment, "There is little that cannot be remedied later, there is much that can be prevented from happening at all" (**50,** 104).

The sanctity of the individual requires for its preservation the trust and respect of the surrounding society and culture. In turn, social institutions require for their perpetuation a corresponding respect and recognition from individuals who depend upon them. The sanctity of the individual is endorsed, then, in his social world. "In order to make the world safer for democracy, we must make democracy safe for the healthy child" (**50,** 145).

Etiology of Human Behavior

Erikson accepts the Freudian model of a psychosexual, energy-laden organism. This energy, or drive, exists from birth, and generates all psychological processes. Erikson, as did Freud, calls this energy, an all-inclusive instinct and motivating force, the *libido*.[2]

---

[2] *Libido*, must be defined as a native, undifferentiated, and unspecified force or energy which in part is sexual (incorporating Freud's interpretation), but is largely an unspecified aspect of the human system which impels its realization. In essence, *libidinal* energy is a term for the as yet unknown

This libido encompasses two dynamically opposed human strivings, creating a fundamental polarity. First, there is the drive to live, to gratify oneself, and to reach out beyond oneself. This concept is akin to original Freudian formulation of the sexual drive to live, to expand, and to be gratified. Second, there is the opposite drive which provides an urge to return to the condition prior to birth, or, at least, to an earlier phase of lesser complexity. This desire to return, or to regress, implies a desire for self-destruction, and can be described as parallel to the Freudian concept of the death instinct, the desire to undo all connection with life. These two opposing drives are ever present, and create a *polarity* which stimulates behavior through each and all of the developmental phases of life. In essence, it is the individual's struggle, which has its societal counterpart in the struggle between progressive and reactionary forces. The psychological components of masculinity and femininity represent another basic polarity within the individual; bisexuality is inherent in all beings. With all behavior originating from the interplay of polarities, Erikson hints at the etiology of conflict and at the recurrence of crises as essential and ever-present components of life.

From the first biological experiences of breathing, resting, and eating, most bodily processes become slowly invested with libidinal energy as a reinforcing emotional charge, and develop and shift with the individual's somatic and physiological maturation. They create different demands for behavioral expressions within the individual via the various libidinal zones[3] and different modes of expression. This is distinctly an Eriksonian concept, and will fully be described in the presentation of each developmental phase. In other words, bodily maturation finds its emotional counterpart in personality development. Sensory experience which, as such, receives little recognition in either Freud's or Erikson's teachings, increases the emotional components of the individual's

force which directs the human system's epigenetic development. At various points in this chapter, the descriptive terms "drive," "desire," and "urge" will be used in place of libidinal energy.

[3] *Zone* refers to a psychological concept of a bodily area which is circumscribed by its neurological coherence, rather than its anatomic vicinity.

erotic zones. These zones, and their behavioral expressions, or modes, serve as prototypes from which all future attitudes, even the most complex in the adult, are developed.

Libidinal forces become attached to various levels of life experience. Erikson, with Freud, defines these levels (or layers) as: (1) *conscious experience*, comprising those life events which remain within the individual's perceptual and/or cognitive awareness; (2) *preconscious experience*, which is beyond the individual's immediate recognition (perceptive and cognitive), but within the realm of conscious recall; and, (3) *unconscious experience* which is entirely beyond the individual's perceptive and rational awareness. The last two become the center of most psychoanalytic investigations, and are seen as the most potent determinants of all human motivation.

Libidinal energies and their manifestations in these three layers of consciousness form distinct psychological constellations, which are known either as *hypothetical structures*, or as the three major analytic *processes*. Both the structures and their respective dynamic processes bear identical names, and can be described as the Freudian triad of *id, ego,* and *superego*. Erikson assumes with Freud that the id comprises the sum of the "pressure of excessive wishes" originating in unexpended, unreconstructed, and unconscious libidinal energy. He further ascribes to the id phylogenetical depositions of unfulfilled libidinal strivings of the organism's evolutionary history. The id is "everything which would make us mere creatures . . . the sum of the desire which must be overcome to be quite human" (**20,** 167). The ego is assumed to be a psychological configuration comprised of, and controlling, the conscious actions—the synthesis and integration of past experience with the tasks confronting the individual in his perceptual-cognitive field in the present. Erikson implies that the ego provides the individual with specific direction, and "forges" the individual's developmental history. The superego is assumed to be composed of personal experience with the ideas and attitudes of significant adults and peers.

Freud proposed that the id undergoes a variety of transfigurations in the psychosexual development of the individual, which, consequently, alter the content of the ego and superego. Erikson converts this assumption by giving equal importance to the ego, the synthesis of past and present experience. The ego ". . . makes it possible for man to bind together the two great evolutionary developments, his *inner life* and his *social planning*" (38, 149). The ego is no longer the Freudian product of id and superego pressures; rather, Erikson points to the relative strength and weakness of the ego which charts the course of psychosexual development and which decides each individual's "destiny"; the direction of individual behavior is determined by the individual's capacity to develop and utilize his ego processes. Freud's defense mechanisms lose their importance for the management of id processes; the major focus is shifted to the nature of the ego processes—play, speech, and thought. These are the *adaptive* manoeuvres to influential inner and outer forces. Adaptation, therefore, becomes not only a way, but also a triumph of human life.

The Core of Human Functioning

Erikson, in full agreement with Freud, assumes that the emotional (libidinal) aspects of life permeate all human functions. The nature of emotional content, or the *quality* of *interpersonal relationships*, determines the basic core of man's make-up. Consequently, Erikson, as well as Freud, is concerned with the emotional relationship between persons, rather than with personality as such. Each individual's life—his manner of perceiving, thinking, doing, and feeling—depends largely upon the relative balance of the three major affective processes—the id, the ego, and the superego.

In the child's development, play is particularly important. Erikson considers play one of the major ego functions. Play usually involves three major dimensions: (1) the content and configuration of its parts which create the underlying theme; (2) the verbal and nonverbal communicative components; and (3) the modes of termination, or *play disruption*. Play deals with life experience which the child attempts to repeat, to master, or to negate in order to organize his inner world in relation to his outer. Further, play involves self-teaching and self-healing; "The child uses play to make up for defeats, sufferings, and frustrations, especially those resulting from a technically and culturally limited use of language" (40, 561). "Playing it out" is a common expression for this form of behavior. In childhood, play activity becomes the child's means of reasoning, and permits the child to free himself from the ego boundaries of time, space, and reality, and yet to maintain a reality orientation, because he and others know that it is "just play." In other words play is the ego's acceptable tool for self-expression just as dreams afford expression for the id. For Erikson, the playing child advances toward new mastery and new developmental stages. Erikson quotes William Blake, "The child's toys and the old man's reasons are the fruit of the two seasons" (20, 195).

In addition to placing Freudian emphasis upon the impact of early-life experience, Erikson recognizes the possibility of constitutional differences in initial sensitivity. Basically, however, the first two years of life, the *formative* years, provide the foundation for all later motivation and personal disposition. Erikson stresses that the same factors which determine healthy interpersonal relations also contribute to pathological relationships. Personality disturbance is an imbalance "in the total libidinal household." Emotional deviation involves neither a product nor an irreversible condition; a deviant personality possesses a different configuration of the same ongoing processes that are found in a healthy personality. Erikson proposes three ego achievements as a prerequisite for a mature, healthy personality: "(1) the reconciliation of genital orgasm and extragenital sexual needs; (2) the reconciliation of love and sexuality; (3) the reconciliation of sexual procreative, and work-productive patterns" (20, 87). A mature, healthy personality may be summarized as *individual happiness combined with responsible citizenship.*

The Newborn

Organically, the newborn baby is not much different from his prenatal counterpart; psychologically, he is already endowed with personality; he has his individual inheritance, as well as all the innate potentials for unique personality development. Without further explanation, Erikson assumes that sex differences type different developmental experiences, and that environment is a heavy influence at birth—possibly even prior to it. Altogether, the individual remains an active participant in the forming of his own destiny. As the child matures, he influences the family as much as he is influenced by it. Society needs the newborn for its continuation, and the newborn needs society for its own nurturing.

The Physical, Social, Cultural, and Ideational Environments

The physical, social, and ideational environmental influences serve as partners to the biological and psychological innate processes which shape the individual's personality development. Much of an individual's future, for instance, depends upon a chance event—such as how a given person reacts to him—or where or when such an event occurs. Environmental forces both limit and free the individual. The typical environment provides ample freedom for individual choice, and the individual wants direction from his society as much as society wishes to direct him. Since advanced civilization provides a division of labor, the present-day child finds himself in the hands of various training, teaching, and curing adults who assume responsibility for a proper balance of his behavior, learning, and well-being. Normally, each adult tends to emphasize and to direct the child's natural development within the range circumscribed by his society and his heritage, and eventually, potential patterns are provoked into a pattern of living; the individual gradually settles into a particular life style. Religion and idealistic concepts, in addition to serving as guidelines for molding the individual, also serve him in his search for a future beyond his life's certainty. Each individual needs a clear explanation of life in the light of an intelligible theory or belief. Religion and ideology provide a needed explanation beyond the individual's limits of reason.

Culture adds the human aspect of living. Man lives by instinctual forces, and culture insists upon the proper use of these instinctual forces. It is the cultural environment, as interpreted by the individual, which selects the nature of each individual's experience. The child and his parents are never alone; through the parent's conscience, generations are looking upon a child's actions, helping him to integrate his relationships by their approval, or dividing them with their disapproval into countless disturbing details (35). The infant first experiences society through his body. Significant physical contacts are the child's first social events and these form the beginnings of the psychological patterns of his later social behavior. A culture, class, or ethnic group's basic ways of organizing experience is transmitted to the infant's early bodily experiences and tie the child forever to his original milieu. Such early cultural indoctrination is, for the most part, transmitted unconsciously.

Erikson assumes that prolonged adolescence, which is found in most of the western world, creates a considerable gulf between psychosomatic and psychosocial maturation, and affects personality development in a manner similar to the formative years of early childhood: "It is human to have a long childhood; it is civilized to have an even longer childhood. Long childhood makes a technical and mental virtuoso out of man, but it also leaves a lifelong residue of emotional immaturity in him" (20, 12).

Erikson assumes that the great variation between cultures and societal groups does not provide independent variables and an explanation of individual differences. He views these differences as reciprocal and interrelated factors. Child training serves to keep the small, dependent individual alive and well; it also automatically serves as insurance to continue and to preserve a society's unique qualities. "The growing child must, at every step, derive a vitalizing sense of reality from the awareness that his individual way of mastering experience (his ego synthesis) is a successful variant of a group identity and is in accord with its space-time and life plan" (20, 208). In short, the developing child needs society, and society needs him.

ERIKSON'S CONCEPTION OF DEVELOPMENT

Development is an evolutionary process based upon a universally experienced sequence of biological, psychological, and social events, and involves an autotherapeutic process to heal the scars created by natural and accidental crises inherent to development.

This development, in itself, "consists of a series of childhoods which call for a variety of subenvironments, depending on the stage which the child has reached and also depending on the environment experienced during previous stages" (49a, 304).

Erikson's first five stages are essentially a reformulation and expansion of Freud's psychosexual developmental stages. Yet, for Erikson, they are phases of constant motion; an individual never *has* a personality, he always is redeveloping his personality. An Eriksonian phase is notable for its own developmental theme, for its relationship to the previous and subsequent phases, and for the part it plays in the total scheme of development. Development proceeds within a zigzag course from phase to phase, yet, becomes known by its *basic* regularity. Life follows an epigenetic sequence, and the awareness of it helps parents to "an almost somatic conviction that there is meaning to what they are doing" (50, 107). Erikson quotes Benjamin Spock: "To be a good parent you have to believe in the species—somehow" (50, 109). Actually, parent and child only sense the real meaning of development, according to Erikson, and parent and child communicate to one another their unconscious comprehension of developmental processes as they relate to their joint developmental history. Even if the presentation which follows does not mention these unconscious communications, their presence must be taken as existing facts.

In general, developmental phases coincide with standard ranges of chronological and sociocultural age groupings. In each phase of development, the individual must face and master a central problem which becomes dominant, and which reveals itself in its clearest form as his dilemma of the phase. The underlying developmental crisis is universal, and the particular situation becomes culturally defined. To illustrate, in many western cultures, weaning is treated as if it were a developmental crisis; actually, it is the first developmental crisis of learning to trust the regularity and the predictability of major life events and to accept change as part of it. When solved, however temporarily, the individual can move into the next. Thus, development is a continuous process with each phase equally a part of the continuum, since every phase finds its antecedents in previous phases and its ultimate solution in those subsequent to it. Each successive stage provides the possibility of new solutions for previous questions, while an element of conservatism is always present because every early acquisition lives on in subsequent phases, in some form.

The developmental stages constitute the ego's timetable and mirror the structure of the relevant social institutions. An individual develops into his next phase as soon as he is biologically, psychologically, and socially *ready*, and his individual readiness is matched by societal readiness. Each phase introduces a new set of the intensive encumbrances of society and, together, these phases embrace a series of encumbrances that are instituted in human life. There are three essential variables: First, the inner laws of development which, like biological processes, are irreversible; second, the cultural influences which specify the desirable rate of development and favor certain aspects of the inner laws at the expense of others, and third, the idiosyncratic response of each individual and his particular way of handling his development in response to his society's demands. It should be pointed out that temporary regression in any of several major areas of development is considered to be a natural by-product of the developmental process. To cite Erikson's faith in the power of the ego, we quote this optimistic comment: "Children 'fall apart' repeatedly, and unlike Humpty Dumpty, grow together again" (50, 83). This power of the ego to integrate provides bridges for stages which would otherwise be inescapably discontinuous. Simultaneously, within each developmental phase, two opposing forces are brought together and demand a joint solution, or synthesis. The coexistence of these opposing forces generates the ego's real challenges and activation toward the opportunities offered in each developmental phase. Successful solution of the conflicts in each phase motivates upward movement on the scale of maturity. Erikson compares the negative counterparts in each phase to the hazards of decay in the body's metabolism (45). Both physical and psychological hazards are always present and must be conquered by the individual to prevent decay and deterioration. Retardation or failure in the development will rob the individual of his potential supremacy and endanger his whole hierarchy of development.

Erikson describes eight epigenetic developmental stages, with the last three falling within adulthood, but the first and last phases of childhood (phases I and V) have received more painstaking attention than the other three childhood phases. His special interest might be due to his personal fascination for these periods and to their strategic importance to our contemporary, western child-rearing efforts.

Each phase can be seen as both a vertical crisis, culminating in an individual psychosocial solution, and a horizontal crisis, calling for a personally and socially satisfactory solution to the problem of motivational forces. Infancy, childhood, and adolescence encompass the first five phases: (1) sense of basic trust, (2) sense of autonomy, (3) sense of initiative, (4) sense of industry, and (5) sense of identity. The three phases of adulthood are: (6) sense of intimacy, (7) sense of generativity, and (8) sense of integrity. Erikson purposefully prefaces each phase's descriptive title with the term "a sense of" because the affective feeling of having achieved or failed to accomplish a stage of trust, autonomy, initiative, industry, identity, etc. is the most important determining factor for development in succeeding phases. The developing individual strives to master the phasal theme (and to overcome its pitfalls). Achieving a positive "sense of"—that is, a notion of competency in the spheres most relevant at that particular point of his development—therefore, becomes the most important question for each individual. Consequently, the reader is urged to insert mentally the term "a sense of . . ." whenever, for the sake of brevity, the author uses Erikson's descriptive labels alone. Furthermore, Erikson employs the word *versus* (vs.) to indicate the vital struggle between the two poles.[4]

It should be noted that the recognition of development beyond

---

[4] The author has substituted a verb for Erikson's *versus* in an attempt to describe more specifically the process that takes place in the developing child, and to avoid the erroneous implication that the counterdirectional pulls could serve to neutralize each other.

the phase and age of adolescence furnishes a unique discovery in itself. In the study of child development, an understanding of the total span of development is essential, particularly since the caring adult is dealing with *his own developmental tasks while he is also instrumental in the child's development.*

Phase I: Acquiring a Sense of Basic Trust
While Overcoming a Sense of Basic Mistrust

Erikson locates the foundation for all later development in this first phase. After a life of rhythmic regularity, warmth, and considerable protection in the uterus, the young infant experiences the reality of life in his first contacts with the outer world. Although he is born naked, meek, and vulnerable,

. . . [he] is endowed with an appearance and with responses which appeal to the tending adults' tenderness and make them wish to attend his needs . . . [and] the vulnerability of being newly born and the meekness of innocent needfulness have a power all of their own. Defenseless as babies are, there are mothers at their command, families to protect the mothers, societies to support the structure of families and traditions to give a cultural continuity to systems of tending and training (38, 150–151).

He develops a sense of expectancy through a mixture of trust and mistrust. His *sense of basic trust*—as opposed to a sense of basic mistrust—becomes the critical theme in his first developmental phase.

For the neonate a sense of trust requires a feeling of physical comfort and a minimum experience of fear or uncertainty. If these are assured him, he will extend his trust to new experiences. In contrast, a sense of mistrust arises from unsatisfactory physical and psychological experiences and leads to fearful apprehension of future situations.

A sense of basic trust helps the individual to grow psychologically and to accept new experiences willingly. Each successful outcome of his trust tends to produce favorable, expectations of new experiences, which, however, always offer occasions for mistrust. Yet the young child must learn to trust even his own mistrust. For example, trusting the experience of mouthing new objects also includes a mistrust of the unknown. Only the trustworthy atmosphere of his immediate environment maintains his overall confident balance. A great share of the unknown and recurrent sources of mistrust can find firm assurance only through various forms of religious beliefs later in life, while during the child's infancy it is his parents' faith and conviction which assures his basic trust in, and genuine dependence upon, the well-being and order of his universe.

The first and fundamental developmental task of establishing a sense of basic trust, in general, coincides with the rapid maturational period of infancy. It is a period when body growth can be overwhelming and can invite much mistrust, unless new modes of body behavior provide adequate compensation. Maintaining the bodily functions of respiration, ingestion, digestion, and motor movements are the young organism's only concerns, and these comprise his immediate purpose for interacting with his environment. Thus, bodily experiences provide the basis for a psychological state of trust; bodily sensations become the first "social" experience, and are generalized in the individual's mind for future reference. Whether the infant is to become a trusting and easily satisfied person in society or a mistrusting and demanding person, essentially preoccupied with bodily needs, is, in large measure, determined by the form of handling he receives during this first phase.

Before further elaboration upon intertwining physical and psychological conditions, it will be necessary to trace the origin of all psychological forces. Psychological energy (*libido*) is present at birth and impels the organism to survive and to ward off destruction. This energy evolves from psychosocial experience, from bodily sensations, somatic needs, and environmental response to these sensations. Libidinal energy is generated by these organic-social events and expresses itself through *id* processes. Other undefined libidinal energy, unassociated to any life experience thus far, exists as *potential* id forces, ready to find expression when and wherever appropriate. While libidinal energy primarily turns into id functions, it also finds its expression in the first traces of *ego* functions. The infant's crying, sucking, visional reflexes, and motor movements are invested with libidinal energy, but become more and more cortically controlled (Erikson recognizes neurological maturation as an important component of ego development) until they become distinctly processes of the ego; superego functions are as yet undiscernible. The infant depends totally upon external care and control.

Libidinal energy becomes closely intertwined with the body zones around which the most crucial life experiences evolve; consequently, these zones become significant erotic centers for id and potential ego processes. During the first three to four months, much of the infant's routine centers around the intake of air, food, light, sound, and around other bodily stimulations. Of these, food intake involves the most regular and most significant contacts between the infant and his social environment; it is his mouth and his sucking activity which establish his primary contact with the outside world; and oral contact and suction alleviate a generalized sense of discomfort, and provide a source of satisfaction in themselves. Thus, the infant meets his society orally; he receives and gives love with his mouth by the modal behavior of incorporation, yet, it is neither the length of oral contact nor the quantity of food and sucking which determines the quality of the experience, but the nature of the interpersonal contacts that regulate these oral contacts and oral incorporation—that is, the quality of physical and psychological comfort inspired by the feeding and its termination—which determines the young organism's feeling about his early social life. The mother, or caring person, brings the social world to him. The environment expresses itself through the mother's breast, or the bottle substitute. Love and the pleasure of dependency, which is so important in this phase, are conveyed to him by the mother's embrace, her comforting warmth, her smile, and the way she talks to him.

Soon the young infant incorporates his oral, olfactory, visual, auditory, and motor faculties as their development becomes acute. Erikson speaks of an *oral-respiratory-sensory stage* in which all social contacts involve an *incorporative* mode. The quality of a sense of trust or mistrust is closely related to the first social modality—the acceptance of the environment as it is. Emotional experience depends on the reciprocity of receiving and giving, and involves the degree of relaxation and confidence which are connected with these acts. The young organism learns to regulate its system in accordance with the way in which the maternal environment is organized in its methods of child care. The infant coordinates receiving and trusting as one experience, according to the way his mother or any other central caring person coordinates giving and trusting in her care of him. As the infant matures, receiving includes reaching for, appropriating, and testing orally everything within his grasp.

The acts of receiving and reaching lead to the next social modality, grasping. Grasping and gripping also occur with the incorporative oral modality of prolonged sucking of the initial object—the nipple, or appropriate substitutes—and with visual perception, the localization of sounds, and tactile experiences. In situations where the initial sense of trust through receiving has been developed unsatisfactorily, the individual tends to employ random activities in an effort to obtain what he feels is lacking in the satisfaction of his needs. His dissatisfaction emanates from a lack of adequate integration, and a sense of distrust of living results from his meager experience of receiving.

As the baby grows, new pleasure is found through more active and aggressive interaction with his environment; this Erikson designates as the second oral stage. The incorporative mode reaches a climax at the time the first teeth develop. Grasping is now under full voluntary control, and visual perception extends to a larger field. In this second incorporative stage, the social mode of gripping is analogous to the process of clamping down (biting) with the new teeth, which it replaces as the essential modal behavior. Psychologically, the child tends to incorporate exclusively, to keep as his own what he acquires or is given. Experience has taught him by now that he can keep his environment through his own efforts. Erikson explains this desire to hold to be a reaction to the somatic experience of discomfort in teething, colic, or other early bodily discomforts. Yet, to hold on through biting frequently causes the withdrawal of the mother and a renewed urge to hold on even more vehemently is thus stimulated in the child. Biting as a sense of frustration is a secondary expression similar to the previously described random activity of reaching for what was felt to be inadequately given.

Oral development is thus the beginning of a continuous, constant experience of regularity and continuity in the child-mother relationship. Through his oral development, the child acquires his earliest experiences of appropriate and consistent satisfaction of his basic needs, and establishes for his developing ego unique patterns and boundaries of behavior. The infant associates more and more his inner stage of well-being with the consistent behavior of the caring person. Adverse experiences may retard his potential ego development; yet if trust has dominated in the child's early experience, he will readily face new situations and overcome any initial mistrust. Erikson locates in this first mutual exchange between mother and child a "cradle of faith [which] . . . permits a mother to respond to the needs and demands of the baby's body and mind in such a way that he learns once and for all to trust her, to trust himself and to trust the world" (47, 101).

Although Erikson sees the young infant as a participant within a social matrix, he recognizes that the infant appears to be totally egocentric, behaving as if he were all that existed and counted. In his very early forms of play, the baby relies entirely upon himself. His activity begins and centers upon his own body, with the repetition of sense perception, kinesthetic sensations, and vocalization. Through play is reflected the developmental theme of incorporation and holding. Slowly, play activities begin to include whatever in his objective world is within the baby's reach.

The continued, dependable child-mother relationship lays the foundation for a prospective identification of the child with his mother, as well as the mother with her child. In other words, the mother herself, and the feeling towards her that she produces within the child, stand for an inner reality and an outer predictability. A healthy identification further increases the mother's incentive to become the significant person in the child's life. The young child assimilates in himself his mother's qualities while he also projects upon the mother some of his own feelings. Children tend to identify with or to project those aspects of their immediate, peopled environment which affect them strongly in any way. The time table of this growing sense of belonging to a central person becomes evident in instances of separation. Erikson suggests that the sense of attachment to a central person becomes pertinent around the sixth month of life. Consequently, separation, however temporary, can be highly influential in an adverse way during this acute formative stage.

It must be noted that Erikson includes joint experience and mutual regulation of frustration as essential components of identification in terms of the basic sense of trust. The very experience of establishing mutual regulation results in moments of frustration for both child and mother. Only when frustration is not eventually solved in trust will frustration lead to feelings of uncertainty and a basic sense of mistrust. Children tend to sense the unconscious insecurities and intentions as well as the conscious thoughts and overt behavior of their parents, even though they do not understand their cause and meaning. In fact, Erikson does not ascribe much importance to individual habits or acts of skill in the mother's care of her child; he points instead to the underlying emotional and attitudinal themes which motivated the parent in her handling, care, and training of her child. Erikson suggests that early training efforts fail when "they become parent training rather than child training" (20, 270).

Adults other than the mother enter into the infant's life with equal influence, as the mother's temporary subsitute or as someone with some nurturing purpose—or as a deterrent to his nurture. The quality of maternal care depends to a degree upon the support that the mother receives from other adults in the household—usually the husband—the family into which the child is born, the society's recognition of the family as one of its basic institutions, and the culture's guarantee for the continuation of fundamental societal mores and values.

Phase II: Acquiring a Sense of Autonomy While Combating a Sense of Doubt and Shame

As the infant gains trust in his mother, his environment, and his way of life, he starts to discover that his behavior is his own; he asserts a *sense of autonomy*. Simultaneously, however, his physical, social, and psychological dependency create a certain sense of doubt of his capacity and freedom to assert his autonomy and to exist as an independent unit. This doubt becomes compounded by a certain shame for his instinctive revolt against his previously much enjoyed dependency, and by a fear of perhaps exceeding his own or his environmental limits. Erikson considers that these conflicting pulls in the child—to assert himself, and to deny himself the right and capacity to make this assertion—provide the major theme of the second phase. In this struggle, the young child experiences an inner urge to prove his own muscular strength and physical mobility, contrasted with an inherent reluctance to experiment with his potential capacities. The child needs sympathetic guidance and graduated support at this time lest he find himself at a loss and forced to turn against himself with much shame and doubt in his existence. The child ". . . must learn to *will* what *can* be, and to convince himself that he *willed* what *had* to be" (38, 155). This period roughly coincides with Freud's anal phase, which occurs between the ages of 18 months and 4 years.

Physically, the young child is undergoing an acceleration of maturation. His movements and mobility become well coordinated and mastered to the extent that reaching, walking, climbing, holding, and releasing are no longer activities in themselves, but rather the means for new endeavors. The youngster finds it increasingly difficult and undesirable to stay within his designated activity space; he wants to explore his world on his own and accomplish new feats. Newly improved and refined muscle control helps the child to regulate his eliminatory functions; he becomes capable of controlling his anal and urethral sphincter muscles. This maturational factor is further enhanced by his diet—now no longer comprised of soft foods—which permits a stool more receptive to control. At this time, the anal zone becomes the center of the child's physical, social, and psychological efforts.

Physical maturation is paralleled by an increase in libidinal energy and the channeling of this energy through the id, ego, and rudimentary superego forms of expression. The desire for autonomy and the negation of autonomy can be traced to the expression of violent id impulses. At times, these impulses are stronger than the child's capacity to cope with them, and they tax, also, the parents' capacity to deal with them. Generally, however, increased id impulsiveness coincides with further ego growth. Greater mobility, more refined perception, improved memory, and a greater capacity for neurological and social integration all point toward added ego strength. This constantly fluctuating balance between the id and ego processes is further influenced by the emergence of superego processes. However rudimentary, these processes increase as the child gains and utilizes his autonomy. As the child becomes relatively autonomous in certain areas of his life, he integrates into himself those controlling and direction-giving guidances which previously, in his utter dependency, were handled for him.

Erikson focuses upon the ego in this psychogenic development of the id, ego, and superego. It is the proper development of the ego which essentially spells healthy growth; it is the ego which permits an awareness of self as an autonomous unit in circumscribed areas of life and the integration of the experience of being autonomous. When the individual can see himself as an organism who can be what he will, and when he starts to perceive the "boundaries" between himself and his parent or parent surrogate, he expands his sense of trust within his expanding self. Although this trust, under ordinary circumstances, can no longer so easily be destroyed by his own strivings for independence or the demands of his controlling environment, the individual senses in himself and his world a danger of being caught in situations beyond his capacity to cope with them. This fear creates some doubt of himself and of his possible failure.

Many of this period's psychosocial contacts center around the newly gained modality of holding on and letting go. The child is preoccupied with activities of retaining and releasing perceptions, interpersonal relationships, desires, and manipulative objects. The alternative of retaining or releasing becomes libido-charged because usually it involves the interference, or the memory of the interference, from the parent. To hold and to let go with the hands, mouth, eyes, and, eventually, the sphincters, become incidents of real ambiguity and ambivalence, for such actions operate under the inner conflict of desire to return to old dependency situations versus the desire to try one's own initiative. Much of this struggle is apt to focus on sphincter control, since proper control of elimination carries considerable cultural importance in societies in most western cultures. Elimination also involves a newly erotic area of the child's body which, until this stage of his growth, has lain dormant. This erotic zone, consequently, becomes associated with the concurrent struggle for autonomy. The whole concern that the child eliminate at a designated place and time centers around the mother's approval of, and trust in, her child; her own self-esteem in doing her job well; and the child's feelings of discomfort, tension, and release of tension as the elimination routine becomes established. Such experiences provide a theme and a test for the child's general notion of self-regulation versus regulation by others. Toilet training leads to greater autonomy for the child, as well as to his subordination to adult direction and in an area of behavior which has heretofore been completely uninhibited. In a social culture where effective bowel training is not an essential concern during this particular developmental age, other behavioral areas may be treated by the parent similarly or analogously to bowel training. Naturally, as the area of concern becomes heavily charged with feeling, the child will transfer the meaning of this struggle into other areas of his life. He tends to treat related activities as if they were retainable, accessible to touch and disarrangement, or as if they needed to be expelled, avoided or cleansed. Many of his activities tend to center around collecting, hoarding, piling up versus discarding, and putting things in their proper places.

It has already been implied that much of the child's initial self-esteem and the release of his infantile sense of omnipotence, depend on his capacity to maintain the reassurance of trust in himself until he finds his ultimate balance of power. The frustration of this real or potential power of self-expression becomes of ever-increasing significance. The child must incorporate the experience of frustration as a reality of his life, and view it as a natural part of life events, rather than as a total threat to his life. Thus, it is important that the child sees, in this period, that an insult to his autonomy (such as frustration) in any one area does not render him impotent in all others.

Play assumes special importance during this phase and provides the child with a safe island where he can develop his autonomy within his own set of boundaries or laws. Doubt and shame are conquered when play proceeds according to these laws. Erikson says, ". . . the small world of manageable toys is a harbor which the child establishes, to return to when he needs to overhaul his ego" (20, 194).

The child's play, and his quick changes of mood from joyful certainty to utter helplessness and despair, provide visible proof that opposites are very close together. This proximity of opposites explains, in part, the proximal qualities of love and hate. This stage, therefore, becomes decisive for the ratio between love and hate, cooperation and willfulness, and the freedom of self-expression and its suppression. From a sense of *self-control without loss of self-esteem* comes a lasting sense of autonomy and pride; from a sense of muscular and anal impotence, of loss of self-control, and of parental over-control comes a lasting sense of doubt and shame (50, 112).

In these early childhood years, the child-parent relationship shifts. Much effort was devoted during the first phase of their joint history to establishing between mother and child a mutual trust and a willingness to face new situations together. In the second phase, the young child violates this mutual trust and tries to establish his autonomy in distinct areas. Vigorously he tries to do all on his own: to feed himself, to walk, to dress himself, and to open and shut things. To live, at this stage, means aggressively to expand, to act on one's own terms, and to insist on one's own boundaries.[5] Toilet training is but a single example typical of all the problems of this age. It reflects most dramatically the theme of child-parent relations, and the establishment of mutual regulations.

"[This sense of autonomy] is fostered by a handling of the small individual which expresses a sense of dignity and independence on the part of the parents and a confident expectation that the kind of autonomy fostered earlier will not be frustrated later (50, 120)." In this give-and-take between child and parent, much depends upon the parent's capacity to grant to the child gradual independence, at least within areas which are relatively safe. The parent's comfortable enjoyment of granting freedom in some areas while maintaining firmness in others will be reflected in the child's sense of tolerance and self-assurance. A parent's firmness, Erikson warns, ". . . must protect [the child] against the potential anarchy of his yet untrained sense of discrimination, his inability to hold on and to let go with circumspection" (50, 112). Most important, the responsibility for establishing wise limits rests with the parent. The child is still pliable; if he knows and fully understands the range of his limits, and what he is supposed to do, his growth will be largely healthy. Conversely, he becomes almost unapproachable when he finds himself involved in activities which he feels he understands and should be allowed to do but which are actually not permissible for him. It is at this point that the adult's tolerant firmness spells the difference between the child's establishment of his own capacity for self-management and self-control or his establishment of a gradually increasing sense of doubt and shame in himself. In the latter case, his self-doubt becomes an intolerable burden, because either he feels inadequate to prove himself, or he senses his unharnessed urges to control. In either situation, he doubts his capacity to become an independent being.

[5] These normal developmental attitudes of the young 2- to 4-year-old remind one of the spirit and proud nationalism usually associated with the life of a young nation.

The child's precarious position—especially in the first beginnings of an as yet very fragile conscience—is readily sensed by the wise parent. This is a period when the child learns to "blackmail" his parent with the threat of his regression (23). At the same time, however, this form of demanding, compared with the one based upon his complete dependency of the previous phase, fosters mutual regulation. The child learns to get somebody to do for him something that he wants done, while he himself learns to give, since all receiving involves some aspect of giving.

Father, and any adults in the child's immediate environment other than the mother, assume an ever-increasing significance in the awareness of the child. In his efforts to find the boundaries of his self, the child constantly comes in contact with different degrees of freedom in different areas of behavior with different adults. He quickly learns to utilize these differences, and he tends to relate to each adult differently. His sense of trust, or mistrust, as far as it has been acquired, is readily extended to others in the household to the degree of safe autonomy he can find with each. Similarly, for the first time, other children assume meaning for him. Erikson suggests that a newborn sibling is experienced as a rival, and is met with jealousy since the intruder necessarily demands a great deal of his mother's attention. This detraction from himself of the attention he has always had is compounded in its effect by the strong desire for dependency which still vies with his desire for autonomy. Other children assume significance only to the extent that they serve as play objects or as additional caterers to his needs for attention.

The child's social setting has direct bearing upon his ultimate realization of his sense of autonomy, or his doubts of it. For the child to release his thoughts and feelings through his behavior is intrinsically neither good nor bad for the child; these values depend on the cultural definition ascribed to the natural urges to assert himself, and will determine the kind of child-training devices used to regulate his behavior. All child-rearing patterns, Erikson points out, lead to some sense of doubt and shame. It is merely the particular behavior to which a positive or negative value is attached which varies from culture to culture, or from family to family. The degree and type of behavior permitted the child, and the way in which the control of his behavior is handled, will have direct bearing upon the individual's attitude toward social organizations and ideals later in his life. It is basic to Erikson's concept that the pattern of child training determines the eventual form of political authority the child finds most satisfactory, and, vice versa, that the political ideology of the time has an influence on the boundaries of acceptable child-rearing patterns.

Phase III: Acquiring a Sense of Initiative and Overcoming a Sense of Guilt

Having learned some measure of conscious control over himself and his environment, the individual can now rapidly move forward to new conquests in ever-widening social and spacial spheres. A *sense of initiative* permeates most of the child's life at a time when his social environment typically challenges him to be active and to master new tasks. This very quest to assume more responsibility for himself and for that which comprises his world (his own body, his toys, his pets, and, occasionally, a younger sibling) convinces him (and his society) that he *is* counted as a person, and that life has a purpose for him. Such a realization starts a flood of new questions which are but obscure variations of "yes, but what am I here to do?" As the child searches for and creates fantasies about the active person he wants to become, he consciously and unconsciously tests his powers, skills, and potential capacities. He initiates behavior the implications of which go beyond himself; he intrudes into others' spheres and gets others involved in his own behavior. This new approach includes considerable feelings of discomfort and guilt because what trusting autonomy he has achieved is necessarily frustrated to some degree by the separate, autonomous behavior of these others, which is not always in harmonious accord with his own, and above all, it negates to some extent previous forms of trusting dependency he had just previously formed with his caring adults. Consequently, he experiences some sense of guilt, with a corresponding desire to curtail all initiative that conflicts with the pull toward a continuance of his searching initiative. This latter pull leads to an even more intensified feeling of guilt stemming from the denial of his own desires and the opportunities offered him by his environment. This polarity of initiative versus either passivity or guilt for having gone too far—that is, living too strongly or too weakly compared to his inner strivings—provides the major theme of this period, usually encompassing the preschool and kindergarten years.

Erikson stresses that psychological mastery of the ambulatory field and organ modes encourages and reflects the child's maturational accomplishments. As far as maturation is concerned, the child has mastered the skills of reaching, taking, holding; he is now mastering those of walking, running, skipping, etc. He can next build upon these acquisitions, moving about with more freedom, knowledge, and energy in an expanding environment. The child discovers that in his greater mobility, he is not unlike the adults of his environment. This leads him to further comparisons, including striking differences which will raise questions and concerns within him. During this phase, his use of language has been improved; he now asks questions through which he begins to understand many old and new mysteries. This reaching out with language and locomotion permits the child to expand his fields of activity and imagination, and inevitably, some of the possibilities will frighten him. He can easily feel and fear, "I am what I can imagine I will be" (50, 127).

The child's innate urges to expand and to live unharnessed—urges which in general have been described as a constellation of id processes—can now find expression through the child's more fully developed body. The individual begins to reveal a readiness to come to conscious grips with his inner urges. Erikson recognizes a two-sided condition. The id processes demand new expression at a time when the ego has developed sufficiently to provide id processes with new modes of expressions. Simultaneously, the young superego has evolved sufficiently to learn from crisis situations. On the whole, the child is faced with the universal crisis of turning from an ". . . attachment to his parents to the slow process of becoming a parent, a carrier of tradition" (20, 225).

Naturally, the first step is to become his own "parent" by supervising himself in the role of his real parents. This process begins to operate during this phase. The child's conscience increasingly assumes the supporting and controlling functions of the significant adults in his environment. The superego is built from external "voices heard firmly enough," which, while they continue to be heard, are being more and more absorbed as the inner voices of the child's conscience. In one sense, the conscience is built from the model parents; in another—and truer—sense, the child's developing conscience is built of the parents' superegos and their sociocultural heritage (34). The parents' superegos— and, subsequently, to a considerable degree, that of the developing child—includes the tastes and class standards, as well as the characteristics and traditions, of the society's culture (26). Thus, the child will incorporate into his conscience what the parent really is as a person, and not merely what he tries to teach the child.

In spite of the powerful push of the id and the integrating functions of the superego, the ego determines major developmental accomplishments. The child invests much in refining his muscular activities, his accuracy in perception, his assessment of others, and his skills in communication. Speech represents more than mere communication; it involves assuming a particular position on a given issue or towards a situation and a verbal commitment to that position. The ego processes reflect the child's behavioral capacities and are directed toward a purposeful existence and a sense of self-identity which replaces the child's previous sense of egocentricity, and represents the child's psychological and behavioral sense of reality within the framework of his skills, knowledge, and emotional readiness in his expanding environment. However, this self-identity includes, also, the mistrust, doubts, fears and the other residues of the polar conflicts with which the child still wrestles as part of his conscious and unconscious efforts to cope with the everyday questions of life.

Psychological development in this phase centers in two major tasks. First, the id, ego, and superego start to find a mutual balance that the individual may become an integrated psychological unit, a personality in his own right. From now on, his development lays stress on his relationship to his parents, peers, and other human beings in his expanding universe. Second, the young individual begins to notice sexual differences among those in his environment, which affect him both in his own feelings (id impulses), and in the course he must pursue according to the social demands of his society; that is, his ego requirements and the social standards of his family frequently vie with his id impulses.

The child now faces a period of energetic learning which leads him through his limitations to future possibilities. The child associates, much of the time, with children of his own age. He enters actively into the lives of others and, thus, into a multitude of new experiences. Above all, he sees himself—he learns, associates, and experiences—as a boy or as a girl. At the same time, the child cannot escape the fact that his learning, his social contacts, and his experience introduce new thoughts, feelings, and imagined or accomplished deeds which will provide a new area for a sense of guilt. The child frequently fears he has gone beyond his rights, which, in fact, he frequently does. He continuously questions his sex role: is his behavior in line with what is expected of his sex? is it all right that, in many ways, he still feels and acts like a child of the opposite sex? is it all right that, in the matter of his sexual desires, he no longer feels like a child? Thus, this phase provides moments of feeling a sense of real accomplishments, and moments when the fear of danger and a sense of guilt are engendered.

During this developmental phase, Erikson, with Freud, locates the *Oedipus complex*, a psychological interrelationship between child and parent which both Erikson and Freud recognize as significant due to its pervading impact upon development in this and subsequent stages. Erikson accepts the Freudian theme that this period comprises a developmental crisis which has implications for the child in the family and for the family as representative of societal mores. Inner id urges to love and to be loved assume a new, more specifically sexual character within the context of the child's family, and they are the first desires for the expression of genital affection. These do not involve incest or incest taboo, but rather the fact that no other real love object other than the parent is available. A boy tends to attach his desires to his mother since it is she who has given him consistent comfort. The mother is apt to accept and to encourage her son's romantic attachment because she, also, senses the maleness in her son. At the same time, society challenges the boy to shift his *identification* to his father. The boy usually finds it easy to admire his father, because the father stands for those symbols of maleness (ego behavior and superego values) which his culture (particularly the specific culture of his home) values as desirable and admirable. A girl, on the other hand, tends to attach her desire to the most trusted and available man—usually her father. Again, this involves a question of propinquity rather than of incest. A girl's Oedipal relationship is one step removed from a boy's, because her desires are not usually attached to the same person upon whom she relied in her infantile dependency. Her Oedipal relationship to father is romantic, while her identification continues with the mother, who stands for all that is embodied in her own strivings for femaleness.

As the boy or girl finds a romantic attachment in the parent of the opposite sex, he or she tends to express mistrust of all those who will interfere with this new relationship. Again, old feelings of mistrust are aroused as the child senses the tenuous character of this new relationship. Naturally, a sense of rivalry develops with the parent of the same sex, which leads to two interdependent sequences. One involves the gradual replacement of the "wanted" parent by other more accessible love objects; that is, in persons who can safely become the recipients of his emotional investment, because the child finds his parent emotionally rather unattainable for him. The other sequence is linked with the child's more appropriate reality perception. Increasingly, he realizes the physical, social, and sexual inequality between himself and his "rival" parent. These factors, then, lead him to find new experiences and satisfactions by relating to those which are closer to his own age. While the parent is successfully replaced as the immediate love object, his or her position becomes enhanced as the ego ideal for the opposite sex. The parent of the same sex becomes the super-ego's model. He tries to achieve this parent's own aspirations, but rarely succeeds. Most important, the parent of his own sex serves as his major identificand.

Boys and girls develop a keen interest in the genitalia of both sexes. Awareness of differences, especially the absence of visible organs in the case of girls, creates specific concerns. Both sexes imagine that something happened to the female genitalia and that it may also happen to the male genitalia. This fear creates uncertainty and presents a potential for all kinds of fears or imagined guilt in relation to this and other unexplained events.

The modality of this stage is different for each sex, although both modalities have an active, aggressive undertone, with conquest as a goal, and both eventually constitute the individuals' expressions of mature maleness or femaleness. Erikson, with Freud, considers this as the genital phase. Psychologically, erotic fantasies and feelings tend to center around the genitals which constitute the major erotic zone of this phase.

The boy's essential modality during this phase involves intrusion—a thrusting forward into space, time, new areas of knowledge, and into people's lives. The last reflects more specifically the boy's basic sexual desire, which translates into such expressions as intense locomotor activities with a penetration of space, curiosity for exploring all unknown spheres, and attacking people and problems head-on. The modality of intrusion finds its most natural expression in dealing with his ordinary life events. His talking and questioning, his activities, and his social relationships all have an intrusive character. As he moves through this phase, which includes resolving his Oedipal strivings, his sexual preoccupation tends to shift its emphases from people to creative play.

The essential modality for girls involves inception, analogous to the biosexual position of the female—inviting or luring an intruder —leading toward the active passivity of the girl and future woman. Now the libidinal sexual drives translate into expressions of making oneself attractive and endearing, of inviting, scheming, teasing, and—above all—to an early adaptation of the maternal mode of incorporation. During this phase, the young girl begins to prepare herself for her future maternal role. Her way of communication, her activities, and her social relations reflect the ever-increasing behavioral and psychological characteristics of getting others to include her into their lives.

Thus, boys and girls, each differently, find new means for solving their conflicting drives of this phase. Play, which serves as the most indispensable and natural autotherapeutic agent, takes two essential forms in this phase. First, the child needs time to himself when he can indulge in solitary play or in undisturbed day-dreaming, during which he can "play out" or "dream out" his conflicts in their resolution. The child also needs the company of other children in order to "play out" together their individual and mutual life crises. At times, small objects are employed to play out the conflicting forces experienced by the child in his life (40); at other times, his play relationship with real people serves as an opportunity for solving previous defeats or unresolved problems. However, the child's greater sense of reality sometimes becomes a liability in play, because he frequently attaches a forbidden (though necessary) meaning to his play fantasies and this leads to a further sense of guilt. In these cases, the child is tensely ready to interrupt his "forbidden" play for fear of being discovered and he often does so at the very moment when the play has reached the autotherapeutic point.

The Oedipal phase has lifted the child-parent relationship into a triangular situation, in which the child has become an independent and active, if not competitive, partner. As we have suggested, only the child who has successfully experienced autonomy can relinquish his romantic possession of the parent. The child who has been less successful has need to cling to such support. He has to be certain of himself as an individual, otherwise he becomes entangled again in the question, "what is me?" versus "what is not me but the other?"

Child and parents work together on problems related to the child's development that are beyond his immediate demands.

Slowly, his concern becomes extended to matters of social trust and mistrust and his relationship to the society that lies beyond his family. When the parents work and play with the child, they can convey common identification with people, ideas, and values beyond themselves. Parents continue to serve as a brake whenever the child's incomplete ego or immature superego needs support or control.

In addition, other significant persons are needed in the child's life at this period, for the child can envisage goals beyond his family. He needs other people in order to experiment with various alternatives of his behavior. The child begins to realize differences between his own standards and those of adults. His parents seem to him to be allowed to do things which he is not so allowed. Rivalry shifts from competition for dependency-satisfaction to competition for full partnership. Older siblings replace younger ones as potential rivals.

The child enters with all his inquisitiveness and adventurousness into his ever-widening social circle. He wants to find out about his world, and he is increasingly encouraged to conform to the teachings of his society in his unfolding world. Nursery schools, kindergarten, and primary grades are the major social institutions which, along with the home and church, indicate to the child the range of initiative appropriate for him at this particular time of life. Gradation of inquisitiveness and permissible aggression by age, sex, and social roles are cultural devices which, ideally, help the individual to develop to his best advantage within the context of his culture.

Erikson draws a relationship between the degree of individual initiative fostered or permitted, and the community's economic system. He implies that the individual's potential capacity to work and to achieve economic success within the framework of his society's economic order depends upon his mastery of this developmental phase.

We have already alluded to the observation that the child seems to grow integratedly into a physical and psychological unit. The young child becomes himself. He tests his forward-surging independence in relation to the many facets of the immediate and expanding environment. The child can gradually gain some insight into the institutions, opportunities, and roles which will permit his prospective responsible participation as an adult. He finds pleasurable accomplishment in manipulating meaningful toys, in wielding tools, and in taking responsibility for himself and younger children. The child's unsuccessful effort to relate to one of his parents and to push out the other leads to eventual successes in different life tasks. His great energy permits him to forget failures quickly, and to start again with better aimed efforts. He finds that he was moving in the right direction, even if at the wrong time. Most guilt and failure quickly become compensated by a sense of accomplishment, ". . . the future is emphasized as against the past. The future absolves the past" (26, 385).

Phase IV: Acquiring a Sense of Industry
and Fending Off a Sense of Inferiority

The child's forward searching has brought him into contact with a wealth of new experience. He soon realizes that he needs to find a place among those of his own age because, as a young school-age child, he is neither capable nor invited to take equal part in the realm occupied by his adults. Consequently, the child directs all his abundant energies towards working on those social problems he can successfully master. The major theme of this phase reflects his determination to master whatever he is doing. The polarity of this phase is, as Erikson phrases it, a *sense of industry* versus a *sense of inferiority*. On one side, there is unceasing energy to invest all possible effort in producing. Opposing this is the ever-present pull toward a previous level of lesser production. The fear of the latter is also supported by the very fact that he is still a *child*, an incomplete person, which tends to give him feelings of inferiority. Roughly between the ages of 7 to 11, the child tries to solve these fears of inferiority; he delves diligently into all opportunities to learn by doing and experiments with the rudimentary skills required by his culture. As he learns to wield his culture's tools and symbols, the child seems to understand that this sort of learning will help him to become more himself.

Physical maturation slows as if to consolidate what has already been acquired. Psychological development reflects a similar pattern. Boy and girl have found, temporarily, their respective psychological and social boundaries. Each can face the opposites realistically without loss of self-esteem, and each can work on filling in the vast gaps within the present limits of his or her own capacities.

The Freudian concept of latency can be rephrased: There is nothing latent in the middle years except the strivings toward involvement with a partner of the opposite sex. The "latent" child continues to invest as much of himself and his libidinal energy as he did before, and works incessantly on his bodily, muscular, and perceptive skills, as well as on his growing knowledge of the world, which becomes increasingly important to him. Above all, he concentrates on his capacity to relate to and to communicate with the individuals who are most significant to him—his peers. A sense of accomplishment for having done well, being the strongest, best, wittiest, or fastest are the successes toward which he strives. The child wards off failure at almost any price. As long as ego tasks are mastered within the spheres of his own age group, the id and superego remain unchallenged and within safe boundaries. Most of the child's efforts are devoted toward improving his ego processes, because his society hints that his very handling of the ongoing situation will determine his future. He senses that if he proves his skills within the areas of his best competence, his successful future will be assured.

Children's pursuits continue to be, in part, even more clearly segregated by sex, although in immediate situations, boys or girls find it easier to express their bisexual interests and to indulge temporarily in activity which ordinarily is reserved for the opposite sex. Essentially, however, all activities and feelings reflect competitive, rather than autonomous, striving. In trying to excel in anything and everything he tries, the child is not attempting a psychological or real elimination of others—on the contrary, the child wants and needs the continued association and cooperation of others—but he needs his contemporaries primarily to measure his own skills and worth. He becomes particularly interested in the operations of the material world which he tries to translate into the modalities of his own social life; the relationship between strength and social power may serve as an example. "He learns to exist in space and time as he learns to be an organism in the space-time of his culture. Every part function thus learned is based on some integration of all the organ modes with one another and with the world image of their culture" (20, 91).

In his play, the child relies much upon the social aspect and he incorporates into play activity real-life situations. Sex is not necessarily the content of play, and the two sexes tend to segregate in separate play habits, although, upon occasion, boys and girls enter into each other's worlds, sometimes participating in play which in general is thought of as particularly appropriate for the other sex. Nevertheless, the basic modalities related to psychosocial sex roles ultimately determine the major preoccupation of an individual's play. Play begins to lose importance at the end of this phase. Beginning with puberty and the onset of adolescent values, the individual slowly ceases his previous habits, and, what once had been an industrious involvement in play, slowly merges into semiplayful and eventually real involvement in work. Adolescents tend to steer a middle course between play and work, between childhood and adulthood.

Child-parent relationships evolve to a realistic level of dependency in those areas where dependency has still been necessary or desirable, while in other areas, the child tends to relate to his parents and other adults on a more equal basis. The child has begun to recognize that he must eventually break with his accustomed family life. By this age, he has overcome—temporarily, at least—his Oedipal power struggle. Since the child sees his parents as representatives of the society in which he must operate, he now begins to measure them against other representatives. Friends of his parents and the parents of his friends assume a new importance for him, his neighborhood and school become significant social determiners for him, and strangers become intriguing and important discoveries. Boys and girls search for other adults to identify with, because their parents can no longer entirely fulfill such qualifications. As long as boys and girls remain free of vocational and marital commitments, they may shift their ideals and personal dedication to any one or to any combination of adult roles, and they will identify with those aspects of people which are most meaningful to them without considering the total personality and situation of the person.

The world of peers assumes a position of equal importance to that of adults; peers are needed for self-esteem, and serve as criteria for the measurement of the boy's or girl's own success or failure, and among them, the child finds another source of extra-familial identification. Interestingly, siblings are no longer significant competitors unless they happen to be members of the peer age group. As the child develops, society seems to become more and more concerned with admitting him on an equal basis, and schools, churches, and youth organizations encourage him toward more advanced participation. The focus has shifted, then, from dependence upon the parent as the child's major influence, to dependence upon social institutions.

Erikson stresses that many of the individual's later attitudes toward work and work habits can be traced to the degree of a successful sense of industry which has been fostered during this phase. Ruth Munroe summarizes best Erikson's contentions:

> Native abilities allow the development of skills prized by his culture, if the wider society, mainly the school, offers good ways of admitting the child to an understanding of meaningful roles in its total economy —then this period of life has enormous functional importance in preparing the child for his later contribution to society and to his own later family in the area of work (80, 220–221).

A stress upon the virtue of skilled craftsmanship lays the roots for later scientific pursuit.

In acquiring a sense of industry and in fending off a sense of inferiority the child must have successfully sublimated many of his previous desires. During this time, the youth is frequently described as being "too big for his boots." The youth devotes his abundant energies to self-improvement and to the conquest of people and things. His drive to succeed includes an awareness of the threat of failure and this underlying fear impels the young person to work harder to succeed, because any half-way measure, any mediocrity, will lead him too close to a sense of inferiority, a feeling the child must combat in order to move on with self-assurance towards his adulthood.

Phase V: Acquiring a Sense of Identity While Overcoming a Sense of Identity Diffusion

A *sense of identity* carries with it a mastery of the problems of childhood and a genuine readiness to face, as a potential equal, the challenges of the adult world. Just as a sense of trust was once necessary for the infant to branch out into new childhood experiences, so is the acquisition of a sense of identity essential for making adulthood decisions, such as the choice of a vocation or a marriage partner. It is interesting to note that the apparent combination of Erikson's special interest in the adolescent phase and public preoccupation with the various facets of this phase's crises lead him to present a more comprehensive schema for this than for any other stage.

Identity Consciousness then is a new edition of the original *doubt*, which concerned the trustworthiness of the training adults and the trustworthiness of the child himself—only that in adolescence, such self-conscious doubt concerns the reliability and reconcilability of the whole span of childhood which is now to be left behind (34, 99).

It is noteworthy, also, that the youth's concerns revolve around the question, "Which way can I be?" He seldom inquires: "Who am I?" because his identity depends upon his *becoming* his identity. A sense of identity requires the subordination of childhood identifications to newly selected identifications and insurance against the resurgence of previous conflicts and confusions. A sense of identity and a sense of identity diffusion make a polarity of both conscious and unconscious strivings. At the one end, there is striving toward an integration of inner and outer directions, and, at the opposite end, there is diffusion, leading to a sense of instability in the midst of many confusing inner and outer demands. This polarity must be solved within the span of adolescence if transitory or lasting disturbances in adulthood are to be prevented. A certainty of his place in the present and future assures the individual of his immediate confidence and his advance beyond the past levels of development. Erikson quotes an aphorism which was found in a western cowboy bar:

> I ain't what I ought to be, I ain't what I'm going to be, but I ain't what I was. (50, 139).

As the child physically matures into the adult, he experiences rapid body growth with important psychological and anatomical changes. His previous trust in his body and his mastery of its functions are suddenly shaken, and must be regained gradually by reevaluating himself. He seeks assurance from his peers who are also in a stage of change and seeking approval. Puberty rites and religious confirmation frequently serve as cultural seals of the individual's new status within the continuity of his developmental self.

Major maturational changes invariably upset the balance in the id-ego-superego integration, and new psychological forces, mostly of id origin, need to be integrated. What were previously temporarily dormant or sublimated psychosexual drives, now demand the full attention of the youth, and desire for sexual fulfillment in a partner of the opposite sex can no longer be diverted as inappropriate or ridiculous, because, finally, they are physically derived from an advanced biological stage, the genital stage. Intensified id processes are balanced, in part, by more universal and age-bound superego processes. Fundamentally, however, it is the adolescent ego which must contain the postpubertal id and which must balance the newly invoked superego. The repetition of the Oedipal theme finds the youth in a different social matrix, no longer confined to his dependent position within his family. Furthermore, his ego processes are no longer dwarfed by powerful id processes. More likely than not, they have reached the point where they help the individual differentiate his boundaries and the problems he can handle in his everyday life from those which are beyond his immediate capacity to solve. Oedipal desires will attach themselves to the youth's remaining ties with his parents, and he will search for new and more satisfactory expression in his relationships outside his family. Now, the child-parent relationship is transitory, solely anchored in its joint history in the past and its mutual anticipation of the youth's future. In other words, the parents enter into the healthy youth's life only by virtue of their joint social and psychological history and their common belief in his future. Otherwise, they remain with others as significant adults in the eyes of the youth.

In adolescence, the ego gradually establishes a synthesis of the past and future. It is this synthesis which is the essential challenge of this final phase prior to sociopsychological adulthood. It could be described as a period of self-standardization in the search for sexual, age, and occupational identity. The youth searches for a sense of self, a commitment to specific roles selected from many alternatives, because identification with an ego ideal or person no longer serves its full usefulness. At this period of his life, the youth integrates all previous identifications. Their gradual but full integration comprises an ego identity. The youth then realizes his fidelity to his new position as a person in his ultimate psycho-social-economic and cultural spheres. He finds promise for an expanded future with the aid of a more universal identity.

Many late adolescents, Erikson points out, are faced with continued identity diffusion concerning their own potentialities and their prospective place within their society. The question of this phase, "Who am I to be?" continues to be everpresent. The individual is apt to solve his dilemma by becoming delinquent, thus choosing the identity opposite to the one society suggests, in preference to remaining a nonentity. Negative identity reflects ". . . a desperate attempt at regaining some mastery in a situation in which available positive identity elements cancel each other out" (34, 88).

Adolescence represents a socially authorized delay of adulthood, as a psychological safety device. Erikson draws the analogy that adolescence as a period of extended childhood provides a psychosocial moratorium, just as latency furnishes a *psychosexual moratorium* (34). The social institutions of various cultures provide status to such institutionalized moratoria as extended formal education, apprenticeship, military conscription, internship, etc. The moratorium incorporates both pulls of the phase's polarity. It sanctions and provides certainty to identity diffusion. It becomes an essential, temporary component of adolescent development. Erikson explains clearly:

> A moratorium is a period of delay, granted to somebody who is not ready to meet obligation or forced on somebody who should give himself time to do so. Here I mean delay of adult commitments, and yet not only a delay. I mean a period that is characterized by a selective permissiveness on the part of society and of provocative playfulness on the part of youth; and yet also a period of deep (if often transitory) commitment on the part of youth and ceremonial acceptance of commitment on the part of society. Such moratoria show highly individual variations, which are especially pronounced in very gifted people (gifted for better or for worse); and there are of course, institutional variations linked with the ways of life of cultures and subcultures (27, 5).

Thus, the individual requires time to integrate himself into adulthood, and society grants him this time. The youth experiments with patterns of identity before he makes more complete decisions. He takes time out from a commitment to a continuous development. It may occur in any combination or simply in any of the following seven dimensions, with each dimension representing a partial polarization of developmental crises on the developmental continuum (29, 30, 136).

1. *Time perspective vs. time diffusion:* A concept of time is essential to identity. If his time perspective is a problem, the youth may demand immediate action or he may immobilize himself completely, in the desperate hope that time will stand still and that feared disappointment will never materialize (136). Intermittently, the adolescent utilizes opportunities to delay planning and to recall the past. Only when he can see his life in a definite perspective does his sense of time lead to a sense of full identity.

2. *Self-certainty vs. apathy:* Self-certainty involves a struggle between identity consciousness and an escape into apathy. In adolescence, the youth can convey an air of total vanity or callousness as if his appearance were all that mattered, or as if it were of no consequence whatever. Only when his awareness of self and the impressions which he conveys to others coincide does he gain certainty of self and a sense of his own identity, while his self-consciousness, with its attendant feelings of doubt and confusion about himself and his autonomy, recedes.

3. *Role experimentations vs. negative identity:* The developing child finds many opportunities to experiment with many roles, while the adolescent finds experimentation is qualified with dangers and commitments. For him, experimentation is critical. Interests in extremes, experiments with opposites, especially those frowned upon by elders, become the center of their role experimentations with their self-images. Eventually identity, positive or negative, depends upon successful experimentation with a wide range of roles.

4. *Anticipation of achievement vs. work paralysis:* The adolescent needs to bring his sense of industry to bear in a persistent pattern in preference to unrelated situational opportunities. A struggle to complete a task, or sometimes even to start one at all, becomes a crucial issue as the youth ponders his sense of the adequacy of his own equipment. "It does not usually betoken lack of ability; in fact, [at times] some of the most gifted suffer from it most extremely" (136, 3). Persistency and integration are essential for forging an occupational identity and for making long-range plans.

5. *Sexual identity vs. bisexual diffusion:* The adolescent needs to resolve his bisexual conflicts and eventually to feel identification with his own sex role. He needs to experience comfort in his range of contacts with the members of the opposite sex. He needs to see himself first as wholly male (or female). The adolescent cannot conceive himself at this point to be a bit of both. Adolescence furnishes situations and attitudes for continued experimentations which need to be resolved if his sexual identity is to contribute

toward a fuller sense of identity and to move him toward behavior prescribed for adults of his sex.

6. *Leadership polarization vs. authority diffusion:* The adolescent's capacity to lead and to follow must coincide with the authority index of his society. A realistically clear appraisal of authority—and a readiness to be in authority, if called upon—are closely linked with the successful mastery of previous developmental phases and with the eventual acceptance of a positive identity.

7. *Ideological polarization vs. diffusion of ideals:* The adolescent must select a basic philosophy, ideology, or religion, which will provide the anchoring trust in his life and society. Adolescence affords many choices. However, "Adolescents tend to be uncompromising in their prejudices and belligerently loyal to their own group's ideas and values. This being against something is one of their greatest needs, for through contrasting themselves and their ideas with an opposite group's, they firm up their sense of themselves" (136, 4).

During adolescence the individual has the opportunity to work on these seven areas and to utilize the many facets of his moratorium. The ". . . extremes of *subjective experience,* alternatives of *ideological choice,* and potentialities of *realistic commitment* can become the subject of social play and of joint mastery" (34, 119). If the moratorium fails, the individual has either defined himself too early and is committed to adult society before he is ready, or he has strong feelings of failure at being left to the danger of this period's crisis, and he finds himself at a loss as a person. In the latter situation, he does not know what he actually wants to be or who he really is in the eyes of others. Ambivalence occurs in the behavioral, as well as in the verbal and cognitive, activities. In fact, articulating and meditating upon alternatives are important. Speech often merely reflects thinking aloud. The adolescent habit of talking things over endlessly with a special friend of the same sex and age group is one of the means of searching for an identity. Once a lasting identity commitment is made, speech is no longer important merely as a means of communication; it also becomes essential in revealing a commitment to the social values consistent with his identity.

Play has already lost importance as a major ego function. The youth no longer has to play at being important. He is now more apt to find himself playing at being younger as an outlet for his regressive pulls, because his society frowns on childish behavior at his age level. Erikson describes role playing and excursions into fantasy in adolescence as an appropriate handling of identity diffusion. Role playing and verbal exaggeration of the "I dare you" and "I dare myself" variety is a form of social play and a legitimate successor to childhood play (49b). "In the healthy adolescent, a great capacity for phantasy is matched by ego mechanisms that permit him to go far into dangerous regions of phantasy or social experiment and to catch himself at the last moment and divert himself in company, in activity, in literature or music" (27, 13). This play, or social experimentation, includes primarily attitudes and roles of adult significance—occupational behavior, preparation for intimacy, the selection of a future life partner, etc. Further, gang, clique, or crowd behavior, with its insistence upon rituals and other conformities for the members of the group, involves a basic aspect of role playing and an urge for self-expression. The youth will select his significant adults, people who have come to mean most to him. They are significant for him either by their past influence or by ongoing pivotal relationships. In this former group, the child might locate his parents, teachers, neighbors, and other well known trust-inspiring persons. The latter are selected for their meaning to the adolescent in his temporary role diffusion rather than for their societal functions. If they are acceptable to the youth, social workers, psychologists, priests, judges, recruiting officers, play managers, dance instructors, or anyone to whom the youth might turn in his search could become a crucially influential person in his adolescent development.

Parents have lost their roles as the essential supports and value givers, and have been replaced by the individual's peer group. Peers absorb most of the prevailing social interest and energy of the developing adolescent. They become age mates and partners.

A shift to competitive partnership with and among age mates began in previous phases and becomes a real fact in the current phase. Such peer relations serve as an essential authority in finalizing ego identity. Adolescent friendships, and loves, and the over-identification with, or complete rejection of, certain heroes are attempts at arriving ". . . at a definition of one's identity by projecting one's diffused ego images on one another" (**20,** 228). Peers stand as intermediaries in a society in which the adolescent must eventually find his inner identity—and the continuity of his identity—to others as an intimate partner, and as a person with an occupational and social career.

Just as the individual is faced with the crisis of this phase, which is to make a choice compatible with himself and with the opportunities of his society, so society is faced with the difficulty of extending sufficient time, space, and social freedom to the adolescent without denying its ultimate range of control and guidance over him. Actually, in spite of the glaringly apparent discrepancies between the standards and aims of the youth and those of his society, there is little danger of him deviating too far from social norms. All of his efforts are directed towards the clarification of his role as a member of his society. Erikson emphasizes that adolescence is not affirmation, but a normative crisis (**34**). "In youth, then the [individual's] life history intersects with history; here individuals are confirmed in their identities, societies regenerated in their life style" (**46,** 23).

The individual slowly moves into society as an interdependent member. He left the heavy dependency upon his family two phases ago; he now requires full status alongside his peers in society. His gradual growth and transformation make sense to those who begin to make sense to him. He finds increasingly new and more inclusive identifications, whether they are with sections of a neighborhood block, a pondered occupation, or an association of kindred minds (**46**). Adolescents ". . . press urgently toward the cultural image of adulthood with much underlying anxiety and reversion to earlier attitudes" (**80,** 410). Their previously developed trust in their environment and their understanding of themselves as creative units sets the tone for their ultimate level of participation in the adult realm. Whenever these foundations have not solidified, there is the danger that his elders will assign the individual an identity which was only a part of him in his identity diffusion. In such instances, society may stamp him as "delinquent," a poor worker, a clown, etc., even though the individual might have only temporarily maintained such a negative identity (30), or, to quote a character from a Faulkner novel: "It ain't none of us pure crazy and ain't none of us pure sane until the balance of us talks him that-a-way" (48, 43). At no other phase of the life cycle, then, is the promise of finding oneself and the threat of losing oneself so closely allied (46).

The youth also looks to his culture's values, religion, and ideology, as a confirmed source of trust. Religion and social ideologies provide a clear perspective for man's underlying philosophy. This counteracts autonomous and individual identities. The youth searches for something and somebody to be true. It is reflected in a ". . . bewildering combination of shifting devotion and sudden perversity, sometimes more devotedly perverse, sometimes more perversely devoted" (46, 6). Such a search induces collective roles and experimentations which will combat individual inhibitions and guilt feelings. They help to solve the desire for self-assertion versus submission to a leader, such as a father figure or a big brother. Above all, they assure genetic continuity of one's identity and self-esteem as a member of one's society and culture (34). A sense of identity assures the individual a definite place within his own corner of society. The youth finds his fidelity (a word Erikson adroitly applies in one of his most recent writings, 38, 46). As the youth blends from adolescence into adulthood, his

. . . progressive continuity between that which he has come to be during the long years of childhood and that which he promises to become in the anticipated future; between that which he conceives himself to be and that which he perceives others to see in him and to expect of him (43, 165).

A horizontal chart of this developmental multidimensional foci is clearly presented in Erikson's *epigenetic chart* (Table 2.1).

TABLE 2.1. *Erikson's Epigenetic Chart of Developmental Phases.*

	INFANCY	EARLY CHILDHOOD	PLAY AGE	SCHOOL AGE	ADOLESCENCE	YOUNG ADULT	ADULTHOOD	MATURE AGE
I. INFANCY	Trust vs. Mistrust				Unipolarity vs. Premature Self-Differentiation			
II. EARLY CHILDHOOD		Autonomy vs. Shame, Doubt			Bipolarity vs. Autism			
III. PLAY AGE			Initiative vs. Guilt		Play Identification vs. (oedipal) Fantasy Identities			
IV. SCHOOL AGE				Industry vs. Inferiority	Work Identification vs. Identity Foreclosure			
V. ADOLESCENCE	Time Perspective vs. Time Diffusion	Self-Certainty vs. Identity Consciousness	Role Experimentation vs. Negative Identity	Anticipation of Achievement vs. Work Paralysis	Identity vs. Identity Diffusion	Sexual Identity vs. Bisexual Diffusion	Leadership Polarization vs. Authority Diffusion	Ideological Polarization vs. Diffusion of Ideals
VI. YOUNG ADULT					Solidarity vs. Social Isolation	Intimacy vs. Isolation		
VII. ADULTHOOD							Generativity vs. Self-Absorption	
VIII. MATURE AGE								Integrity vs. Disgust, Despair

SOURCE: Reprinted with permission from E. H. Erikson, "Identity and the Life Cycle: Selected Papers," *Psychological Issues* (Monograph), New York, International Universities Press, 1959, I:1.

*Phase VI: Acquiring a Sense of Intimacy and Solidarity
and Avoiding a Sense of Isolation*

With his childhood and youth at an end, the individual begins life as a full member in our western society. Now it is time for him to settle seriously to the task of full participation in the community; it is time for him to enjoy life with adult liberty and responsibility. For Erikson, the achievement of psychological adulthood entails continued growth and sociopsychological time devoted to study or to work at a specified career, and social intercourse with the other sex in order to select a partner for the extended intimate relationship of marriage.

Ego-identity acquires its final strength in the meeting of mates whose ego-identity is complementary in some essential point and can be fused in marriage without the creation either of a dangerous discontinuity of tradition, or of an incestuous sameness—both of which are apt to prejudice the offspring's ego development (26, 381).

The major developmental theme now involves psychological readiness and a commitment to mutual intimacy in marriage. Readiness includes the ability and willingness to share mutual trust, to regulate cycles of work, procreation, and recreation for each partner's fullest and most self-satisfying participation in society to prepare a foundation for the healthy development of their potential offspring. To find *a sense of solidarity* in choosing a mate who represents the ideal of all past experience with the opposite sex is a hazardous undertaking and this is reinforced by a counter developmental crisis of a sense of isolation and distance in remaining single. This counter crisis is infused with feelings of social emptiness and of being an isolated unit within a world of family units. Moreover, the crisis involves a mode of genitality, which was sublimated earlier, the solution of which is afforded through marriage. To use Freud's words, he demonstrates his capacity for a healthy adulthood by his ability in *Lieben und Arbeiten* (love and work). He achieves a personalized pattern of living which guarantees him an "individual identity in joint intimacy" (38, 159). Curiously enough, in the worlds of work and love we speak of finding a career. In work and in marriage, career efforts are directed towards improving and interpreting patterns of cooperation with varying allowances for competition, and for patterns of love, friendships, and other associations. If these efforts are not satisfied in marriage, an individual must isolate himself and find solutions which deviate from the accepted norm into more formal interpersonal relationships, and in rather disjointed love associations. This holds true for the spheres of both work and love. Graduation from adolescence requires a sense of identity; graduation from the first phase of adulthood requires finding a *sense of shared identity*. The solidarity of marriage is an evolutionary and individual achievement of the selectivity of sexual love, ". . . for the mutual verification through an experience of finding oneself, as one loses oneself, in another" (38, 158).

Phase VII: *Acquiring a Sense of Generativity and Avoiding a Sense of Self-Absorption*

Establishing a new unit based upon mutual trust and intimacy includes the preparation of a home to begin a new cycle of development through a division of labor within the shared household. A healthy marriage union serves as the foundation for promising new offspring a satisfactory development. This very concern for the next generation embodies the theme of the second developmental phase of adulthood, a sense of generativity versus a sense of stagnation. It should be noted that "generativity" and "stagnation" do not refer to the procreating individual, but to the course he pursues to establish with his mate for the next generation, and to provide care for the next generation which will stem from all the virtues and wisdom he has accumulated. A sense of generativity within an individual includes parental responsibility for his society's efforts and interests in supporting measures for child care, education, the arts and sciences, traditions which soon will enter into the newly developing individual's life span. Each individual's life involves a career amalgamating love for his children as well as his work and ideas. His personal, creative, and ideational life, and his community, have to become one, unless self-absorption drains and estranges his efforts and himself from his community. Each adult accepts or rejects the challenge of accepting the next generation as his responsibility and of assuring this new generation the trust outlined in the first Eriksonian developmental phase.

Phase VIII: Acquiring a Sense of Integrity and Avoiding a Sense of Despair

Finally, as the adult procreates and assures development to this new generation, he gains a fuller perspective of his own cycle; he develops a *sense of integrity*. He accomplishes the fullest sense of trust as the "assured reliance on another's integrity" (20). Thus, the first developmental theme evolves into the final one, while the final theme clearly has its roots in the first one. Integrity rests upon an acceptance of mankind's collective and individual life cycle as ". . . something that has to be and that, by necessity, permitted no substitutions: it thus means a new, different love of one's parents. It is a comradeship with the ordering ways of distant times and different pursuits" (20, 232). If it is acquired, a sense of integrity provides a successful solution to an opposing sense of despair and disgust of the many life styles, and of fear of death as the end to an unfulfilled life. In other words, this final phase involves a sense of wisdom and a philosophy of life which often extends beyond the life cycle of the individual, and which is directly related to the future of new developmental cycles. To quote Erikson, ". . . healthy children will not fear life, if their parents have integrity enough not to fear death" (20, 233).

AMERICAN CULTURAL INFLUENCES ON DEVELOPMENT

Throughout Erikson's writings are sprinkled a number of concepts which he defines as distinctly culture-bound, and which are of particular importance to child and family development in the interacting subcultures of America.

First, Erikson stresses the rapidity of the ongoing changes of all social and cultural practices. As he states it, "One can become an American to some extent in one's own lifetime even if one started elsewhere. And once an American, one has to continue becoming an American even if he was one at the beginning" (33, 136).

Second, throughout life the individual is confronted with polarities. Unique to the American cultures, every truly American trait has its equally characteristic opposite (20). It can be stated that the American, on the whole, lives with two sets of truth. To illustrate, either or both of the following two contradicting statements convey distinctly American attitudes and expectations: "Respect his point of view" and "Tell him off and let him know what you think. It's a free country!" Erikson himself experienced such a polarity when he and his colleagues at the University of California were asked, in 1950, to take a special loyalty oath to affirm "the validity of their own oath of office." As the question of the "loyalty oath" in this author's opinion is still a crucial issue on the contemporary American scene, Erikson's own penetrating comments on this vexing question might be most relevant. He reflects in an open statement to his colleagues of the faculty of the University of California:

> . . . I may say that the constitutional oath still seems to me to cover admirably and fully my obligations to country, state, and job. I still resent being asked to affirm that I meant what I said when I signed the constitutional oath. One could accept such an additional affirmation wherever and whenever it might seem effective in a special emergency. To me, this contract is an empty gesture toward meeting the danger of infiltration into academic life of indoctrinators, conspirators, and spies. For a subversive person need not have a party card; a conspirator is not bound by declarations; a party member may be unknown to any but a few; a would-be commissar would not ask you for a hearing; and a fanatic indoctrinator may not feel that he lies when he says that he represents objective truth.
>
> One may say, then, why not acquiesce in an empty gesture, if it saves the faces of very important personages, helps to allay public hysteria, and hurts nobody? My answer is that of a psychologist. I do believe that this gesture which now saves face for some important people will, in the long run, hurt people who are much more impor-tant: the students. Too much has been said of academic freedom for

the faculty; I am concerned about certain dangers to the spirit of the student body, dangers which may emanate from such "compromises" as we have been asked to accept.

For many students, their years of study represent their only contact with thought and theory, their only contact with men who teach them how to see two sides of a question and yet to be decisive in their conclusions, how to understand and yet to act with conviction. Young people are rightfully suspicious and embarrassingly discerning. I do not believe they can remain unimpressed by the fact that the men who are to teach them to think and to act judiciously and spontaneously must undergo a political test; must sign a statement which implicitly questions the validity of their own oath of office; must abrogate "commitments" so undefined that they must forever suspect themselves and one another; and must confess to an "objective truth" which they know only too well is elusive. Older people like ourselves can laugh this off; in younger people, however—and especially in those most important students who are motivated to go into teaching—a dangerous rift may well occur between the "official truth" and those deep and often radical doubts which are the necessary condition for the development of thought. . . .

I would find it difficult to ask my subject of investigation [people] and my students to work with me, if I were to participate without protest in a vague, fearful, and somewhat vindictive gesture devised to ban an evil in some magic way—an evil which must be met with much more searching and concerted effort.

In this sense, I may say that my conscience did not permit me to sign the contract after having sworn that I would do my job to the best of my ability (19, 244–245).

The preceding statement presents, clearly, Erik Erikson's own attempt to relate himself to conflicting demands. He also incorporates in practice his own theoretical formulation that it is the generation of elders which must demonstrate to youth an "objective truth" which to this younger generation might yet appear only as a vague and elusive motion.

Third, only in the American context of child-rearing does the individual ego receive so much opportunity and recognition. The American idol still is cradled in a log cabin, according to the American dream. A new idol is cherished by the fact that he establishes his place by his own labor, by conquering inner and outer temptations. It is this "self-made ego," with its unequalled development of ego functions to work, to think, to play, to love, to remember, to laugh, and, above all, to integrate, that is admired as a genuine and healthy person.

Fourth, Erikson finds his concept of a moratorium ". . . at worst, a no man's land between childhood and maturity, and at best, a normal time of sports and horseplay, of gangs and cliques and parties" (20, 298), nowhere as universally accepted as by the American cultures. Fluctuating adolescent attitudes towards authority and conflicts which result do not overtly focus upon the father as the authority, because the American adolescent has a composite father ideal, made up of many male figures. In fact, son and father, or, girl and mother, identify jointly with some of the same ideals. Furthermore, adolescent mood swings are focused on the peers, and not on the family, because at this point of development, it is largely in the peer group where questions pertaining to the family are tackled.

Fifth, and most significantly in America as nowhere else, the *mother* stands as a symbol of the family. She is an "historical phenomenon" as the defender of decency and morals of frontier days. It was the mother who once made or broke the frontiersman (20), and who still continues to do so on the screen in western films. In contemporary, everyday life, she continues to use her influence in political parties and special interests. She is the authority in questions of mores, yet she can remain extremely feminine in her emotions and secretly invite standards she openly denounces. The latter is particularly true in the area of sex, where she denounces free expression of sensual and sexual pleasures, while she accentuates sex in her dress, her use of cosmetics and her choice in pictures, in books and magazines. In cases of conflict, she tends to blame the children and not herself by claiming there is a strict separation of childhood and adult status.

Sixth, there is a decisive change in the psychological position of the father as well as the mother. Until the last two generations, mothers, historically, had to play the roles of both mother and father. They assumed total care for the young except for the father's share in training freeborn sons. Only when father became "Pop" to *all* the children, did mother become "Mom." "Momism," Erikson proposes, "is only misplaced paternalism" (**20**). This recent change places mothers and fathers in a new position for which they have neither a prototype nor an image of their own. Rapid change suggests to the parent that he does not want to be like his own parent. He cannot turn to his own parent for advice and support on questions of child rearing and family matters.

Seventh, the man's activities within the family, as well as in his social life, have changed with the events of two major wars. The man can now admit his bisexual tendencies. The man can now admit such feminine interests as child care, homemaking, and the culinary arts. Man proved his masculinity by his successful survival as a soldier in two major wars; he now may feel free also to exhibit his more feminine interests without their threatening his masculinity.

Eighth, in the absence of tradition among the elders of one's own family, one of the major cultural regulators, the family in the American culture, therefore, tends to depend upon *mutual* regulation within the family which restores self-control in both child and parent. On the one hand, the American family as a group, has lost its importance as a regulator of family standards. Furthermore, the American family lacks control from within because each family member seeks autonomy and substitutes authority from outside the family. In the family unit, the child is seen as the adult's *partner*. In the American family the rights of the individual members, adults and children alike, are guarded against domination by any other member or group of members, i.e., parents, children, older children, all males, etc. As stated, mutual regulation for self rather than family preservation comes into play. Erikson employs the analogy of a miniature Congress with an undefined consensus that no one pressure group must be eliminated by any combination of others. In short, the family is tolerant of different interests, because "nobody can be sure he is right, but everybody must compromise—for the sake of his future change" (**20**, 277).

SUMMARY

Erikson's contributions must be studied and understood for their totality, as an integration of many interlocking concepts and propositions. His developmental blueprint can be most graphically

TABLE 2.2. *Erikson's Worksheet of Developmental Phases.*

	A PSYCHOSOCIAL CRISES	B RADIUS OF SIGNIFICANT RELATIONS	C RELATED ELEMENTS OF SOCIAL ORDER	D PSYCHOSOCIAL MODALITIES	E PSYCHO- SEXUAL STAGES
I	Trust vs. Mistrust	Maternal Person	Cosmic Order	To get To give in return	Oral-Respiratory, Sensory-Kinesthetic (Incorporative Modes)
II	Autonomy vs. Shame, Doubt	Parental Persons	"Law and Order"	To hold (on) To let (go)	Anal-Urethral, Muscular (Retentive-Eliminative)
III	Initiative vs. Guilt	Basic Family	Ideal Prototypes	To make (= going after) To "make like" (= playing)	Infantile-Genital, Locomotor (Intrusive, Inclusive)
IV	Industry vs. Inferiority	"Neighborhood," School	Technological Elements	To make things (= completing) To make things together	"Latency"
V	Identity and Repudiation vs. Identity Diffusion	Peer Groups and Outgroups; Models of Leadership	Ideological Perspectives	To be oneself (or not to be) To share being oneself	Puberty

TABLE 2.2. (*Continued*)

	A PSYCHOSOCIAL CRISES	B RADIUS OF SIGNIFICANT RELATIONS	C RELATED ELEMENTS OF SOCIAL ORDER	D PSYCHOSOCIAL MODALITIES	E PSYCHO- SEXUAL STAGES
VI	Intimacy and Solidarity vs. Isolation	Partners in friendship, sex, competition, cooperation	Patterns of Cooperation and Competition	To lose and find oneself in another	Genitality
VII	Generativity vs. Self-Absorption	Divided labor and shared household	Currents of Education and Tradition	To make be To take care of	
VIII	Integrity vs. Despair	"Mankind" "My Kind"	Wisdom	To be, through having been To face not being	

SOURCE: Reprinted with permission from E. H. Erikson, "Identity and the Life Cycle: Selected Papers," *Psychological Issues* (Monograph), New York, International Universities Press, 1959, I:1.

summarized by means of his diagrammatic *Worksheet* (Table 2.2). It is truly a worksheet, for Erikson sees his work as still progressing. His formulations are still subject to changes and expansion as his work continues.

Erikson, as researcher, writer, and creative thinker, always approaches individual questions in relation to the total situation. His work deserves to be hailed as a major breakthrough in psychoanalytic theory, since Freud. Erikson, with his vast appreciation of human potentialities, conceives the developing individual as a creative enterprise in his efforts to utilize his own inner drives and enmesh them with environmental opportunities. At the same time, the developing personality falls victim to the hazards of living by a combination of instinctive, parental, communal, cultural, and environmental forces which fail to undo successful development because success depends upon channeling innate tendencies in a direction which will serve the need of the individual and his community and will assure both a continued cultural heritage. Development is a process of maturation meeting a process of education. In technical terms, it is the growth of the ego combined with the quality of the ego experience afforded to the child by his immediate environment. In the true sense of the meaning of the term, Erikson is an ego-psychologist.

3

The Cognitive Theory of
Jean Piaget

PIAGET'S LIFE AND WORK

SEARCHING FOR and formulating a genetic theory is the life work of Jean Piaget. His scientific efforts and penetrating insights have added a new dimension to the understanding of child development. Born in 1896 in Neuchâtel, a French-speaking Swiss university town, Jean Piaget describes his home and childhood as having been dominated by the combination of an intelligent, energetic, but somewhat neurotic mother, and a scholarly father, who had an air of detachment from his wife's emotional outbursts and from his son's abortive scientific studies. Piaget traces his own later interest in intellectual rather than emotional development to these lonesome days of his childhood:

I started to forego playing for serious work very early. . . . Indeed, I have always detested any departure from reality, an attitude which I relate to . . . my mother's poor mental health. It was this disturbing factor which at the beginning of my studies in psychology made me intensely interested in questions of psychoanalysis and pathological psychology. Though this interest helped me to achieve independence and to widen my cultural background, I have never since felt any desire to involve myself deeper in that particular direction, always much preferring the study of normalcy and of the workings of the intellect to that of the tricks of the unconscious (89, 238).

At the age of 10 Piaget published his first article, concerning a rare albino sparrow, in the *Journal of Natural History of Neuchâtel*. He reports with much amusement that this article brought him an invitation to consider the position of curator of the Geneva Museum of Natural History. This invitation was quickly withdrawn when the director of the museum discovered that the scholar of this article was still a pupil in knee pants in secondary school. Later, as a *gymnasium* student, his research on mollusks introduced him to the scientific approaches of the biological sciences. He continued his studies of mollusks and sciences at the University of Neuchâtel (1915–1918), although, by this time, he had achieved recognition beyond the borders of Switzerland. This work culminated in his doctoral dissertation on *The Mollusks of Vallais* (1918).

During his university years, Piaget discovered philosophy and psychology. The writings of Bergson awoke in him a feverish interest in the idea of identifying God with life. This notion, he writes:

. . . stirred me almost to ecstasy because it enabled me to see in biology the explanation of all things and of mind itself . . . [However] instead of finding science's last work therein . . . I got the impression of an ingenious construction without an experimental basis: Between biology and the analysis of knowledge I needed something other than philosophy. I believe it was at that moment that I discovered a need that could be satisfied only by psychology (89, 240).

Thus, in addition to his studies in the natural sciences, Piaget applied his energies to the reading of philosophical and psychological publications. He writes that during this period "I began by reading everything which came to my hands after my unfortunate contact with the philosophy of Bergson: some Kant, Spencer, August Comte . . . Durkheim, Tarde . . . and, in psychology, William James, Th. Ribot and Janet" (89, 241). Young Piaget must have found himself in a constant turmoil in his search for a scientific explanation of the psychological existence of man. He

REPRODUCED BY KIND PERMISSION OF PROFESSOR PIAGET

Jean Piaget

wrote incessantly and systematically as if he were writing articles for scientific publications, but these remained a private communication with himself, never to be published. In a philosophical novel, he formulated rudimentary concepts of intellectual development, which anticipated strikingly his research of the following thirty years. His exposure to the psychological laboratories at the University of Zurich (1918) brought him to the experimental laboratory of Alfred Binet in Paris (1919–1921) where he pursued clinical psychological research. During these years, he attended lectures of Pfister, Jung, and Freud, all of which acquainted him with the theories and methods of psychoanalytic investigation.

At 25, Piaget started his professional career with the desire to find a logical link between psychology and biology. He searched for systematic patterns of thought which would correspond to the biological hierarchy of cell, organism and species. Moreover, he searched for a research methodology applicable to qualitative research. His work at Binet's laboratory led him to the observation that a child's answers to standard questions served as the opening wedge for new and more probing questions. In other words, the child, rather than the questions, became the source for data. A child's spontaneous questions were additional sources for getting at the real significance of a child's thoughts. For the following thirty years, Piaget and his associates created over fifty new—and, at times, most ingenious—research techniques which built upon these earlier insights that the child, the child's interpretations of his own comments, and the child's questions provide the "key" to research on intellectual development. His research methodology combines psychoanalytic techniques with standard procedures of experimental research. Piaget postulated that a study of intellectual development would yield the embryology of intelligence. In his own words:

I made plans which I then considered final: I would devote two or three years more to the study of child thought, then return to the origins of mental life, that is, study the emergence of intelligence during the first two years. After having thus gained objectively and inductively a knowledge about the elementary structures of intelligence, I would be in the position to attack the problem of thought in general and to construct a psychological and biological epistemology (89, 246).

His research for the years 1921–1925 led to five major publications during the years 1924–1932 (91, 92, 95, 96, 98). These early publications introduced him to the university centers of Europe and the United States. In fact, these publications found a wider audience in this country than any of his later writings. Much of this country's present-day criticism of Piaget's research is leveled at his early works, a criticism which he himself was the first to acknowledge and to correct:

I well knew that thought proceeds from action, but I believed then that language directly reflects acts and that to understand the logic of the child one had only to look for it in the domain of conversations or verbal interactions. It was only later, by studying the patterns of intelligent behavior of the first two years, that I learned that for a complete understanding of the genesis of intellectual operations, manipulation and experience with objects had first to be considered (89, 247).

Important personal and professional experiences paved the way to the second period of Piaget's work. The births of his three children (1925, 1927, and 1931) brought him into a continuous and intimate contact with developing individuals that was unparalleled by the most ideal laboratory arrangements. He designed, and followed through, detailed observations of the *manipulative* behavior of children, recognizing perceptual and conceptual processes as being interrelated rather than independent operations. His study of perceptual development concentrated upon optical illusions and their implications for intellectual development; that intellectual development evolved *differently* in the conception of objects, space, causality, and time. Further, he paid renewed attention to the affective phase of human behavior in his studies on play, dreams, and imitation (100). His three major publications of this period (1925–1929) included a revision of his earlier study on developmental stages, which was more restricted in terms of age boundaries (99, 93, 100).

The years 1929–1939 he later described as the time devoted to the formulation of the psychological concept of *groupings* which was to tie together his theory of cognitive development. Later, during the immediately post-World-War-II years, Piaget continued his research, lecturing, and writing in three capacities: as the professor of the History of Scientific Thought at the University of Geneva, as Assistant Director of the Institute of J. J. Rousseau, and as Director of the Bureau of the International Office of Education. In 1949, he fulfilled his driving ambition with the publication of *Introduction a L'épistemologie Génétique*—the manuscript he anticipated when he first came to Geneva in 1921, and an area of study to which he has been devoting most of his energies and scientific inquiries during the past decade.

Piaget's membership in a wide range of professional organizations,[1] his appointment at the Sorbonne—first professor chair occupied by a non-Frenchman since Desiderius Erasmus (1530)—and his reception of five honorary degrees in four different countries,[2] clearly point to his close contacts with the scientific and academic circles of his time. His feeling and respect for people is reflected in his devoted leadership as Director of the International Board of Education and as member of the Executive Board of UNESCO. His more recent studies in logic and mathematical concepts and his collaborative research on perception are beyond the scope of this chapter; these widely varying ventures in research characterize clearly his indefatigable and creative mind, and give essence to his own observation that the widening of one horizon serves to open new frontiers of knowledge. Basically, Jean Piaget's work is that of a genetic psychologist and philosopher. Piaget might be compared to an explorer who sets out to investigate unknown territories, but who ends up discovering a new continent. His studies and findings generate zest and excitement.

PIAGET'S THEORY IN RELATION TO OTHER PREVAILING THEORIES

Although the first to acknowledge the limitations of a one-dimensional theory, Piaget is nonetheless inclined to be parochial and to rely upon his own system of logical thought. At the same time, he maintains contact with contemporary psychologists and applies their teachings to his work. E. J. Anthony refers to Piaget's power to integrate: ". . . [he is a] creative borrower of genius,

---

[1] Société romande de Philosophie; Société de Sociologie de Genève; Société Suisse de Psychoanalyse; Société de Neurologie and Société française de Psychologie (81).

[2] Harvard University, 1936; Sorbonne, Paris, 1946; University of Brussels, 1949; University of Rio de Janeiro, 1949; The University of Chicago, 1953 (89).

transposing and amplifying all that he borrows while generously acknowledging the sources" (5, 34). At a round-table research gathering in 1953 Piaget suggested:

We still know very little about how independent, or dependent, the two systems [human action system and the physiological system] are. At one stage they may seem very independent, but this may prove to be only a question of how long it will be before the physiologic background will show that there is much more dependency between the two systems than there seemed at first? Interpretation in terms of structures, that is of similar structures in one system or another, is really only a working hypothesis. It is a precautionary measure, leaving the way open to further relationships between the two when the advancement of physiologic science has progressed (102, 168).

Piaget's interest in others' work has not been fully reciprocated, and this is apparently due to the difficulties associated with reading his writings and following his complex reasoning.

Piaget's theory and general psychoanalysis share an attempt to explain human behavior within one system and to avoid quantitative data. E. J. Anthony describes Piaget's theory as an ego psychology, leaning upon the cognitive, conflict-free side, of human behavior (5). Piaget's interest in the genesis of the whole and its parts occurred without an awareness of Gestalt psychology, which he did not know until he had completed his initial research on this question. The striking absence of any reference to learning-theory research is best explained by John H. Flavell: "It is probably safe to assert that Piaget is by no means entirely ignorant of the metatheory of the Hulls, Esteses, and Skinners, and it is important to recognize that it is his philosophy of science, rather than laziness or experimental naïvete, which dictates the informal quality of his research" (52, 3–4). Piaget concerns himself with the organizational activities *within* the individual rather than with the stimulating environmental cues which are the major concerns of most learning theorists.[3] Wayne Dennis writes: "We turn to Piaget for ideas, not for statistics . . . the writer [Dennis] expected to refute his theories, became convinced that many of

[3] W. Mays makes the comparison that Hull uses logic to discover psychological theory, while Piaget employs logic to understand what is discovered (75).

them were sound" (14a, 161). In summary, Piaget readily reflects the formulation of other theories. At times he has been misunderstood and misquoted; understanding his use of words is no simple task. His scientific terms lack definitions and frequently he applies them differently, depending upon the period of his work. He also openly anticipates, accepts, or disputes the teachings of others, while he keeps strictly within his own field. He leaves the interpretation and the application of his findings to us.

ASSUMPTIONS BASIC TO PIAGET'S THEORY

Prior to considering Piaget's developmental theory, it is advisable to examine the basic assumptions which underlie it, and which can be summarized under the following sub-headings:

1. Approach to Theory Formation
2. The Order of the Cosmos
3. Etiology of Human Behavior
4. Fundamental Human Values
5. Core of Human Behavior
6. The Newborn
7. The Physical, Social, and Ideational Environment

Approach to Theory Formation

Basic to the formation of any theory is its author's approach to science and his selection of scientific tools. Piaget's life history clearly reflects his early training in the biological sciences, when he was collecting and classifying data. Piaget, the scientist, is complemented by Piaget, the philosopher, who seeks logical systems with internally consistent explanations for all their parts.

Piaget proceeds with the assumption that a detailed investigation of any small sample of a species will yield basic information inherent to all members of that species.[4] The children of Geneva,

---

[4] After Piaget had developed a theoretical framework of his own, his subsequent research (since 1939, approximately) shows a consistent increase in the number of subjects used for the testing of each new hypothesis. His research in the past decade has an *n* of 1500.

for example, and his own particularly, are representative of children everywhere. Until very recently he made no allowances for sexual differences; his samples were segregated only according to the desired age span.[5] Furthermore, he assumes that the reliability of any findings is directly related to the completeness of the data furnished by the informant. He measures validity by the degree of inner consistency his findings hold with his theoretical propositions. In other words, Piaget sees empirical research as a tool to substantiate or to refute facts which were previously established by logic.[6] Once facts are established, they can be generalized upon. These findings serve not only as bases for inductively acquiring new data, but also as a source for the hypothetical deduction of new concepts. For Piaget, the logical consistency of all findings is the most decisive criterion for their potential usefulness.

In recent years, Piaget has explicated his eclectic methods of research and theory construction. He proposes two essential approaches, much akin to those utilized in the nuclear sciences (102). They are:

1. The step-by-step analysis based upon an investigation of cause and effect, which forms a network characterized by hierarchical relationships and combined connections.
2. The analysis of implications by considering both the field as a whole and the coordination of its parts. In mathematics this is comparable to the group, and in logic, to the propositional operation.

Empirical investigations and the inductive mode of reasoning is akin to the first approach, while reasoning by logic and constructing hypotheses by deduction is similar to the second. Symbolic logic, Piaget stresses, can be applied scientifically as a research tool as much as can the more commonly used statistical techniques.

[5] In a round-table discussion (1955), Piaget comments that he is now aware that boys and girls consistently approach problems related to questions of space in a different manner (107c, 114).

[6] John H. Flavell challenges the validity of some of Piaget's work in his observation that at times Piaget forces the findings of his empirical research in order to validate his theoretical hypothesis (52).

The Order of the Cosmos

Piaget believes in universal order. He suggests a single unity of all things: biological, social, psychological, and ideational, in living as well as nonliving systems. All science is interrelated. A theorem established in one branch of science, he feels, is directly relevant to the laws and principles of other branches. Altogether, Piaget insists upon cosmic unity, which provides one explanation for his notion that his samples are representative; he assumes that any deviation, whether cultural or hereditary, is an inconsequential variation to the regular process of development. Occasionally, his position becomes more tenuous, and he refers to a parallelism based on an isomorphism between psychological and biological processes (102). The spontaneous organization of all activities provides the foundation for all prevailing logic and natural order. Conversely, the biological models of hierarchy, of nesting, and of lattices provide the key to understanding the cosmic order and the relationship between parts, as well as the relation of the parts to the whole. Four spontaneous actions are always present:

1. The action of the whole on itself (producing the law of preservation and survival).
2. The action of all the parts (producing the law of alteration and preservation).
3. The action of the parts on themselves (producing the law of preservation and survival).
4. The action of the parts on the whole (producing the law of alteration and preservation).

Spontaneous action, and inherent and constant dynamic change, sustain each organism's evolutionary development with movements in the direction of greater mobility, complexity, versatility, and increased unity for all actions of the parts involved, the last of which tends to gravitate the whole towards a sense of equilibrium. Piaget recognizes three possible forms of equilibrium:

1. Predominance of the whole with alteration of parts.
2. Predominance of the parts with alteration of the whole.
3. Reciprocal preservation of the parts *and* the whole.

The ultimate goal of the evolutionary process is the third level of equilibrium which is achieved only by the most evolved organism —the human being at the time he approaches intellectual maturity.

Etiology of Human Behavior

Piaget sees himself as a researcher of human development; questions of behavioral etiology are beyond his field of investigation. Nevertheless, as a philosopher-scientist, he deals with etiological questions. His theory of cognitive development rests upon a chain of assumptions which find explanation in two different aspects of his developmental theory: First, biological growth points to all mental processes as continuations of inborn motor processes; and second, in the processes of experience—the origin of all acquired characteristics—the organism discovers the separate existence of what he experiences. In experiencing his own native reflexes, the individual is led to use them and to apply them, resulting in the acquisition of new behavioral processes. Consequently, Piaget establishes the basic assumption that human systems of organization are not acquired purely socially, but evolve from an individual's natural patterns of living. In Piaget's words, they constitute a "law of nature" and the evolution of cognitive organization is explained by two different assumptions which Piaget alternately implies:

1. The organization and interrelationship of objects, space, causality, and time presume *a priori* the existence of definite patterns of intellectual development.
2. The intellect organizes its own structure by virtue of its experience with objects, space, causality, and time, and the interrelationship of these environmental realities.

Consciousness, judgment, and reasoning—in fact, all attributes of personality—depend primarily upon the evolving intellectual capacity of the individual to organize his experience. Concomitantly, the totality of experience shapes the interests of an individual and the specific experiences he tends to pursue.

Adaptation, Piaget postulates, is the cognitive striving of the organism—the thinking person—to find an equilibrium between himself and his environment, and it depends upon two interrelated Piagetian processes: *assimilation* and *accommodation.* Assimilation involves a person's adaptation of the environment to himself, and represents the individual's use of his environment as he would conceive it. Experiences are taken in only as far as the individual himself can preserve and consolidate them in terms of his own subjective experience. Thus, the individual experiences an event as he conceives it. Accommodation is directly converse to assimilation, and represents the impact of the actual environment. To accommodate is to conceive and to incorporate the environmental experience as it truly is. For instance, a loud noise of a door falling shut unexpectedly is *assimilated* according to its impact upon the individual hearing it; the nature of the noise experienced is determined by the way the individual interprets it. However, the individual also, in varying degrees, adapts to the noise for what it *actually* represented; that is, he *accommodates* the experience. Thus, both processes always act together. They are interlocked and simultaneously involve conflicting force between opposite poles; that is, assimilation is always balanced by the force of accommodation, while accommodation is possible only with the function of assimilation. An environmental object is never experienced unless it has a personal, assimilative impact. Piaget stresses that an object can never exist unto itself, it always involves assimilation and accommodation on the part of the experiencer (99). To repeat, processes of both assimilation and accommodation provide complementary, but opposing pulls. A pull to think, to feel and to act as previously experienced is challenged by a pull to think, to feel, and to act according to the realistic demands of the new situation. Although Piaget's theory is built upon these biological models of homeostasis, he warns us as recently as 1953, "We describe behavior in physiologic or behavioristic terms. We describe *in toto*, but we do not know the underlying processes" (**102**, 151).

Fundamental Human Values

Piaget's assumptions concerning fundamental human values can be traced to his concepts of cosmic order and to his own philosophy of life. He suggests that basic values may be explained either by the assumption that they follow an evolving scheme or by the assumption that evolution follows a system of values. Under either assumption each individual can be viewed as unique, and as possessing a wide range of potentialities. Piaget's scientific assumption of "normal distribution" of all basic traits suggests a democratic outlook concerning the potentials of each individual. He assumes a democratic form of human interaction as the natural state. Moreover, he claims that men have a sense of solidarity as soon as they achieve a certain level of maturity. His concept of "distributive justice, as the pinnacle of men's sense of justice," implies that reciprocal equality presents the natural, ultimate goal of mature individuals.

The Core of Human Functioning

Primary processes, as defined by Piaget, refer to two original expressions of the individual. First, primary processes specify all original activities of the organism and all immediate forms of human functioning which unfold from them. He then applies the term to all early, undifferentiated mental processes up to the age of 7, at which time a child starts to apply the logical mode of reasoning to his thinking. In primary processes, opposites appear to be in proximity, with no sense of logical contradiction or time. The fact that Piaget employs the same terms for the totality of early human behavior and for the development of early mental processes suggests that, for him, intellectual functions provide the core of all human activities.

There is no doubt that, for Piaget, the story of intellectual development is also the story of personality formation. He suggests that the faculty of knowing serves as the coordinator, and occupies a position parallel to the synthetic function of the ego in an analytic formulation.[7] *Consciousness* lacks definition in the Piagetian system. By inference, it may be viewed as a state of awareness with no counterpart, such as the analytic unconscious, ordinarily the counterpart of the conscious. At the same time, however, Piaget accepts the analytic concept of unconscious processes, and explains them as the sphere of interest of another field. In Piaget's system, *unconsciousness* refers merely to one end of his continuum of consciousness. Unconscious thought is "a series of operations, not actual but potential, not manually performed, but none the less outlined in the organism" (**95,** 145). It is thinking outside or beyond one's awareness.

Identification, as a cognitive process, is closely related to the mental capacity of conceiving another model in relation to one's self. Similarly, imitation is accepted as an intellectual function with neither affective overtone nor a stress upon repetition of perceptive experiences. *Play,* an essential part of the evolution of intelligence, begins with a predominance of assimilation in an adapted activity. Language is a product of mental activities. In spite of its pivotal position later in life, language, like play, emerges as part of the continuum of intellectual development. In contrast, *perception* assumes a subordinate status. Perceptual experiences are not on a continuum; they are centralized from moment to moment. As the lungs furnish oxygen to the body, so perceptual impulses furnish impressions to the intellect which must be translated into life experiences.

Piaget assumes that human *affect* (emotion) evolves from the same primary processes as its intellectual counterpart. He vacillates in his assumptions as to whether affect assumes an equal rank or a subordinate position to intellectual organization. At one time affect regulates the energies of actions and intellectual structure determines the techniques, while in other instances intellectual processes determine the capacity of emotional receptivity. Altogether, however, it can be stated that the two functions, intellect and affect, are like two sides of a coin. "Both are always together as one. Both serve the adaptation to the environment" (**103,** 275). "Reason and

7 See Chapter 2, "The Psychoanalytic Theory of Erik H. Erikson."

feelings are not independent faculties, they are always united in the facts" (3, 3). "We do not love without seeking to understand, and we do not even hate without a subtle use of judgment" (100, 207).

Thus, Piaget's theory rests upon the assumption that human personality evolves from a composite of intellectual and affective functions, and also from the interrelation of these two functions. The intellectual processes provide direction by organizing and integrating these functions of human personality.

Piaget maintains that achieving a near equilibrium in a constantly changing situation is the goal of all human functions: biological, affective and, above all, mental. He defines equilibrium as a state in which ". . . all the virtual transformations compatible with the relationships of the system compensate each other (97, 41). Life finds itself in a field of constant motion, and ". . . intellectual operations proceed in terms of structures-of-the-whole. These structures denote the kinds of equilibrium toward which evolution in its entirety is striving at once organic, psychological and social, their roots reach down as far as biological morphogenesis itself" (89, 256). Any state of equilibrium is entirely theoretical and, at best, only momentarily attainable. The efforts towards a state of equilibrium is the paramount and essential problem of psychology. Piaget thinks that psychology should work out the laws of equilibrium, which are primarily descriptions of the processes of change governing the states of equilibrium (104).

Piaget recognizes two pulls in opposite directions. The individual seeks a balance by striving toward a new, more advanced equilibrium. In other words, Piaget assumes the same struggle as suggested by Freud (54) and others, to the effect that the individual tries to reconcile his personal desires with the demands imposed upon him by the environment. Cognition recognizes the quality of *desire* activated by the affective side of behavior; it also recognizes the opportunities and limits furnished by the environment. Rapaport observes that these assumptions could be readily translated into the psychoanalytic index of pleasure vs. reality orientation (110).

Piaget assumes a state of permanent striving towards an equilibrium similar to the activities in constructing an ever-expanding pyramid. Life is a progressive series of attempts to balance forms; each attempt rests upon previous acquisitions, and each—with increasing complexity—creates new forms which furnish in turn the foundations for later balances.

The Newborn

Piaget assumes that the infant is born as a biological organism with a series of reflexes whose psychological make-up can be described as "protoplasmic consciousness" (5). The following three phylogenetically inherited drives (or instinctual behavior) are attributed to the newborn:

1. A hunger drive plus a capacity to seek and to utilize food.
2. A drive towards a sense of balance (balance as to position, light, heat and sound as well as reactions to a sudden disturbance in this sense of balance). The newborn's diffused reflex reaction to the disturbance of his balance can readily be denoted as original emotion.
3. A drive for independence from, and adaptation to, the environment plus a certain hereditary capacity to gain much independence.

The Physical, Social, and Ideational Environment

The foregoing Piagetian assumptions are supplemented by those related to the surrounding environment to which the individual is adapting himself. Piaget's position can be summarized by his acceptance of Durkheim's theorem that all *social* realities—values and processes—are created by men (98). The social and ideational world represents no entity without man. Such a world is the reflection of the socialization experienced by each individual in his cognitive development. The universe is undifferentiated to the newborn. Piaget postulates that the individual and his environment represent a syncretic whole. One's concept of objects, that is, all things (or persons) to which actions, thoughts and feelings are directed, or vice versa, and his ideas emerge simultaneously with the individual's awareness of self. Curiously, these man-made phenomena become part of the individual's environment, consequently, and activate his adaptive processes. In other words, social, psychological, and ideational aspects, as well as physical objects, appear as environment and comprise one field for the individual.[8] The field of each individual can accelerate, retard, change the order of succession of the individual growth process (102). This assertion, basic to Piaget's theory, justifies his major concentration upon the *phases* of development which are irrevocable in their sequence. Piaget refers to his theorem when he discusses the findings of Dennis, Deutsche, and others who had found different data in repeating some of his research. He suggests that their findings of different average ages could be traced to environmental (cultural, socioeconomic, etc.) variations between the two groups of subjects. More important, Piaget maintains, is the fact that the *sequence* of developmental phases remains the same (100).

PIAGET'S CONCEPTION OF DEVELOPMENT

Piaget views development as an inherent, unalterable, evolutionary process; yet within this developmental process he locates a series of distinct developmental phases and sub-phases. Whenever Piaget locates distinct sub-phases within any one of his major developmental phases, we shall specify them as *stages*. This approach, we trust, will add further clarity to his notion of a regular, definable, sequential development. The highlighting of sub-phases, that is *stages* occurs in a review of Piaget's first developmental phase. As will be seen shortly, he divided the *sensorimotor phase* (the first developmental phase) into a progression of six distinct stages. Piaget and his interpreters use both terms: "phase" and "stage" indiscriminately. We shall employ the term *phase* when we deal with one of the five major Piagetian developmental periods of cognitive development. A *phase* is a homogeneous pat-

---

[8] *Field* is used here in the terms of Gestalt psychology.

terning of an individual's life style for the duration of that period. Although Piaget's developmental phases are frequently cited as his major teachings as if they represent an entity, they are actually no more than points of reference to understand the sequence of development. They serve only to demonstrate the course of development, and do not represent development itself. Piaget describes phases as indispensable tools for the analysis of developmental processes and compares them with the biological method of classification (106, 56). Piaget's developmental phases serve as a convenient "handle" for a presentation of cognitive development.

Each phase reflects a range of organizational patterns which occur in a definite sequence within an approximate age span in the continuum of development. The completion of one phase provides a passing equilibrium, as well as the beginning of an imbalance for a new phase. Each phase suggests the potential capacity and probable level of behavior. It should be noted here that Piaget intentionally avoids a statistical approach; his concern is with the pattern and order of sequence rather than with a quantitative analysis. Piaget deals with a tendency toward patterning without relying upon a statistical measure of tendency.

Whether or not the individual will predominantly employ his potential capacity remains a separate question. An individual's rate of development tends to coincide with Piaget's obviously arbitrary ranges. The important thing, as Piaget stresses, is the order of succession of these phases. The succession remains always the same. Developmental phases, then, are age-bound on the basis of Piaget's preliminary, cursory observations. They are also age-free in terms of their order of sequence.

Piaget's concept of development can be summarized by the six following generalizations:

1. There is an absolute continuity of all developmental processes.
2. Development proceeds through a continuous process of generalizations and differentiation.
3. This continuity is achieved by a continuous unfolding. Each level of development finds its roots in a previous phase and continues into the following one.

4. Each phase entails a repetition of processes of the previous level in a different form of organization (schema). Previous behavior patterns are sensed as inferior and become part of the new superior level (107a).
5. The differences in organizational pattern create a hierarchy of experience and actions.
6. Individuals achieve different levels within the hierarchy, although ". . . there is in the brain of each individual the possibility for all these developments but they are not all realized" (104, 156).

PIAGET'S DEVELOPMENTAL THEORY

Piaget's writings introduce a variety of developmental divisions. For instance, in Piaget's works of 1956 (105) he illustrates a developmental continuum by a division into three major phases:

1. The sensori-motor phase, (roughly, ages: 0–2)
2. The period of preparation for conceptual thought (roughly, ages: 2–11/12)
3. The phase of cognitive thought (roughly, ages 11 or 12 and up)

Here Piaget's theory is analyzed within the framework of his most traditional and most inclusive developmental phases: the sensory-motor phase, the preconceptual phase, the phase of intuitive thought, the phase of concrete operations, and the phase of formal operations. The aptness of the names for these five phases will become apparent in the presentation of each.

The Sensori-Motor Phase

Sensori-motor fittingly describes the first period of the developmental continuum which depends predominantly upon sensori- and body-motor experience. This phase covers a period from birth to approximately the age of 24 months, during which time the child is considered to be a baby because of his dependency upon his body for self-expression and communication. In Piagetian terminology, *sensori-motor* indicates the infant's creation of a practical world entirely linked to his desires of physical satisfaction within his immediate sensory experience. The major developmental tasks of this period are the coordination of his actions or motor activities, and his perception or sensori perception into a tenuous "whole." In other words, the new organism must find himself an active part of his environment and must be able to perceive his environment within the horizon of his immediate experience.

Piaget must have attributed great importance to this first period of human development. He devotes more detailed analysis to the first two years of life than to any subsequent period. His detailed studies (93, 99, 103) analyze this period on the basis of six distinct *stages* of development. Similar to the major developmental *phases*, these stages also build upon one another. Sensori-motor development can be explained in terms of these six successive stages of organization:

1. Use of reflexes
2. Primary circular reactions
3. Secondary circular reactions
4. Coordination of secondary schemata and its application to new situations
5. Tertiary circular reactions
6. The invention of new means through mental combinations.

The use of reflexes prevails in the first stage of the sensori-motor phases. Exercising reflexes, a continuation of prenatal developmental activities, characterizes the infant's first month of life. At birth the infant's individuality is expressed by crying, sucking, and variations in the rhythm of breathing. These behavioral responses are the beginnings of his personality development. The very nature of reflexes, the *spontaneous repetition* by internal or external stimulation provides the necessary experience for their maturation. Repetitive experience establishes rhythm and a *quality of regularity*. It also furnishes the first traces of *sequential use* and a sense of order. For instance, the sucking reflex depends upon practice for proper functioning. The location of the nipple and the immediate experience of having something to suck provide an experience cycle fundamental to all later development. It should be noted that this concept reflects vividly the dynamic as well as the environmental aspects of Piaget's theory. Change, or development, comes about by "living." The organism never is something; he always is becoming something by the very fact that he is confronted by an environment which also makes its demands upon the individual by the fact of his mere existence in the environment.

Repetitive use of reflexes, combined with neurological and physical maturation, tend to form habits. Further, repetition necessarily involves accidental variation and differing contacts with the environment. Piaget omits further explication of habits and the shift from reflexes to voluntary movements.

As stated earlier, human functioning rests primarily upon the process of adaptation which comprises the interplay of the processes of assimilation and accommodation. Adaptation, as the central Piagetian process, has its start in these very early variations of reflexive actions and the ever-increasing repertoire of behavior. First, it involves a generalized assimilation, with the infant incorporating more and more of his momentary, immediate environment. This incorporative process is nonselective and includes all stimulation to which his sensory equipment is capable of responding. Repetition and sequential experience prepare the way for rudimentary generalization and recognitory assimilation. The generalization of practical experiences into such abstract categories as palpable, tactile, or visual experience implies *ordering*. It also initiates a process of differentiation in an acting environment previously undifferentiated. The 1-month-old infant is in a purely autistic phase. He adapts (assimilates) his environment entirely according to his organic demands. He experiences all objects to his own satisfaction. He initiates general organizational patterns of behavior basic to his unfolding life. The importance of these patterns becomes more evident in the following stages.

Primary circular reactions mark the beginning of the second stage when reflexive behavior is slowly replaced by voluntary movements. Maturational readiness is requisite to this development. The infant must reach a certain neurological maturity before he can comprehend his own sensations. The infant's *psychic life* starts when maturation ". . . no longer alters assimilated objects in a physico-chemical manner but simply incorporates them in its own form of activity" (104, 8). In about his second month, the child can consciously repeat this action. His activities primarily involve repeating voluntarily what was previously merely automatic behavior. This repetition of behavior is now a deliberate response to the recognized stimulation of a previous experience. Accidentally acquired responses (such as reaching or pushing by means of hand) become new sensori-motor habits. They open new *parts* of these ever multiplying environment*s* (the plural of environment has been employed purposely in order to stress Piaget's concept that the young child knows many environments; the child is yet incapable of coordinating the parts of his experiences into one or several integrated units).

Reactions become closely linked with the stimuli. Experience is closely tied to the environment which stimulates the reaction, and repetition—especially sequential repetition—leads to the realization that a repeatedly experienced stimulus has a signal-value. Here is the start of a new cycle in the behavior sequence. For instance, stimulation of the palm and grasping become a willful, a *cognitive* behavioral unit. Piaget calls it a primary circular reaction. Primary circular reaction refers to the assimilation of a previous experience *and* the recognition of the stimulus which triggers the reaction. Piaget describes the latter as the emergence of the accommodative process. The child incorporates and adapts his reactions to an environmental reality. A synthesis of assimilation and accommodation occurs, which, in essence, is adaptation.

Primary circular reaction, however simple, provides an organizational pattern, a *schema* by which two or three factors are organized into a relationship pattern, superimposed upon the previous action patterns of *reproducing, repetition,* and *sequentiality. Schema,* for Piaget, is an established pattern of a meaningful, repeatable psychological unit of intellectual behavior or its prerequisites. It is a behavioral event which can be repeated and coordinated with others. Piaget chose the Kantian term because, in his theory, it assumed a similar position to the one given by the philosopher Kant in his discourse on human reason. Piaget also defined *schemata* as a product of the intellect, where the understanding is able to apply its categories.

New sensori-motor functions now can be utilized by the growing individual. Vision, for example, becomes a continuous experience. Sucking, prehension, and hearing provide experiential episodes with newly evolving circular-reaction patterns. Objects, as stimuli, become closely related with the ongoing behavior pattern. Each object, and the space involved in an action sequence, become distinct but yet isolated units of experience, and each experience occurs as a momentary life event. To elaborate, the grasping of the mother's finger outside the field of vision and the sucking of the nipple provide two centers of experience, while smelling the nipple, touching it with the oral cavity and the seeing mother's face become part of one experience (reaction) sequence in the child's world, which is experientially heterogenous. Most important, eye-hand coordination begins to emerge as an essential developmental achievement.

Two new areas of organization find their roots in this stage. First, a notion of causality can later be explained in terms of this early recognition of the sequence of events. Food, as an extension of sucking or of grasping, is related to these early intuitive experiences. "A child's first sense of causal relation, then, is simply a diffuse connection between an action on the one hand and a result on the other, without comprehension of spatial relations or intermediary objects" (90, 50). Second, a notion of temporal space finds its genetic roots in the seriation of experienced events. For years, however, the child senses all seriation as the extended present. Sequentiality also leads to increased incorporation of a relationship between action and the stimulation of action. This suggests that laws of S-R theories gain importance with development but do not operate as such during the very early developmental periods.

The infant slowly relinquishes his autism and acknowledges

sections of his environment. Yet he is incapable of distinguishing between external and internal stimuli, since either type, to him, represents a separate environment. The major theme of this period is the child's capacity to incorporate the new results of his behavior as part of his continuing behavior. New or past experiences have no meaning unless they become part of a primary circular reaction pattern. The infant has to experience any new object through his accustomed repertoire of sensory activities—sucking, touching, etc. For example, he will coo happily to a new baby-sitter if she will handle him in much the same way as he has been handled by those with whom he is thoroughly familiar.

Secondary circular reaction, a phrase aptly descriptive of the third stage of development, incorporates a continuation of the circular reaction patterns combined with a secondary function which lifts the primary circular reaction beyond its basically organic activity. Between the infant's third and ninth month his behavior continues with familiar forms of experience. His sensori-motor apparatus is capable of "tuning in" (being aware of) only those events to which he has become accustomed. The major aim of his behavior is retention, not repetition. The child's efforts are to make events last, to create a state of *permanency.* This effort results in further awareness of the environment *and* accommodation to it—the child's first real acknowledgement of environmental forces.

Primary circular reactions are *repeated* and *prolonged* by the new secondary reactions. The grasping reflex, for instance, evolves from a sequence of to grasp and to hold, into such unified activity as to shake, to pull, or to tug. Activity remains the primary motive of experience. Increasingly however, the infant also widens the scope of his activity by relating two or more sensori-motor activities into *one* experiential sequence, or *schema.* The infant will combine visible, tactile, or other differentiated experiences into a single experience. This ever unfolding intellectual process of combining occurs predominantly by using vision as the prime coordinator. Visible fractions of an object can serve to trigger an action sequence. To illustrate, the sight of the end of a familiar string can be sufficient to induce a child to pull, perhaps to shake the carriage hood over his head. The string, the shaking and the motion of the hood are one universe although the infant is not yet aware that he himself belongs to this same universe (93). An action sequence, however, contains the potential for many intellectual accomplishments. Most roots for future cognitive understanding are acquired during this early sensori-motor phase, which can be summarized as follows:

1. The child reacts to distant objects and although he still considers ends and means as one, the beginning of the differentiation between cause and effect takes place.
2. Qualitative and quantitative evaluation find their roots in these simple experiences (i.e., "more" or "less" shaking).
3. The various and distinct reactions and response patterns are ultimately unified into a single, unified action sequence.
4. This coordination of separate experiences into one schema leads to an awakening awareness in the infant that he, too, is a part of the sphere of action.
5. The notion of time finds a cursory introduction into the infant's mind, as he gains a dim awareness of a "before" and "after" in each action sequence.
6. The recognition of a particular stimulus as a part of an entire action sequence introduces the use of symbols as a kind of shorthand to comprehension and leads eventually to communication. This early awareness of stimuli as symbols also serves as an introduction to a sense of future.
7. Variety in available patterns of action, the dawning recognition of symbols, rudimentary projecting of time, as well as increased accommodation stress the *intentional* aspects of the child's prospective behavior.

Each of these seven beginnings has significance for the developing infant; only the synthesis of all, however indicates actual intellectual development. Once achieved, this development, in turn, stimulates three new processes of human behavior: *imitation, play,* and *affect.*

Imitation depends upon the capacity to differentiate among several events and to react to those selected. *Repetition* referred to self-imitation with no alternative behavior, but the second half of his first year the infant is capable of the systematic imitation of observed movements and of some sounds. Imitation starts with the repeating of already acquired primary and secondary circular reactions, and involves no new model.

Play, Piaget maintains, is hard to describe in its beginning, but once it has made its appearance, its antecedents are readily revealed in repetition, cyclical activities, and in the acquisition of new skills. The skill of shaking, for instance, can become play at the moment the skill as such is mastered. There is no doubt that an activity is play if an individual repeats it as the happy display of comprehended behavior (100). However, the exact boundary between ordinary behavior and play behavior is hard to establish. It is noteworthy that play comprises part of the child's activities in his third sensori-motor stage. The child starts play within his first year of life.

Affect (or emotions), originally seen as an indivisible part of primary intellectual development, emerges as a distinguishable and separate, but related, function at this phase. The increase in environmental contact, particularly in those actions which are beyond mere organic expressions, introduces a hierarchy of potential actions. Affective processes emerge in relation to these differences in experience. Piaget locates here the genetic roots of *interest* which later provide the affect, or the direction-giving force in human behavior.

In the first 6 months, affect has little significance because the child has no sense of permanency. An infant believes in an object only for as long as he perceives it. He ceases to be aware of it once it is beyond his perceptive range. The child's early preference and dependence upon the mothering person is treated by Piaget only to the extent that he ascribes it to a desired "affective permanence without localization" (93). In other words, in these instances, affect dominates the primary processes without historic foundation or rationale.

The secondary schemata stage, and its application to new situations, comprises the fourth sensori-motor stage, and tends to coincide with the infant's first birthday. During this stage, the infant uses previous behavioral achievements primarily as the bases for adding new ones to his expanding repertoire. Although transitional, Piaget considers this period sufficiently important to designate it as a separate stage.

Familiar modes of sensori-motor activities are applied to new situations. Increased experimentation, facilitated by the child's greater mobility, directs his interest to an environment beyond his heretofore limited functioning. He now experiences new objects; he tests and experiments with new ways of dealing with them. For example, he begins to discover that hiding an object occurs prior to finding it. The moment a child is aware of the continued existence of an object once it is beyond his immediate perception, he is capable of reasoning to the degree that the obstacles to his perception of the object can be removed. Ends and means are further differentiated by experimentation with, and discovery of means originally not intentionally related to the desired end. Thus, during this period the child is involved in continued and repeated experimentation—despite the fact that, to the casual observer, the emergence of new skills and awareness often appear to have been learned spontaneously.

Towards the end of the child's first year, he has refined his capacity to generalize and to differentiate to the degree that specific experiential episodes are generalized into classes of experience. Each is distinguished from the others by recognized signs, and each evokes different sets of action sequences. When the child can read these signs, anticipate action, and perceive his universe beyond the boundaries of his sensori-motor sphere of action, the capacity for intelligent reasoning has begun to emerge. Trial-and-error behavior is extant during this phase of development, employing previous behavioral patterns in new ways, and selecting those results most useful to the achievement of desired goals. Piaget recognizes that, during this period, adaptation is one result of random experimentation. In adaptation, the child fits new activities and objects of experience to previously acquired schemata. These new behavioral acquisitions are important for two reasons: First, the developing individual can distinguish objects from the related activity and can perceive them as objects; and second, he has acquired a developmental level of organization in which he can distinguish end products from their means.

This level of intellectual organization opens new dimensions. The ability to recognize signs and, the capacity to anticipate appropriate responses to them, create in the child a sense of independence from the action in progress. The center of activity becomes removed from the child's own actions. For example, delayed search for a missing object, as well as trial-and-error experimentation, reveals a child's capacity to remain apart from his action sequence. The child can experience action by *observation*. He lets things happen and observes the results. This is an important advancement. He observes in order to understand that which is beyond his immediate active involvement. For example, he watches the ball roll and then responds with delight or with pained cries. Here intellectual activities are clearly present. Yet, thinking remains entirely within the order of the child's range of classifications. To illustrate, to "go bye-bye" might mean to him that "mother, father (or anyone else) is going away," to "go for a walk," to "take a drive," to "go outside," or that "an object has been removed," or "has disappeared."

The discovery of new means through active experimentation refers to *tertiary circular reactions* introduced in the fifth stage. This stage generally occurs in the first half of the second year of life. Accommodative processes provide more balance to the processes of infancy which were originally purely assimilative. Active experimentation continues to compose a large share of the day's activities including the progression of primary, secondary, and tertiary circular reactions as a cyclic repetition of previous processes, with the addition of newly acquired capacities. It almost seems as if the child were saying to himself, "Let's try it this time in a new way!" This experimentation entails the application of old means of secondary circular reactions to new situations. The child incorporates into his knowledge the actions of this new experimentation *and* its results. Piaget locates in this cyclic repetition the roots of rational judgment and, ultimately, intellectual reasoning:

It involves an application of familiar means to new situations or the invention of new means constitute, from the same functional point of view, actual reasonings since, as we have already emphasized, the schema used in the capacity of means (it makes little difference whether it is familiar or invented on the spot) is subsumed under the schema characterizing the final end in the same way that judgments are put into a state of mutual implication in the framework of the conclusion (99, 268).

Reasoning must be given credit for this cyclical repetition. The individual tries to grasp the ongoing situation as it is and begins to observe its components. The child can now enter into an action sequence at any point without reproducing the total sequence.

With an awareness that objects are independent from their action sequence, the child gains an intensified interest in his environment. Piaget observes that sensory cues, perception, and continuous perceptive awareness entail three distinctly separate acquisitions. Sensory cues do not necessarily indicate perception just as perception does not necessarily guarantee awareness of that perception. Not until the present developmental level is achieved is the child capable of forming a beginning concept of "thing"— a beginning awareness of an object as an entity with its own distinct properties. Prior to this period, the sensory cue has been only a necessary part of the whole action sequence. A more important development is the child's ability to observe that the discovery of new objects or new methods of behavior and the utilization of this discovery present two distinct steps. The first precedes the second, but the second does not necessarily follow immediately or, for that matter, at all. Throughout life, the awareness of the *availability* of an activity does not imply its *utilization*. This distinction is a separate accomplishment which is acquired as a new mode of behavior.

The awareness of relationships between objects forms the early traces of memory and retention. Piaget attributes to the younger child the capacity to retain previous behavior patterns so long as they have become part of a behavior sequence. Now, with the capacity to separate objects from the ongoing action, the child can continue to envisage an object beyond his sensori-motor perception of it so long as he understands its immediate relationship to what remains after the action sequence. In other words, the awareness of an object's *relationship* to other objects (including its use) is essential to the remembrance of the object. The failure to remember, therefore, is due to a failure to understand relationships. Of course, during this early period of the child's development, only immediate relationships are understood and reflected in actions.

The discovery of objects as objects introduces the awareness of their spatial relationships. For example, the filling and emptying of hollow objects with smaller objects, or the fitting of differently shaped blocks into corresponding openings are typical experiments of children of this age. The recognition of spatial relationships between objects, and of rotations and reversals of objects in space, leads to an awareness of one's own movements and the movements of other people.

At this point, causal relations begin to assume a new dimension. The child recognizes the existence of causes which are completely independent of his activity. Other people become autonomous centers of action. Moreover, the child distinguishes himself as the actor, as the power behind the movement of inanimate objects, from other people's ability to cause action. This new outlook is essential for the evolving capacity to relate to different people; Piaget maintains that these developments are necessary to the affective behavior of competition and rivalry.

Earlier, primary and secondary reactions were mentioned as essential components in habit formation, which entails the continuation of a previously acquired behavioral pattern in a subsequent developmental phase. From the second year of life, however, increases in accommodative processes constantly threaten previously established habits. In Piaget's words:

. . . the external environment imposes a constant enlarging of the subject's reactions and that new experience always causes the old framework to crack. That is why acquired habits are sooner or later superposed on reflex schemata and on the former are superposed the schemata of intelligence. And, of course, it can also be said that the subject accepts this necessity with pleasure since the "circular action" at all levels is precisely an attempt to conserve novelties and establish them by reproductive assimilation (99, 265–266).

The capacity to imitate depends upon systematic accommodation, upon the ability to discern differences between objects. The capacity to imitate, to be or to act like another person, does not emerge, according to Piaget, roughly until the second year of life, and even then, it remains confined to the action phase of its model, because the child is as yet incapable of retaining a model as a mental symbol in itself, designating a class of actions or objects, which can be utilized at will despite the absence of the actual model to his perception.

Play increasingly becomes an expressive function of the developing child, primarily involving the repetition of his learned behavior as a self-satisfying occupation. Of note is the fact that play repeats the *action* phase which is not meant to represent any particular concept. For instance, a child playing at "going to sleep" imitates the action of "going to sleep," not the concept of "bed-time" or of "night-time." Play is termed *ludic*, as it is an activity calculated to amuse and to excite the playing individual, while assimilation takes over with a progressive differentiation between the signal, the signifier and what is signaled. Piaget employs the term *signifier* to mean the mental signal for subsequent action. Play becomes progressively less involved in the context of the existing environment, and begins to have meaning only within the context of the *child's* own fictitious, personal world. Ludic play denotes the personal, therapeutic aspect of play, as if play were to "legalize" a predominance of assimilation.

The stage of invention of new means through mental combinations is entered sometime during the second half of the child's second year of life. A gradual shift in focus occurs from the actual sensori-motor experiences to an increased reflection about these experiences. The phrase, "through mental combinations" suggests an advanced level of intellectual behavior. Obviously, this developmental stage climaxes previous acquisitions and builds a bridge to the next developmental phase. For the present, the infant tends to act in set ways until his patterns of action become solidified. Eventually, they develop into his scheme of behavior by the very process of his experiencing them. These first beginnings of mental operations appear as if by *intuition*, a term which Piaget applies, at times, to this stage (100). Only later does his behavior reveal a clearer comprehension and a reliance upon previous experiences.

Thus far the child has been limited to knowledge of his environment only so far as it concerns his action sequences. Towards the second half of his first year, the child becomes clearly aware of objects as independent, autonomous centers with their own properties beyond his intent and action. "When do objects become permanent?" is a question which permeates all of Piaget's research related to infants and young children. During the second half of the second year a child indicates an awareness of the permanency of objects and he simultaneously discovers a new approach to his environment. Most important, the child perceives and utilizes objects for their own innate qualities. He can use them differentially, apart and beyond his immediate experience with them. First, the individual discerns himself as one object among many. He then discovers that objects can endure in the passage of time. It is then possible for newly acquired mental images of objects to be retained beyond immediate sensory experiences with them. In other words, the child is slowly becoming capable of perceiving an object by its telling part and remembering this object beyond its perceptual presence. Further, he begins to relate the object to new actions (or vice versa) without actually perceiving all the actions. Closely linked with the remembered image of an object are its properties: its uses, its form, its size and its color. The comprehension of each property of the object requires a separate level of intellectual maturity. In this way, a child's "permanent" image of an object might be composed of only one of the object's properties. The child sees and remembers as much of an object at any given period as he can understand at the time. He has already begun to anticipate action, however, by his capacity to respond to signals and, with the acquisition of retained images and the ability to relate them to past experiences, he starts to formulate new images of his own. In short, he thinks.

Notice must be taken of the child's new relationship to his environment. He not only experiences himself as one among many, he also understands himself as a single entity. In simple situations he can think of himself in relation to past and immediate future situations as well as to those in the present. He can also conceive of objects without having a detailed personal experience of them. His previously acquired capacity to perceive cause is extended to a point where he can envisage himself as the *potential* cause or initiator of action.

This new vista of mental functioning also affects previously learned behavior. Sensori-motor patterns are slowly replaced by semi-mental functionings. The child has a beginning ability to recall without having to repeat an activity with his sensory motor system. He perceives simple causality by perception alone; he can initiate detours or alternatives to most simple forms of action without actually performing by trial and error. Still, the child will depend, for some time, upon his sensori-motor approach. He is slow to utilize his new *organizational* pattern of thinking.

Imitation now proceeds with the attempt to copy either the action itself or the representative *symbol* of the action. For example, a child might imitate a parent's work, or, he may imitate the same action in order to convey the idea that he is "going to work" like his parent. In either case, the imitative process involves a predominance of accommodation of an environmental model. This mode of behavior is of import to the imitation of sounds in language development.

Previously, *play* had been purely functional. It involved the repetition of life activities to no aim other than the pleasure of sheer self-satisfaction. The acquisition of representative symbols, however, opens new possibilities in the sphere of play behavior.

So far this discussion has avoided the Piagetian concept of

egocentricity, the state of confusion of self and the external world. *Egocentrism* is the term given to the undifferentiating state of awareness that exists prior to that of multiple perspectives. In essence, all infant and early childhood behavior rests upon a lack of differentiation between the child himself and his environment. Egocentricity is due to an ignorance of social perspective rather than to a failure in social sensitivity.

Identification as a mental process becomes evident towards the end of the child's second year, although it has formulated its roots during earlier developmental stages. Through this process, the child imitates and remembers the model's imitable characteristics. The ability to imitate, however, depends upon the level of the child's intellectual development, and the choice of the model is related to the child's interest in assimilating the model's behavior. In other words, successful identification relies upon the intellectual capacity to differentiate and the affective incentive to imitate. Piaget states:

> When the subject sees objects as distinct from himself and sees models as objects, models can no longer be assimilated wholesale; they are seen to be both different from and similar to the child himself. It is no longer only identity, but also similarity which becomes a source of interest. It is true that as yet it is only those models which have some analogy with the child's schemas which give rise to imitation. Those which are too remote from the child's experience leave him indifferent (**100**, 50–51).

The Preconceptual Phase

Jean Piaget's material concerning the 2- to 4-year-old is elusive; his research and his writing about this period have been limited. For Piaget, these years involve a period of transition sandwiched between life patterns of purely self-satisfying behavior and rudimentary socialized behavior.

The life of the child in the 2- to 4-year-old period appears to be one of continuous investigation. He investigates his environment and the possibilities of his activity within it. Every day he discovers new symbols to use in communication with himself and others. These symbols have primarily a personal reference for him, still. He cannot at this time comprehend the more general system of meaning they hold in the adult world. Thus, even though the child and the adult employ much the same language, they do not necessarily have a mutual framework for their communication; the child's thinking is largely preconceptual in content.

Yet, the egocentric approach of this phase reflects a decisive advance over the autistic behavior of the previous phase: "The interplay of practical relationships in the world of reality teaches the child to shift centers of space and its objects from his action to himself, and thus locate himself at the middle point of this world which is being born" (101, 38). The child knows the world only as he sees it; he knows no alternatives. Further, he sees his physical and social worlds only as he has previously experienced them. This limited view of things leads to his assumption that everyone thinks as he does and understands him without his having to work to convey his thoughts and feelings. Necessarily, during this phase, assimilation continues as the paramount role of the child; otherwise he could not incorporate the new experiences which will lead to his more expanded view of his world.

Play occupies most of the child's waking hours, since this activity serves to consolidate and to enlarge the child's previous acquisitions. Play, with its emphases upon how? and why?, becomes the primary tool for adaptation; the child quickly turns his experience of the world into play. For instance, a child will behave as if he had mastered the routine of dressing as soon as he can put his clothing on in one way or another. Then "getting dressed" becomes play, even if his method of dressing varies considerably from his elders' standards. For the young child, "getting dressed" is a subjective activity and, therefore, it can be play. Through play the child is actually pretending that he is performing real-life tasks and it may involve activities ranging from the simplest to the most complicated. Imaginary or symbolic play is prominent for its rich egocentric character; for the child, play has all the elements of reality, while to the uninitiated by-stander, this play appears to be sheer fantasy. To illustrate, a wooden block might represent a rabbit eating, another block as its carrot. The child in this phase may be said to play his way through his life. Symbolic play and the playful repetition of actual events bring the child in contact with the questions and objects of everyday life. In a spiral-like fashion his contacts evolve more and more into realistic experience with his social world.

Language, as play, also serves as a vehicle of development. The child repeats words, and connects these words with visible objects or perceived actions. With his recent acquisition of proper phonation and approximately correct use of words, the 2- or 3-year-old employs his language in order to convey his own experience. For example, "soup is hot," means to the child that his own soup is hot; he cannot yet understand that this phrase might be applicable to all soups. As in play, the child experiences his world purely from his egocentric vantage point. His language not only repeats sensori-motor developmental history, it also replaces it. The more a child verbally expresses desire, experience, or thought without having to act them out, the more it is indicated that he accepts speech as a conveyor of meaning; he has translated from the mental symbol, into words. This is the necessary step before the child can learn to generalize and comprehend objective concepts. Communication by verbal or nonverbal language establishes a bond between thought and word, while it negates the autistic world of imagery and ludic play. Language becomes possible the moment the child relinquishes his autistic world and his primary circular response of self-imitation.

The imitation of others and symbolic imitation are mostly spontaneous processes in children of these ages. An instance of symbolic imitation might be that of a child who, by sitting crouched with a pen in one hand, means to imitate the entire action sequence of his father writing a letter; similarly, the mere wearing of a sheriff's badge might be adequate for a child to consider himself in the entire act of being a sheriff. The child imitates as he perceives, with little concern for accuracy. He considers a model as important to him and tries to incorporate often in one gesture his own perception of the entire action sequence, demonstrated by the model. Imitation furnishes him with a wealth of new symbols for objects and also enriches his repertoire of available behavior. The process of shifting his attention from himself to others and then back to himself further helps him to refine his imitation to more closely approximate the action sequence of the model. Above all, during this phase, his interests and awareness place a greater emphasis upon objects and actions in his environmental world.

The child is constantly forced to evaluate and to reevaluate his perception of his environment. Piaget does not construe these processes to be the child's attempt to sharpen his perception, but rather the results of the psychological processes of accommodation and of the child's developmental readiness to relinquish some of his subjectivity. The latter schematic change allows for the formulation of more accurate perception and of a more representative use of language.

It is noteworthy that the absence or severe retardation of play, language, or imitative behavior, leaves a child in his autistic world and less subject to the impact of his environment. Play, involving language and imitation, leads to communication with an outside world and to a gradual process of socialization. David Rapaport states:

The mere fact, then, of telling one's thought, or telling it to others, or of keeping silence and telling it only to oneself must be of enormous importance to the structure and functioning of thought in general, and of child logic in particular. Now between autism and intelligence there are many degrees, varying with their capacity for being communicated. These intermediate varieties must therefore be subject to a special logic, intermediate too between the logic of autism and that of intelligence. The chief of those intermediate forms, that is, the type thought which like that exhibited by our children seeks to adapt itself to reality, but does not communicate itself as such, we propose to call *Ego-centric thought* (110, 158).

Thought and reason in the 2-year-old are entirely ego-centric with a predominance of self-reference. These processes go on automatically in the child as he is involved in one particular inci-

dent or another without his associating the events with their overall meaning. In his use of his newly learned language, the child
merely replaces his earlier reliance on pure sensori-motor behavior. The use of language in itself does not necessarily indicate
that the child has achieved a more advanced intellectual organization. With the aid of words, the child places his experiences in
verbal proximity. On the basis of previous experience with sequential relationships, however, the child relies upon his subjective
idea of proximity; that is, whatever occurs in proximity with
something else has a relationship to it. The child reasons that one
event followed by another must have a causal relationship. The
child begins to think in terms of relationships and establishes his
own view of cause and effect. For example, the young child is apt
to interpret the acts of walking past a stool and tripping on a leg
of that stool as interrelated events. He sees the stool as the cause
of his fall and blames it because of its association with his fall. The
implication here of *animism*, the attribution of life and consciousness to inanimate objects, is evident and will be considered later on.

The repeated experiencing of events in sequence is coordinated into the child's perceptual configurations:

> Any change in configuration modifies the predictions accordingly;
> that is why there is no generalized conservation . . . [reasoning is still
> essentially and characteristically nonreversible] . . . There is only
> consciousness of perceived or factual relationships, but not yet aware-
> ness of any system of possible transformations of these relationships
> . . . [Later on, however,] the change from one configuration to
> another becomes more important. Such changes . . . [Then become]
> understood as parts of actions, but of reversible actions (**102**, **138**).

The child orders his concept of space and spatial relationships by
his subjective experience; life to him is logical within his own
frame of reference. This is the same level of behavior that is at
times continued in adult life when a point of view or action can
only be explained and justified by self-reference and only within
the terms of the person's own history. Piaget's observations stress
two essential phenomena characteristic of this age. First, events
are reasoned and judged by their outward appearance, regardless

of their objective logic. Reasoning—or "simply a reflective level of internalization and of symbolization on permitting reasoning but originating at the sensori-motor level, before the development of language and inner thought" (**107b**, 61)—is based entirely upon subjective judgments. For example, a child will select a glass filled to the rim in preference to a three-quarter-filled glass twice its size, basing his selection upon his own idea of fullness. Though he may have witnessed a greater amount of milk being poured into the latter glass, he judges as he sees things.

Second, in preconceptual thought, a child tends to experience either the qualitative or quantitative aspect; he does not perceive both at once or any connective relationship between the notions of quantity and quality. The child has not reached the point where he is able to merge concepts of objects, space, and causality into temporal interrelationships with a concept of time.

Close to the preconcept of causality and the perception of phenomenalistic characteristics are the tendencies of the child to bestow power upon objects. On the basis of his own reasoning process, this is justified since he no longer considers all actions as emanating from himself. "He thereby invests another person [or physical objects] with an exaggerated power over the universe, a sort of artificialization due to projection of personal activity onto those new centers of forces constituted by the other 'selves' " (**93**, 308). Basically, the child's thinking reflects a failure to differentiate between his own actions and those of the object.

Investing a model with unusual desirability and/or power leads to *identification*. Piaget explains the emergence of identification as follows:

He [the child] feels close to those who satisfy his immediate needs and interests. He selects them as his model. These spontaneously selected models become frequently for years the measuring stick for value judgments. In spite of unavoidable conflicts, particularly during the period of negativism around the age of three, the spontaneously selected model, usually the caring adult, remains the object of identification and obedience. Under ordinary conditions the young child maintains a sense of respect and awe for the superior powers of his caretaker(s). He places him in an omnipotent position. The child's sense of obedience and awe . . . is derived out of a combination of love and fear and provides the foundation for his conscience. Obedience to the demand becomes only then a moral obligation when the person requesting obedience is held in awe. Respect for the caretaker requires obedience to the values established by him (translated from 103, 308).

Identification on the present level emerges from a combination of imitation and a sense of awe for the model. This sense of awe flows from the child's continuous experience with this model, usually his parents, because they have been continuously associated with his most self-satisfying behavior sequences. They are also the only models the child knows and can incorporate into his intellectual and affective schema (100). The individual's original focus of interest in his own body has been expanded to interests in his immediately experienced environment. Episodes related to family feelings now provide him with most of his affective-laden experiences. This spontaneously developed identification becomes a guidepost for all judgment. With an increased capacity for refined differentiation of affect, the child builds up his system of values, his conscience. Identification also is strengthened by the child's accommodation to the pressure of the environment. Adult restraints and demands for obedience are as real to his experience as are episodes of self-satisfaction.

Long before the child has a conception of obedience, he comprehends the activity of "doing as he is told." He equates this with pleasing his parent and uses a causal relationship between the two. He complies with verbal commands in his behavior and regards being a "good child" as one who fulfills his parents' commands. The young child takes orders literally, as if words were objects or actions. Consequently, he frequently finds himself in a dilemma since he is unable to carry out orders as he perceives them. For instance, the command "be good" only confuses the child. He does not know what to do in the absence of a demand for specific behavior. A generalized concept of "goodness" does not as yet exist for him. The child carries his wish to obey into his play behavior. Just as obedience to adults is in the order of things, so the rules of games are sacred and untouchable. In the play of 3- or 4-year-olds, the child's own activities are the center of play. Consequently, "to win" means to carry out his activities successfully. Unless his winning necessitates elimination of the other child, he sees no inconsistency in several simultaneous winners. All that matters is the successful completion of his play.

The Phase of Intuitive Thought

Most important for the 4- to 7-year-olds is their widening social interest in the world around them. Repeated contact with others necessarily reduces egocentricity and increases social participation. Piaget, in a recent publication (97), indicates that this phase is an extension of the previous one; both actually cover *preoperational thought* and, together, they form a bridge between the child's passive acceptance of the environment as it is experienced and his ability to react to it realistically. In this second transitional period, the phase of intuitive thought, the child begins to use words in his thought. At first, his thinking and reasoning are still acted out. Just as the child had to coordinate sensorimotor experience on an earlier level, so on this level of intuitive thought the child has to coordinate perspectives of different individuals, including himself. He must coordinate his own subjective and egocentric versions of the world with the real world around him. During this phase, he increasingly acts in a consistent pattern of reasoning. He tends to behave similarly to his elders, as if he knew intuitively what life were all about; he exhibits the first real beginnings of cognition.

When the child is old enough to begin school, his thinking is largely the verbalization of his mental processes. Much as the child once employed his motor apparatus to act out his thinking, he now employs speech to express his thinking, yet his thinking remains largely egocentric. His perception and interpretation of his environment are continuously colored by his personal preconceptions, and will, naturally, be at variance with the thinking of his elders and with the real world. Furthermore, he can think only of one idea at a time.

The child still struggles to find a better equilibrium between assimilation and accommodation. He tries to adjust his new experiences to his previous patterns of thinking. "Those parts of reality which are again encountered are fraught with a multitude of new shades and elements which can at first be ignored in assimilating occurrences to the habitual schema, but which in the long run must be taken into account" (**100**, 83). Increasing interest in occurring events brings assimilation on a broader scale. Or, stated inversely, accommodative processes are extended to verify, to stabilize, and to generalize the various models in order that the individual can assimilate more universal precepts. Simultaneously, current development entails the generalization of symbols as images of a more encompassing concept. His organization of his expanding knowledge aids the child to gain the capacity to generalize his mental experience. For example, a child having two large red marbles and three small blue marbles envisages them as "a collection of five marbles." The symbols "two plus three," figuratively speaking, can be manipulated mentally and altered into the representative symbol "five." Or to wear a sheriff's badge —which in the preconceptual period meant "I *am* a sheriff"—means for the child in this phase that he is playing the part of what, in his opinion, a sheriff represents. In other words, assimilative processes build upon the early images, frequently beyond the conscious awareness of the child involved. It must be stressed, however, that the child must first understand the preconcept of being a sheriff before he can realize that the concept of sheriff stands for law and order.

It is still difficult for the child to entertain two ideas simultaneously, which calls attention to one of Piaget's major concerns: The capacity to see the parts concurrently, and to relate these parts to the whole. At this point, the child is still incapable of thinking in terms of the whole; he is preoccupied with the parts. If he attempted to think in terms of the whole, he would lose sight of the parts and their relationships which he is just beginning to grasp. This loss, or childish amnesia, frequently occurs when the environment is altered or when other events or a force which he cannot comprehend intervenes in a situation. A summary of Piaget's experiment of matching in two parallel lines serves to illustrate this problem. A child will think of two identical sets of buttons as being the matching quantity as long as each additional button is placed in close proximity to the others in a given group. If, within the child's view, each row is rearranged into two piles, each of different dimensions, the child will indicate the larger *appearing* heap as that with the most buttons, even though actually each pile contains the same number of buttons. Thus, the concept of an unaltered "whole" cannot be considered without an inspection of its parts. As long as the piles or rows of buttons looked equal, the child would explain that no buttons have been taken from or added to either group, and he would deny a difference in the quantity contained in each group (94). The alteration of the perceptual field, the change from a matched line of buttons to uneven though still identical piles of buttons, created an environmental intervention and a new situation beyond the intellectual grasp of the child, obliterating his previous ideas.

It is noteworthy that the child increasingly employs appropriate language without fully comprehending its meaning. For example, a child in the early years of this phase knows his right arm from his left, but has no notion of the concepts "right" or "left." In this phase, the child's knowledge is specific but he applies it universally. Further, the child can think only in terms of the ongoing event. Any experience is judged by its end stage, or product. Speed, gifts, amount of work or other accumulative events are evaluated by their appearance at the time of completion. For instance, any work he might complete first he pronounces the "easiest," or a toy car which arrives first in a race is the "fastest," regardless of the shorter distance it may have covered in comparison with that covered by the others. The child judges by a single, usually spatial, clue. His reasoning proceeds from the premise to the conclusion in a single jump. The outcome justifies the "logic" applied. A certain event *had* to happen. The child attempts "logical" reasoning, though spuriously, and such reasoning is a step forward.

Actually, the child continues an earlier pattern of relating all things, with one important addition; he now selects an objective point of reference. In one sense, his reasoning is transductive; that is, it relates particular to particular. In another sense, it is syncretic in its depiction of things as a whole, for these things do not cohere. The child is unaware of this contradiction. As long as the child reasons primarily from his own vantage point, he is not capable of assigning *fixed* laws to causality, nor does he see a need for it. Visual representation and personal experience, however, permit him to perceive simple relationships and to establish his precepts. A child of this age explains dreams in a manner similar to that in which he explains his objective world. Dreams are assumed to exist outside the dreamer, and the occurring events are attributed to "real" persons and creatures that appeared in the dream. Later, a dream is explained as it was visualized during the time of dreaming.

Naturally, increased accommodation during these years calls for added attention to events beyond the child. Attention to other points of view widen the child's perspective, and at the same time, reduce his egocentricity. His widening perspective also includes an extended understanding of his objective world, and objects are observed for their multiple properties of form, color, utility. Each property or attribute of an object or a person, however, is seen as an absolute; it is common for a child of this age to see the night as always "black" or the hero of a story as always "brave." The child does not have a notion of valuation or rank, nor of relativity, except in terms of opposite absolutes; there is always "a best" and "a worst." This explains his common lack of appreciation of the true value of others. In the absence of a hierarchy of values, the child senses no difference in alternatives between all good or all bad, and he is essentially egocentric in his understanding of what pleases or displeases him. Piaget characterizes this approach as an "immediate, illegitimate generalization" (95).

The new awareness of such multiple properties as form, speed, or moral value does not necessarily suggest a comprehension of the basic concepts related to these properties. At the same time, however, the child is acquiring the prerequisites for such under-standing. He slowly becomes aware of the fact that one property —for example, height—does not exclude the simultaneous presence of a second one, such as width. Once aware of this much, he will detect further patterns of relationship, and will eventually realize that total quantity or quality can be maintained even when one attribute is reduced or another increased. It should be stressed that the child can evaluate only those relationships which pertain to one object or precept. Relationships between two or more objects or ideas are still beyond his comprehension, because he cannot conceive of several points or ideas beyond those of a single object, as part of a still larger whole.

Although it may seem self-evident, it is important to state that a child of preschool age may know how to count, even though he has no concept of numbers. A year or so later, he usually acquires a concept of numbers regardless of his capability in counting. Piaget maintains a child must master the principles of conservation of quantity, such as permanency and continuity, before he can develop a concept of numbers. The former is a logical notion and brings the child into the next phase of intellectual organization.

During this phase of intuitive thought, the child retains his pre-conceptual notion that his thoughts and body are one. This was illustrated by a child who tripped over a "bad" chair. Correspond-ingly, early in the intuitive phase, the child considers everything that is active as alive. Towards the latter part of this phase, how-ever, life is attributed only to objects which are capable of motion or of the production of energy. Furthermore, in the absence of a better understanding of causality and natural laws, the child will reason along two lines. In some situations, as in ludic play, his explanations are without any recourse to apparent facts. For in-stance, he explains that the sky has been made by men. Or, he may say that the clouds are alive and traverse the sky on their own. This is due to the continued predominance of assimilation in his developmental process; his physical and psychological worlds are still intertwined, from his vantage point—thoughts, things, and persons are experienced as if on one plane. This may explain the observation that a child's respect for a toy is equal to his respect for people.

All of this serves to illustrate an important Piagetian theorem: The understanding of different objects may occur at different times in the child's life, but this understanding follows a similar cycle in each instance. Familiar objects in immediate proximity are fully perceived for what they are in the preconceptual phase; distant objects of more casual familiarity are fully comprehended only later in life. The child, for example, is apt to speak of a "new" sun which appears every day. Thus, though he grants permanent existence to his ball even when it may be missing, he will not grant such permanency to the remoter sun. And, even though his ball is recognized as an object which must depend upon an outside force for its motion, the sun continues to be vested with animism. The child believes new sun "wakes up" on its own every morning.

Intuitive thought introduces a rudimentary awareness of relationships which eventually can be schematized into a conceptual hierarchy, but usually such early understandings are related to concrete events. For the child of preschool age, the family consists of all living things in his immediate physical proximity and frequently includes the family pets; the family is not yet separated in time and space. It is almost impossible for the child to understand fully that he belongs to a *particular* family, and likewise to a *particular* town and country, all at the same time. These observations have important implications for understanding a child's sense of belonging.

Language at this level serves a threefold purpose. First, as an important tool of intuitive thought, it is employed to reflect upon an event, and to project it into the future. Self-conversation is a common occurrence at this age and is popularly described as "thinking aloud." Second, speech remains primarily a vehicle of egocentric communication, with assimilation as its most potent adaptive process. Speech is limited to a few communicative expressions because, in general, until he is 7 or 8, a child assumes that everyone thinks as he does. Arguments are simply conflicts of contrary affirmations with no understanding involved and with no motivation present to bridge any lack of understanding. Verbal arguments become vehement, because words are readily accepted as thoughts and deeds. For example, two children may argue about their preference for a Ford or Chevrolet. Having perhaps heard their fathers engage in a similar discussion, neither child has any real knowledge of the merits of his championed car, although each child affirms what he accepts as correct. Each child presses the argument, because he thinks that the affirmation, the power of words, makes it so. Similarly, a child might cry for having been called "dumb" because he feels being called "dumb" makes him, in fact, dumb. Finally, speech is a means of social communication in the accommodative sense. It serves as a means to understand the external environment and to adapt to it. Conversation is an extension of thinking aloud, and projects individual thoughts into the social plane and encourages collective thinking.

Play reflects much of the evolutionary intellectual development of these early childhood years. On the surface, play becomes noticeably social, while its underlying thinking processes still maintain their egocentric tone. In his play, the child now uses a more extended symbolic imagination; for example, the understanding of "being a sheriff" progresses from the mere wearing of the sheriff's badge in the preconceptual phase, to playing "as if I was a sheriff" in the present phase, to playing the role of sheriff, as a guardian of law and order, in the next phase. Games which depend on finding missing objects, such as in Hide and Seek, or guessing games, appear at this age in a child's play repertoire. Also, genuine make-believe play appears which indicates that the child has achieved a new level of organizational thinking; he can now think in terms of others. Most important, however, is the fact that the child's play becomes more social. Social disciplines, such as collective rules, one by one replace individual ludic symbols, while traditional games, such as tag, which are typical of the age group, replace spontaneous games. In fact, most play is now done in relation to other people. Consequently, collective considerations and rules become a necessity. Intellectual and social development from preschool age on occur in an inverse ratio to symbolic distortion and ludic play. The more accommodation to reality there is, the more opportunity there will be to adapt without recourse to play. Play and work ultimately find themselves together without clear boundaries.

In an earlier phase, imitation was manifested as an end in itself, and the child employed imitation without full awareness of his model's intrinsic values. At that point, activity and objective were confused. In this phase, with a conscious awareness of some of the relationship patterns of his social world, the child tends to imitate others in order to capture their values or the status which they represent. Piaget emphasizes that this effort of imitation must not be confused with identification. The organizational pattern for identification varies from phase to phase. Identification provides an interesting mixture of the assimilation of simple mental images of desirable objects to a child's established patterns of thinking and behaving. The child's newly widened social dimensions open opportunities for new relationships, and for investing them with previous feelings. The transfer of feelings, in an analytic sense, depends upon the current understanding of environmental factors and their relationship to each other for expression. (*Transference*, in psychoanalytic theory, refers to the inappropriate shifting onto another person of one or more revived emotional fixations—usually originally attached to a parent—that were not successfully outgrown or assimilated in early childhood. In this process, a less significant person in the child's life usually becomes the unrealistic object of the fixated person's love or hate.)

Moral values for the young child, it must be remembered, are generalized as they are learned. The child, so far, tends to view moral laws as absolute values in real things. Rules, moral obligations, and their phenomenalistic sources are seen as one. Just as its name and its attributes are part of an object, so moral values and rules exist as an indivisible part of the object. For example, the command "Do not touch the scissors," becomes a property of the scissors. Or, father, and obedience to father, are perceived as one. Increased social contacts, combined with more accurate imitation, gradually result in new understandings. Adult rules are observed to be elastic and are no longer absolutes. This puts the child in a situation of conflict, because he has no new ways of dealing with this new problem, nor can he find a solution until he combines a higher level of thinking with an understanding of the relativity of social obligations. As before, the first change will occur in behavior which is related to daily practice and well mastered habits. Values less related to daily life are not challenged until later. Altogether, obedience to adults remains the prevailing moral code for the 4- to 7-year-old. Obedience to adults still means "being good," while disobedience means "being bad." A child in this phase regards all adult actions as fair. Children conform through their unilateral respect and constraint towards adult authority and prestige.

In his play and fantasy, the child enacts the rules and values of his elders. He may behave as if he had adopted their social conventions as his own. A sense of mutual cooperation and social responsibility may be reflected in his play and speech, but it does not exist in his pattern of thinking; consequently, to hold the group responsible for the behavior of a few makes little sense to a child of this age. Mutual responsibility and group solidarity are still beyond his comprehension. The young child judges a lie by the degree of disobedience involved; motives or underlying circumstances are not considered. The child judges a lie for its accepted value rather than for its intended purpose; he does not see the implications of deceit, since he thinks primarily about himself: "[A child] . . . lies as he romances, so that the obligation not to lie, imposed upon him by adult constraint, appears from the first in its most external form: a lie is what does not agree with the truth independently of the subject's intentions" (98, 143–144). In this phase, disobedience is an interruption of adult authority rather than a violation of moral obligation. For instance, so called "naughty words" are linguistic taboos. Using them is called "bad" because they break adult-imposed taboos. The sense of propriety involved in avoiding unpleasant terms cannot occur until the child sees himself on a similar social plane with others, and until he understands a need for mutual cooperation which will replace restrictive, unilateral adult respect. Piaget warns that unilateral respect for authority is slow to give way to more advanced patterns because of its *guilt* component. Piaget never traces the development of guilt and its underlying dynamics. Although he questions the Freudian assumption of guilt prior to memory, he seems to accept the Freudian formulation that guilt is a product and expression of the conscience for later ages. The child sees noncompliance as an insult to adult authority even if his noncompliance is unavoidable, as in situations of involuntary awkwardness. If he feels responsible for an incident, he feels little relief in escaping an adult censor. "The sense of guilt is proportional not to the incidental negligence . . . but to physical acts themselves" (98, 177). Reproof is expected by the young child as a natural consequence of an assumed misdeed. The child perceives punishment as a necessary sequence following any transgression against adult standards. He sees a necessity for atonement and punishment in due proportion to the gravity of the misdeed, regardless of the underlying circumstances. Indeed, until the age of 5, a child sees a need for an act of punishment to take place, which could take the form of punishment of the innocent, and just as well fill the child's expectations. The expectation of punishment during these early years is also reflected in the child's belief in automatic punishment and immanent justice. *Immanent justice* is employed by Piaget to describe a subject incurring upon himself a verdict of guilty and subsequently inflicting punishment upon himself whenever he commits a wrong. This notion remains with the child until the end of this phase.

As we have suggested, unilateral respect for adults slowly gives way due to an awareness of many adult authorities whose rules vary, and to the inconsistencies even within one adult's rules. Simultaneously, the child slowly turns from his single authority, usually a parent, and tends to cooperate with other authorities, even without full awareness of the meaning of social cooperation. A 6-year-old might be very apt to participate with others in a minor exploit which goes contrary to adult wishes. But the 6-year-old is merely cooperating on the plane of action, and in thought he fully accepts adult authority, even though the incident may appear to the adult to be a deliberate act against authority:

> Thought always lags behind action and cooperation has to be practiced for a long time before its consequences can be brought fully to light by reflective thought.
> The idea of autonomy appears in the child about a year later than cooperative behavior and the practical consciousness of autonomy . . . We may therefore advance the hypothesis that the verbal and theoretical judgment of the child corresponds, broadly speaking, with the concrete and practical judgment which the child may have made on the occasion of his own actions during the years preceding the interrogatory [gathering of data] (98, 114–115).

The Phase of Concrete Operations

In the previous phase, the child became aware of relationships by a more accurate appraisal of his social position in relation to his environment. In the present phase, he manages to see an event from different perspectives. His manifold perspective leads the individual to an awareness of reversibility, a term which is deliberately employed because, since he has acquired sensori-motor intelligence, the individual has practiced reversibility in his daily contacts with objects. *Reversibility* is ". . . the permanent possibility of returning to the starting point of the operation in question" (105, 272). In other words, reversibility is the capacity of relating an event or thought to a total system of interrelated parts in order to conceive the event or thought from its beginning to its end or from its end to its beginning. Reversibility is achieved either by canceling an operation (inversion or negation) or by reciprocity (reciprocal operation as an equivalent). The child achieves a new level of thought; namely, *operational thought*. Operational thought refers to the mental capacity to order and relate experience to an organized whole. On the basis of his later work (after 1929), Piaget separates operational thought into two distinct phases: *concrete* and *formal* operational thought. Concrete operations presuppose that mental experimentation still depends upon perception. The individual, in the 7- to 11-year age range, cannot perform mental operations unless he can concretely perceive their inner logicality.

In reviewing organizational patterns of concrete thought, all patterns of behavior will here be considered to be a total process. Assimilation and accommodation become less an experience of opposing pulls than one of "mobile equilibrium" (97). This is due partly to the child's new perspective of time. Until this level of maturity, assimilation and accommodation have always competed for dominance; yet the new capacity of considering several points of view simultaneously, and of returning each time to an original state, indicates major organizational gains. The child can explore several possible solutions to a problem without necessarily adopting any one, because he can always return to his original outlook. His awareness of manifold approaches to one object elasticizes his previously rigid and intuitive approach, and permits him to order his sense data along two levels of cognitive thought.

First, as any whole becomes known for its parts, the child studies these parts and classifies them in relation to each other, which eventually leads to his understanding of their whole. This form of understanding grows from the realm of experience; yet his experiences with his physical and social environment, and the abstractions he learns to make from concrete experiences with objects, lead him to mathematical methods of conceptualizing. For instance, the acquisition of the concept of weight proceeds from an ordering of actual experiences related to sensations of "small," "medium," and "large." On this level, the child essentially is pondering about relationships as if he were to set up equations. He relates his behavior to the consequences it will create. For instance, a child, while strolling in the woods, wants to crack open a walnut. He will select a stone which is large enough to do the job. His thinking tends to proceed as follows: Large stone equals cracked walnut. His thinking focuses upon both ends of the equation. He is now attempting to solve both sides of the equation; that is, he wants to know *which means can accomplish which ends?*

Secondly, at this point of his development, the child becomes equally preoccupied with establishing for himself *systems of classifications*. He will tend to see to it that he can conceptualize and classify each object as part of a larger total system. He will organize his parts into a larger whole by the hierarchical systems either of *nesting* or *lattices*.

Nesting is a descriptive term for classifying an internal relationship between smaller parts and their all-inclusive whole. This term is used similarly to that of describing *nesting blocks* which is a toy of boxes fitting tightly into each other. In either case, in its conceptual use or in its description of a child's toy, nesting specifies that all classes are additive. Each larger whole sums up *all* previous parts. Children, by means of nesting, add together their world into a "fitting" whole. Suddenly, the animal kingdom or sundry previously unconnected ideas make sense to them.

Lattices, on the other hand, refer to a special form of classification in which the focus is upon the connective link and the parts which are linked together. Ordering conceptually by means of a hierarchy of lattices places stress upon creating subclasses of *related* objects. Related classes are conceptually linked together in order to create a coordinated whole. Noteworthy, as in the lattice work of a fence, so in mentally binding together the reversible relationship between subclasses and a larger whole. The lattices establish the "whole"—the fence or the interconnected orderly world. At this point in the child's life, relationship between pieces of knowledge is established by their logical relationship to each other rather than merely by proximity in experience. Most important, cognition by two different systems of ordering highlight a child's increasing awareness that each object has several reference points and can be ordered accordingly. The child can now envisage any object in relation to one or several wholes which, in turn, become part of a still larger unity or system. His life, from now on, proceeds in an ordered world where he can organize his experiences separately or as part of a unity.

The ability to order experiences and to be aware of their realistic relationship to each other helps to create a *notion of certainty*. The child can explain his experiences or thoughts in relation to others. He can order his experience as he sees fit. At present, all ordering must be done for him singly with the aid of a concrete model. If offered a choice, a child cannot choose unless he can weigh each choice and perceive the relationships between them. Piaget stresses that the child first masters the seriation of small aggregates with small quantitative units of familiar classes. Ordering by seriation involves the active manipulation of symbols or objects into new hierarchies. Previously, because of his ego-centric perspective, the child knew only irreversible hierarchies; with his present outlook, he can start to reason on the basis of an objective hierarchy. For instance, the previous pseudoparadox of simultaneous membership in family, city, etc., can now partially be resolved. It must be noted that this entire process is gradual, and that egocentric perspectives continue longer in matters further removed from his daily life. Again the principle of proximity remains in evidence.

Classification, seriation, and hierarchical arrangements bring together a number of previously independent reference systems into unified and interrelated larger systems. The new organiza-tional schema of reversibility emerges directly from the cognition of reversible activities. They have been performed all along. How-ever, only with more accurate accommodation and understanding of relationships has the child become aware of their meaning. To return to a previous example, the child is now aware that the milk poured into a smaller container represents the same amount of milk that was contained in the original container. The concept of constancy, regardless of phenomenalistic appearance, opens the way to new vistas of understanding. Reversibility establishes a mobile equilibrium. Any mental operation can now be returned to its starting point, be approached from opposite ends, and be related concurrently to the same whole. A mental operation can be repeated in a different direction, or be altered by the inclusion of new questions ("detours"). All these variations can take place without obliterating the logic or the original content of the thought. The question can be raised: "Is thought reversible and can a person ever return to his unaltered original premise?" Gestalt psychology and the theorem of *circular response* by M. P. Follett (53) would negate this possibility.

Basically, at this point the child shifts from inductive to a *deductive* mode of thinking. In all of his mental operations, his reasoning takes cognition of a larger whole and the logical relationship to it; a developmental acquisition which has relevance for his learning and his relationship to his social and ideational world.

It must be stressed that the mental capacities for concrete operations evolve one by one, and proceed from the very simple, to the ordinary, and eventually to the more removed experience. The different properties of space are mastered in a definite sequence. First, the child appraises size in terms of length, then after a year or more, size in terms of weight, while size as an expression of volume is usually not comprehended until near the end of this phase. The previous order for mastery of objects is also repeated. Concepts related to objects precede the learning of concepts related to space, causality and time. The child also comprehends the laws of his environment in this sequence. For instance, a child's comprehension that a flower maintains its identical size and shape under a magnifying glass does not necessarily imply that he will comprehend correspondingly that fifteen minutes of watching TV actually involves the same time span as fifteen minutes of chores. It is still common for a child to confuse different perspectives in one event in his reasoning. Mental operations ". . . develop separately field by field, and result in a progressive structuralization of these fields, without complete generality being attained" (97, 15–16). Each field or combination of fields form islands of knowledge without full awareness of logical relationships and a unified approach to life.

As the child becomes more accustomed to operational thinking, he can conceive two hypotheses and understand their relationship without being able to communicate this understanding by words or actions. Again, knowing precedes a capacity to verbalize and to apply this knowledge.

As previously stated, thinking can be equated to mental experimentation with the symbols of relationship within the field of perception. This process evolves from past experience. Previous consciousness of repetition and rhythmic regularity have pointed towards ordering experiences. Generalization and differentiation of such experiences as playing, using, and studying introduced classes which held potentials for hierarchical relationship. These experiential steps are essential to conceptualization. The child has learned to generalize and to deduce from simple experiences. Each new understanding occurs at the expense of his personal (egocentric) beliefs which cannot be easily shaken off. Increased objectivity in one area does not necessarily exclude egocentric thinking in others. Every new acquisition of more advanced objective behavior initially involves only surface behavior. When threatened, the child automatically returns to his previous intuitive and egocentric mode of thinking and reasoning.

To this point a concept of time has included only a notion of sequentiality in which "before" and "after," as well as differences in time, were measured by spatial distances. On this level, such concepts as "past," "present," "future," and their interrelatedness are understood to be a part of the temporal continuum. Now, time becomes independent of perceptual data. Slowly, time comes to imply a progressive structurization of such concepts as "equal distance," "duration," and "speed." Naturally, in its beginning, conceptualization necessitates the use of symbols within the perceptive awareness. The concept "time" becomes fully understood with the coordination of the concepts of "equal distance" and "speed." Eventually, after repeated experience, the child, by now a young adolescent, can explain his understanding that an hour of work has equal duration regardless of the content of the work assignment.

In his acquisition of language, the child adopts word definitions without full awareness of all they convey. Symbolic speech has been employed without a full understanding of its meaning. On the current level of mental organization, language continues to be a tool of communication while it also serves as a vehicle for the thinking process. Curiously, verbal impressions which are communicated correlate with the individual's conscious conceptual judgments of his actions. Both conscious communication and conscious conceptual judgments lag a year or more behind the time when the individual actually manifested such behavior without full awareness of its significance and the necessary symbols for explaining this new understanding. Again, thoughts and words follow the potential action and the action phase. Similarly, a child's evaluation of stories lags behind his evaluation of life, because the content of such stories usually deals with events which are more removed from their everyday experience. Experiences more distant are understood later.

The child's contacts with his physical world become more productive. First, increase in accommodation stimulates a real desire for verification of the accommodative process which is accelerated by a decrease in egocentricity. Second, more accurate perception and an awareness of the process of perception extend his present understanding of his experience with the environment. Some of these expansions are connected with an increased comprehension of the multiple dimensions of an object and their permanency in space and time. Above all, the child knowingly applies his interpretation of his perceptions of the environment. He has points of reference and he can anchor his experiences in a rational and communicable system.

The child can now use an actual measuring stick rather than self-reference, such as his own body. Objects become known for their internal parts. Objects and events tend to be defined by their use. The child remains primarily concerned with his practical success or failure without much consideration of the means involved. Notions of animism continue, because objects with spontaneous movements are considered to be alive. In fact, underlying most objective interpretations is an animistic formula. During this phase, the child still conceives natural phenomena to be made by man for man. Furthermore, more complicated events still receive a circular explanation. In other words, a child's immediate explanation for his environment does not coincide with his own reasoning and ultimate conviction. Only later in this phase do physical and natural explanations contribute to more realistic understanding. Loss of animism forces the child to face the concept of death and to apply a biological interpretation of all life near him. Events beyond his reach are still centered in a socialized egocentrism. For instance, he may think that the sun rises because we need light.

Piaget stressed that intellectual advance finds expression also in involuntary behavior. The child now explains that dreams are perceived only by the dreamer. Dreams are in the head, and become visible while one is asleep. The latter explanation hints at the remaining confusion of things and symbols.

Piaget stresses that the widening awareness of physical factors always precedes an awareness of social factors. The child has first to experience his new perspective of physical phenomena before he can extend this pattern, or schema, to his social sphere. To illustrate, awareness of the left and right sides as objective reference points in space must precede a recognition of two points of view as different reference points in social relationships.

Emancipation from parental dominance and participation as an equal in his social world bring about a shift in the child's models of imitation. Desire for verification also finds expression on the social plane. Observation, comparison and comprehension of others assume an important part in the child's life. He is eager to avoid self-contradiction, a notable phenomenon in previous phases, and attempts to understand the various patterns of social behavior. Play and conversation, no longer primary means of self-expression, become media for understanding the physical and social worlds. Eventually, an important new level of social behavior is obtained by understanding others in terms of their social position. The incorporation of the principle of reversibility and the mental manipulation of symbolic images is self-evident. This accomplishment also helps to develop the notion of mutuality on the previous level into a concept of mutual respect toward the end of the present phase. Mutual respect necessitates the acquisition on a widened social perspective. "It is indispensable that there should be established between them (the children) and oneself (the adult) those simultaneous relationships of differentiation and reciprocity which characterize the coordination of view points" (104, 162). Inversely, different points of view can be coordinated only to the degree that the persons involved are willing to participate in the process.

Recognition of seriation and hierarchy of nesting also place the child's understanding of his family in a new perspective: the family is now comprised of those immediately related in "blood," which means that pets lose their immediate status as members of the immediate family. The understanding of relationships, interpersonal and "blood," provides the schema for this new awareness.

Imitation proceeds in two directions. The child's increased interest in the mechanics and verification of the parts lead to the imitation of details. On the other hand, consciousness of the model's manifold relationships encourages the imitation of the symbolic aspects of the model, such as mental role-taking. Imitation becomes reflective of, and subordinate to, the ends pursued. Its former purely accommodative nature is balanced by the accommodative faculty. "The reversibility characteristic of the operations of logical intelligence is not acquired *en bloc*, but is prepared in the course of a series of successive stages: elementary rhythm, more and more complex regulations, . . . and, ultimately, reversible operative structures" (89, 256). Imitation continues because the child fully understands the importance of the model and the process of imitation.

The imitation of details also has impact upon play when intricate and complicated constructions furnish satisfaction equal to that earlier furnished by ludic play. Collective games emerge from symbolic play, although they still carry many of the symbols and self-fulfilling characteristics of symbolic play. Collective games quickly accumulate representative rules. For instance, neighborhood children spontaneously playing ball are apt to form a highly structured game with some rules which are universal for the entire neighborhood. Just as imitation finds its equilibrium, play loses its assimilative characteristics and becomes a balanced subordinate process of cognitive thought. This process is further substantiated by the fact that curiosity no longer finds its expression in active play, but in intellectual experimentation.

Affective behavior is also coming closer to the Piagetian state of equilibrium. The awareness of obligation is equated with awareness of necessity in a manner not much different from the earliest schemata of primary circular reaction. When once *to hold*

was equal to *keep hand closed,* now the request to maintain social
play is equal to the moral obligation to keep a mutual agreement.
Knowledge of feelings in relationship to various value systems
encourages the balance and constancy of behavior. For the present, the child finds himself in the active process of ordering his
impulses with implicit interest focused on obtaining an equilibrium.

Conscience finds its anchoring points in newly acquired centers
of mutual respect and awareness of necessity for collective
obedience. In this new level, cognitive thought manages to in-
ternalize all sense of morality. The new concept of time tends to
free moral standards from temporary and specific situations. The
child brings together into several systems the standards he has
acquired and practiced in the past. He also incorporates his elders'
comments, standards and expectations. Basically, he relates frag-
mentary practices, hear-say, and knowledge into one related,
practical system, although the theoretical implications of the
system will not be comprehended until later. These processes of
integration will be strengthened by the appropriate interpretations
of key adults. On the other hand, a lack of fitting explanations
and guidance by elders, combined with adult domination retards
the growth of moral outlook.

In general, children from the ages of 9 to 12 are interested in
rules which will regulate their mutual activities. They examine
rules for all their details. They inquire into the meaning of the
parts, in order to establish verifiable relationships as well as to
guarantee themselves a sense of permanency. Social reciprocity
leads to a sense of equality which is carried over into concepts of
fair punishment. Equality in punishment, to compensate exactly
for the damage done or to do to another exactly what was done
to oneself, constitutes fair judgment. A sense of equality hints at
a sense of autonomy. The child sees himself and others as autonomous, independently acting persons. He strives towards complete
objectivity in the enforcement of rules and disciplinary actions. A
boy or girl of preadolescent age insists upon a shift in emphasis
from adult authority to respect from all for peer standards. Violation of reciprocity seems to be the worst crime. Furthermore,

lies are defined objectively. The more a lie attempts to deceive and to deny mutual respect, the worse it is. Such an attitude represents a reversal of the views held by the younger child. At the same time, it becomes permissible, in the teen-agers' eyes, to lie a little to adults.

Expiatory judgment continues in more remote relationships such as in stories and on the theoretical plane. A sense of equality appears first in daily interaction with peers. However, unilateral respect continues much longer in such habits as manners and cleanliness, in religion and in relating to special authoritarian groups, such as policemen, where previous beliefs are constantly reconsolidated by adult constraint, as if they were "World-Order decrees" (98).

The Phase of Formal Operations

The last phase of intellectual development occurs between the ages of 11 and 15; childhood ends maturationally and youth begins. Moreover, the nature of thought undergoes a change, which Piaget, in a 1958 publication (107c), links to the maturation of cerebral structures. Unlike the child the youth becomes ". . . an individual who thinks beyond the present and forms theories about everything, delighting especially in considerations of that which is not" (104, 148). He acquires the capacity to think and to reason beyond his own realistic world and his own beliefs. In short, he enters into the world of ideas and into essences apart from the real world. Cognition begins to rely upon pure symbolism and the use of propositions rather than sole reality. Propositions become important to him as a form of reasoning in which relationships are hypothesized as causal and are analyzed for the effects they bring. Assimilative and accommodative processes receive little concern in this final phase. Both found their equilibrium by integrating into unconscious and spontaneously carried out processes of human functioning.

Cognitive random behavior is replaced by a systematic approach to problems. Seriation involves more than adding like phenomena; it serves to order systematically and to control an established order. Not until this present level does the youth begin to comprehend geometric relationships and questions dealing with proportions. These questions carry implications beyond the mastery of geometric and mathematical problems; they affect problems of social relationships. They deal with relativity, balance, and equality between concepts, actions, and reactions. The objective cognition of proportions opens the way to understanding relativity in ordinary situations. Just as increased objectivity and socialization previously changed the focus from egocentricity to mutual social reciprocity, so do acute objectivity and the awareness of relative relationships bring about a new level of organization and a new approach to the physical and social environment.

A concept of relativity emerges from two other essential accomplishments of the formal operational phase: first, reason by hypothesis, or the application of propositional statements, and second, the use of implication.

Piaget states that systematic ordering and reasoning by hypothesis is an endeavor

. . . to formulate all possible hypotheses concerning the operative factors [of the phenomenon under consideration], and then arrange [these] experiments as a function of these factors.

The consequences of this new attitude are as follows. In the first place thought no longer proceeds from the actual to the theoretical, but starts from theory so as to establish or verify actual relationships between things. Instead of just coordinating facts about the actual world, hypothetico-deductive reasoning draws out the implications of possible statements and thus gives rise to a unique synthesis of the possible and necessary (97, 19).

Obviously, the youth is now concerned with establishing hypotheses. He tends to think and to reason with propositions rather than with symbols.

It must be emphasized that it is not simply a case of new linguistic forms expressing, at the level of concrete operations, already known relationships between objects. These new operations, particularly those which concern the mechanism of proof, have changed the whole experimental attitude.

The logic of propositions is especially helpful in that it allows us to discover certain new kinds of invariants, which fall outside the range of empirical verification. For example, in studying the movements of balls of different weights and mass on a horizontal plane, some adolescents are able to state the problem in terms of factors of resistance or rest (97, 19–20).

The ability to reason by hypothesis furnishes the youth with a new tool to understand his physical world and his social relationships within it. One of these new tools is logical deduction by implication. As a child, he has already managed the deduction of relationships on the basis of juxtaposition, proximity, transduction and other irreversible relationship patterns. Now, propositional statements of groupings allow the formation of new concepts. The latter ones are the product of deduction by implication. Reasoning by implication permits the youth to introduce simple, logical assumptions by taking a third position without resorting to verification by means other than logic. The youth undertakes a search for general hypotheses which can account for the observed and possible events which have occurred to him. Each partial link is grouped in relation to the whole which is a set structured from all subsets (105) with an integration of all parts into this whole. Reasoning acts continually as a function of a structured whole, with all deductions anchored in the possible, and not merely in observed empirical facts. In fact, "reality becomes secondary to possibility" (105). Reversibility permits thought to branch out into the realm of possibility without losing the sense of reality.

Deduction introduces the possibility of bringing contradictory and apparently unrelated wholes into logical relationships. It is a new means of generalization and differentiation especially applicable to the eventual integration of hitherto unintegrated and different wholes. Piaget's world finally finds its ultimate homogeneity. The importance of this new pattern of thinking is stressed by Piaget's suggestion that hypothetico-deductive reasoning serves as the major criterion for denoting the fifth and final phase of development.

All intellectual efforts prior to this level tended to expand and to intensify on a *horizontal* plane. Thought was verified in terms of its horizontal relationships, its logical relation to its parts and in terms of an integrated whole. Adolescence is known as an age in which the youth thinks beyond the present. He establishes *vertical* relationships. He forms notions, ideas and, eventually, concepts about everything from the past, through the present, into the future. The youth separates variables and combinations of variables so far unavailable to him through direct observation. His interests center around broad issues and around most minute details. Around the ages of 14 to 15, the youth reflects maturity in cognitive thought, when he can depend solely upon symbolism for operational thought. In brief, he thinks by applying symbols of thinking; he develops concepts of concepts.

It is noteworthy that the youth is no longer satisfied with empirical events which are solely on the surface. He regards his observations of life events merely as points of departure, or as proofs of the larger domain of the possible. With the aid of his new mental capacities, and his ability to formulate hypotheses, he structures a wide variety of possible combinations of events as they might occur. Simultaneously, he attempts to prove empirically which possibilities could materialize. Once he has established a range of hypotheses, he does not proceed to any final ordering, but rather views these temporary findings, or new insights, as starting points for new combinations of possible approaches to life's problems.

Interestingly, Piaget locates, in a much earlier work (100), a similar development in the child's interpretation of his dreams. At this final level of cognitive behavior the youth justifies dreams as instruments of thought; dreams are internal thoughts, or thoughts with oneself, and only seem to be real.

Language continues to develop more fully, and it encourages cognitive thought and behavior, by the fact that ". . . language conveys to each an already prepared system of ideas, classification, relationships, an inexhaustible stock of concepts which are reconstructed in each individual after the age-old patterns which previously moulded earlier generations" (104, 159).

The youth's physical environment appears in many new shadings. Objects become relative in terms of their appropriate use, while their properties assume relevance to the demands of the situation. The youth conceives the value of objects to be related entirely to man's value system. Even the names of objects are finally explained as being imposed upon the object immaterial to its ultimate existence. Furthermore, even distant objects, such as the sun and the moon, find explanation in a rational system. The recognition that life is restricted to man, animals, and plants, Piaget links to a new sense of inadequacy and awe in the presence of an all-powerful nature. The youth finds his place along with other living organisms in an ever evolving world.

Since his position in the family has been established, already, the youth sees his family and its members in relation to other families in his society. His major interest, however, centers in weighing, classifying, and reevaluating different social points of view. The adolescent finds pleasure in this new power of manipulating ideas without seriously committing himself to any one. The tenuous character of his manipulation of ideas and social practices can be compared with his former practice of imitating others' behavior with no real intention of adopting any of their behavior permanently. Just as he finds pleasure, during his leisure time, in anticipating all possible cases and codifying them into complicated rules, so does he toy with new concepts, common and extreme, to anticipate all possible eventualities. His manipulation of social concepts, as well as other ideational expressions—whether they are ethical or religious intangibles—follows progression similar to his comprehension of physical properties. As we stated before, the youth no longer needs mere rudimentary reality. He can "dream," in popular language, about all potential implications without establishing what is practical and socially real, at least for the present. First he visualized the permanency of ideas through space and time. Later, he saw the permanency of relationships between ideas, and, finally, each group of ideas was organized in relation to others for classification, comparison, and final integration into one meaningful system.

Forming a social and ideational position is closely linked to the acquisition of moral values or to the exercising of the conscience. Deduction by hypothesis, and judgment by implication, furnish the youth with opportunities to reason beyond cause and effect. For example, in the case of two youngsters who fight over taking turns, cause and effect judgment would base its decision on the question "who was first?" Judgment by implication would necessitate a total evaluation of each child's situation in relation to a larger context. A new logic of moral values emerges from the latter approach. Piaget's very early empirical research on lying (98) points toward this new level of cognition. Around 11 or 12 years, the youth starts to define lying quite differently than he did in his childhood. Anything intentionally false is a lie, because of its intentional aspect, its implicative meaning. This new concept also reflects the socially autonomous perspective of the maturing adolescent. Individualization has been traced to the adolescent's more adequate perspective. It may also be related to his new awareness of relativity. His previous sense of equality evolves into a sense of equity which Piaget defines as "nothing but a development of equalitarianism in the direction of relativity" (98, 316). The child slowly incorporates subtle concepts of fairness and justice which tend toward equity. These developments can be described as a state of

... never defining equality without taking account of the way in which each individual is situated. In the domain of retributive justice, equity consists in determining what are the attenuating circumstances. ... In the domain of distributive justice, equity consists in taking account of age, of previous services rendered, etc., in short, in establishing shades of equality (98, 284).

In contrast to earlier childhood attitudes, punishment of a group in order to punish unknown offenders is now viewed as an injustice to the innocent members.

Adolescence is known for its acquisition of new values which eventually will come into balance near the end of adolescence. This equilibrium, according to Piaget, can be explained by four developmental accomplishments:

1. The social world becomes an organic unit which has its laws and regulations and its divisions of roles and social functions.
2. Egocentricity has been "dissolved" by a sense of "moral solidarity" which is consciously cultivated.

3. Personality development from now on depends upon an exchange of ideas by social inter-communication in place of simple mutual imitation.
4. A sense of equality supersedes submission to adult authority (98).

Around the ages of 14 and 15, Piaget sees the individual finding his equilibrium, because the youth can envisage potential operations which will compensate each other (105). Basically, he ties together propositional operations into structured patterns of relationships and systems which eventually are structured into a single unity. Piaget concludes that *"the structured 'whole,'* considered as the form of equilibrium of the subject's operational behavior, is therefore of fundamental psychological importance" (97, 45). At this point, Piaget's analysis of development ends. Although Piaget does not commit himself, he does imply that the individual's basic pattern of thinking and reasoning has been established. The individual has reached intellectual maturity.

It must be repeated that the charted course describes *potential* development. The actual rate and degree of completion of each phase varies with each individual. Very likely an individual will achieve completion (maturity) in one area while reflecting incomplete development in others. Therefore, it is not surprising that egocentric thought and mature intelligence concerning physical perspectives can exist side by side. Such divergence is apt to appear in many areas. Also, developmental phenomena may continue beyond their usual approximate age levels.

SUMMARY

From the beginning of his professional life, Jean Piaget dedicated all of his creative energies to uncovering the nature and direction of intellectual development. He can best be described as a scientist researching the nature and logic of human development. He established that intellectual development follows a predictable pattern:

1. All development proceeds in a unitary direction;
2. Developmental progressions are in order and can readily be

described by criteria marking five distinct developmental phases;

3. There are distinct organizational differences between childhood and adult behavior in all areas of human functioning;

4. All mature aspects of behavior have their beginnings in infant behavior and evolve through all subsequent patterns of development;

5. All developmental trends are interrelated and interdependent; developmental maturity means the final and total integration of all the developmental trends.

In reviewing Piaget's research and teaching, we find that he presents us with a great variety of developmental themes which can serve as guiding principles for the study of and research in cognitive development or for more knowledgeable approaches in dealing with individuals on questions pertaining to their affective functioning.

Piaget recognizes a number of basic trends which transcend all developmental processes:

1. All development proceeds in identical sequence. At the beginning of life there is a kind of metamorphic transposition of organic processes into volitional ones.

2. All developmental phenomena reflect a natural trend of change from the simple to an ever-increasing complexity.

3. Each developmental aspect begins with concrete ordinary experiences or problems. Only after complete mastery of a concrete experience does development proceed toward the mastery of its corresponding abstraction.

4. Personality development proceeds from experience with the *physical world* to the *social* and finally to the *ideational* world. Every new dimension is first experienced by its physical realities before social and later ideational, considerations can be absorbed.

5. Personality development starts with an egocentric orientation, moves through a period of pure objective appraisal, and a sense of relativity emerges while moving toward maturity.

6. Intellectual behavior evolves descriptively from activity without thought to thought with less emphasis on activity. In other words, cognitive behavior evolves from doing to doing knowingly, and finally, to conceptualization.

7. An object is first known for its use, then for its permanency, its representative symbol, its place in space, its properties (weight, etc.) and finally for its relativity in space, time, and utility.

8. Actions of all objects are first attributed to *animism*. Later, animism is limited to moving objects, and eventually, only to self-perpetuating objects. Only the acquisition of cognitive thought permits an explanation by natural or mechanical realities.

9. A sense of ethics and justice (conscience) is anchored first in complete adherence to adult authority, to be replaced by adherence to mutuality, to social reciprocity, and finally, by adherence to social integrity.

10. Previous developmental acquisitions are retained as active ingredients throughout life. Various forms of earlier behavior patterns will find their expression in instances when the individual faces new problems or feels compelled to revert to previous patterns.

Altogether, Piaget's theory furnishes us with a frame of reference. His developmental trends describe individual potentiality. The actual developmental profile of each individual resembles a barogram showing peaks in some areas and depressions in others. In addition, variations may exist at any one point in an individual's approach to everyday problems. Basically, however, his theory pointedly demonstrates that there are regular patterns in cognitive development which are experienced by everyone. In turn, such understanding allows us to predict for an individual his mode and range of comprehension all along on the course of his development.

4

The Learning Theory of

Robert R. Sears

SEARS' LIFE AND PROFESSIONAL HISTORY

ROBERT RICHARDSON SEARS—the only native American of the three theorists presented in this book—employs an experimental, rather than clinical, approach to child development. Born in 1908 in Palo Alto, California, Robert R. Sears spent much of his childhood in and around Stanford University, where his father was a professor of education. Sears himself graduated from Stanford at the age of 21 with a major in English and a minor in psychology. Stimulated by Professor Lewis M. Terman of Stanford, Sears moved East to continue his psychological studies at Yale. Upon completion of his doctoral thesis, *Effect of Optic Ablation on the Visuo-Motor Behavior of Goldfish*, in 1932 (72), Sears embarked upon an academic career and, within ten years, he had achieved a full professorship. His first academic post was a joint appointment to the University of Illinois and the Institute of Juvenile Research in Chicago (1932–1936). Later appointments at the Institute of Human Relations, Yale University (1936–1942); at the Iowa Child Welfare Research Station (1942–1949); and at Harvard Laboratory of Human Development (1949–1953) took Sears over most of the United States. Ironically, the years since 1953 have found Sears back at Stanford University, where he became executive head of the Department of Psychology and where he has been Dean of Humanities and Sciences since 1964. His professional stature was acknowledged by his election to the presidency of the American Psychological Association in 1950–1951, and again in 1960–1961.

Sears' special interest in learning theory can be traced to his close association with Clark L. Hull, of whom Sears was both a student and a colleague during his years at Yale. Other important influences on Sears were Dollard, Miller, Doob, and Mowrer, with whom Sears collaborated in a joint research undertaking of the application of learning theory to immediate social problems (**17, 78, 117**). More recently, Sears' research and writing reflect a fascination for the learning theory and terminology introduced by B. F. Skinner (**114, 121**). By 1943, Sears' research in psycho-analytic concepts had convinced him of the significance of parent-child relationships and their rich potential for learning-theory research. Since then, his major research projects, and the theories which stem from them, have concentrated upon early-childhood development. In 1944, he described the challenge he saw before him:

> It seems doubtful whether the sheer testing of psychoanalytic theory is an appropriate task for experimental psychology. Its general method is estimable but its available techniques are clumsy. Instead of trying to ride on the tail of a kite that was never meant to carry such a load, experimentalists would probably be wise to get all the hunches, intuitions, and experience possible from psychoanalysis and then for themselves, start the laborious task of constructing a systematic psychology of personality but a system based on behavioral rather than experiential data (**116, 329**).

Somewhat eclectic in his work, Sears has attempted to reconcile psychoanalytic psychology with behavioristic theory, and a wealth of psychoanalytic concepts can be found in his theory of learning. As a result of his experimental work in these divergent areas, Sears has contributed much to the formulation of learning theory, particularly as it bears upon the development of dependence and identification during the early years of childhood.

SEARS' AMPLIFICATION OF LEARNING THEORY

As an empiricist, Sears focuses upon those aspects of behavior which are overt and can be measured; for him, personality development can best be measured through action, and through social interaction. Active behavior can be evaluated from two perspectives: (1) with an emphasis on the sequence of events in an action continuum of a particular theme and the causes and effects of the events; and (2) with an emphasis on the learning experience of an individual that results from an action sequence—that is, the learning effects of the stimulus-response (S-R) sequence, in which each effect of an action can become the learned cause of future behavior. It is the latter with which Sears is primarily concerned. His emphasis on reinforcement and secondary-drive (learned) motivation has its roots in Hullian learning theory, but it derives further elaboration from his own work with Dollard and Miller and others on the frustration-aggression hypothesis (17; 69).

Action is instigated by a drive strong enough to impel the individual to respond to a cue, or stimulus. Initially, all stimuli are associated with primary, or innate, drives, such as hunger, etc.; the satisfaction or frustration that results from the behavior prompted by these primary drives leads the individual to adopt additional behavior. During this interactive process, the individual learns new modes of behavior, the satisfactory results of which serve to reinforce the achieving behavior. Constant reinforcement of specific actions, in turn, gives rise to new, or learned, drives and to primary-drive equivalents; these are the secondary drives. For example: "The individual does not wait for the onset of the primary drive (stomach contraction or changes in chemistry of the blood) before engaging in the appropriate adaptive response (eating). Rather, he responds to the secondary drive stimulation

Robert R. Sears

which may be linked to time, place, or verbal command" (77, 429). In other words, secondary drives arise from the social influences on his development.

Thus, the frame of reference to which Sears always adheres is the S-R sequence. The stimulus, or cue, that activates the individual's response also determines when, where, and how he will respond, and, in triggering an action sequence directed toward a given goal, it concomitantly serves to reduce the intensity of the drive. Sears is particularly concerned with the quality, or the reinforcement value, of each goal-directed response. It is the kind of behavior and the results it brings—as experienced by the individual—that determines whether an action sequence will prove to be an insignificant, transitional event, with little or no reinforcement value; or whether it will contribute permanently to the individual's repertoire of behavior, thus having strong or effective reinforcement value. The latter tends not only to entrench the behavior itself, but also to integrate secondary drives within the individual's motivational system. Behavioral differences among individuals can be traced to the reinforcement value derived from even minute variations of similar action sequences. It should be pointed out here that, in a given individual, reinforcement of behavior or of secondary drives can occur only if there is some variation in the reinforcement techniques. For example, a child accustomed to constant praise will cease to be affected by praise unless he is exposed to notable variations in the pattern in which praise is awarded him.

But, in any S-R sequence, the response of one individual can serve as the stimulus for another; for instance, the wails let out by a child in response to a tumble become the stimulus for the mother's response to assist and to comfort her child. Thus are the bulk of human actions in some way social and interpersonal. Recognizing the importance of human interaction, Sears pointed to the fact that child development occurs within *dyadic* units of behavior, rather than within the *monadic* units of behavior of a single individual with which much of the field of psychology has been concerned. Adaptive behavior and its reinforcement in an individual must therefore be studied in terms of the actual or anticipated response of another individual. This dyadism of Sears introduces for research purposes a practical separation of antecedent and consequence. Each S-R sequence can be studied with respect to the interrelated behavior of two or more individuals, while the stimulus and the response, in themselves, receive only secondary consideration.

Sears experimentally tested many psychoanalytic concepts. His familiarity with them led him to utilize in his theory of learning such analytic concepts as repression, regression, projection, sublimation, and the psychosexual developmental stages of oralism, analism, Oedipalism, and latency. It is significant that, in his latest research (125, 130), these analytic concepts are presented as major motivational systems within the structure of a learning theory. The work of Sears has done much to apply and to test jointly the wisdom emerging from psychoanalytic and learning-theory concepts. He opened up new avenues for understanding and guiding child development.

A true representative of the prevailing American approach to theoretical construction, Sears maintains that, in the behavioral as well as in the physical sciences, theory must be based upon empirical and well-controlled research: "A theory stands or falls by its effectiveness in ordering empirical observations" (130, 382). His experimental research is limited exclusively to native-born Americans. Involving essentially dyadic situations, his studies deal, for the most part, with the mother-child relationship. Sears bypasses the father-child dyad, as if the mother-child dyad were the all-inclusive one. He makes one notable exception to this in his study of Mark Twain's relationship to his father, when his biographic research focuses upon both Mark Twain's relationship to his father and mother (121).

Sears employs standard research techniques, with properly controlled variables, for the prediction of behavior. In interpreting his findings, however, Sears sometimes makes inferences beyond the scope of his research data, and he often incorporates into his conclusions inferences made from merely preliminary, and at times statistically insignificant, findings.

BASIC ASSUMPTION OF SEARSIAN THEORY

The Order of the Universe

Sears, as any scientist by virtue of his field, believes in the discernibility of knowledge of the universe. Yet his interest and scientific work focus upon selected aspects of human behavior. Only occasionally, as in his collaborative efforts on the frustration-

aggression theorem (17, 78), in his more recent work on identification (118, 119), and the conceptual equivalence of transcultural
variables (1960), does Sears venture to apply his findings to more
generalized concepts and a formulation of universal principles of
human behavior.

Fundamental Human Values

Sears judges man by his actions; to him, actions represent the
core of one's individuality, creativity or one's vulnerability. Sears
is optimistic about man's universal social nature and infinite
capacity to learn (118). Sears places stress on the influence of
parents in the development of a child's personality. It is the
parents' child-rearing practices that determine the nature of a
child's development. In turn, personality differences between
individuals are largely, according to Sears, related to differences
between parents in their access to various forms of information
about child-rearing practices. It is therefore important that the
parents have access to the latest knowledge. Sears feels that every
parent could do better if he knew better.

Etiology of Behavior

Sears maintains that, for the present, it is unimportant to understand the source of human behavior. However, although Sears
does not deal explicitly with etiological questions, he seems to
proceed on the basis of the following assumptions.

First, behavior is both the cause and the effect of other behavior; Sears considers primary drives only as instrumental for the
beginning of behavior in a social world. It is the environment
which shapes behavior. For instance, very early in the infant's life,
a parent tends to react differently to a son than to a daughter.
Therefore, from very early in life, each sex experiences different
child-rearing practices and, consequently, develops differently
Second, behavior is self-motivated by its tension-reduction effect.
Beyond this assumption, Sears holds that the final cause is unimportant as long as the ongoing reduction of immediate needs can
be related to the prediction of subsequent behavior. Third, every

unit of behavior preceding a goal achieves a reinforcement potential, either by its having been repeated before the achievement, or by the subsequent repetition of the behavior as a result of goal achievement. Fourth, all reinforced behavior with drive-equivalent characteristics forms secondary motivational systems. These socially learned desires motivate all human behavior. They comprise the culture-conforming behavior, because socially relevant acts are based on motives which are gradually conditioned through social experiences (123). Fifth, frustration, aggression, identification, and social habits—each has its own mode of development.

Frustration is always the product of an anticipated or previously experienced interference with a goal achievement or with an instrumental act which leads to achievement of the goal (117). Frustration creates an internal drive for aggression which eventually requires outward expression. Therefore, aggressive feelings are anchored to a powerful motivational system within each individual. Equally, identification has its roots in the early experiences of spontaneous imitation of behavior and reinforcement through recognition received for imitating and personal satisfaction in finding behavior of others in one's own actions. Habits find their explanation in persistence in behavior without imitation of new and different patterns. In one way, habits can be explained as behavior which weathered (or resisted) either change or extinction (116).

Behavioral changes find their source and impetus in (1) physical maturation; (2) cultural conditioning; and (3) the expectation of forthcoming behavior as conveyed by others.

The Core of Human Functioning

Sears views personality as a product of a "lifetime of *dyadic action* which has modified the individual's potentiality for further *action*" (126, 476). Consequently, all human functioning must be seen as the result of the *interactive* effects of all the influences, both constitutional and experiential, that have impinged on the individual (130). Since all behavior is constituted of goal-directed responses, behavioral events must find their explanation in sub-sequent action sequences. The individual is the constant enactor of his behavior. A child's inherent desire to learn and a mother's urge to do right create a dyadic situation where the proper knowledge of actions produces the proper balance of human behavior. To quote Sears: "If a mother knows the effect of a particular practice, she can decide whether to use it or not. She can base her judgments on a knowledge of the product she will get" (**130**, 17).

Emotions affect the degree of reinforcement which any action might receive. Emotions are seen as qualitative-quantitative responses to anticipated or experienced actions. At no time are emotions viewed as entities. To illustrate, Sears recognized aggression as a goal-directed response. An aggressive act can be explained as counter-aggression, elicited or anticipated by a previous dyadic action.

As long as all behavior essentially represents reinforced actions, development may be readily viewed as a training process. A child's behavior, consequently, is the outcome of *how* he is reared. Adaptive behavior depends upon reinforced learning.

Sears gives little consideration to play.[1] At one point he designates play as learning by trial and error. Trial-and-error learning serves as a means of discovering perceptual orientation (how things feel, taste, or perform). Play also serves as a means of rational orientation (discovering what things do, what they stand for, and what space and time they occupy (**120**). On another occasion, Sears ascribes an irrational component to play. Play, like fantasy, occurs "when some of the laws of the physical and social universes have been rescinded, and hence it is the product of the child's drives and habits when these have different constants in the behavior questions" (**115**, 498). All human functions follow the same behavioral laws. In play or fantasy a person tends to apply behavioral antecedents (constants) different from those

[1] Sears' position on play is cited because for Erikson as well as for Piaget play is assumed as a major human function in development. Sears' position is not known. Thus far, he has only concerned himself with play in isolated research projects.

found in usual, everyday interaction. Social behavior depends almost exclusively upon the impact of others, rather than upon any internal developmental processes.

The Newborn

The newborn infant has various biological needs which result in primary drives; hunger, thirst, sex tension, sleep, fatigue, needs for activity, waste elimination, and optimum temperature maintenance are interrelated with primary drives. These drives make up a complex and are the instigators of social learning:

> The child is endowed, at birth, with a potentiality for securing many forms of gratification from his world. He can eat, he can eliminate when need be, he can be warmed or cooled, he can be fondled and loved. These experiences are not only gratifying; they are also the sources of learning (113, 68).

Therefore, the family is the cause of all subsequent learning for the infant, and a study of a child's family leads to a description of his early-childhood development.

The Physical and Social Environment

Physical and social environment is dealt with on the basis of previous contacts with environment. Both are known only so far as they are previously experienced by the individual as a part of his behavior sequence (122). Eventually, society implants "appropriate" motives, interests, skills, and attitudes in the child as he learns to act accordingly to environmental expectations; thus, stimuli vary with each culture. Each society and culture sees to it that certain actions are reinforced; only those actions which are reinforced incorporate values which become a part of a person's social heritage. Most important for its implications is the assumption that all socialization, however permissive, necessarily contains some frustrating elements, or will lead to frustration by its eventual generalization and application to new and wider action sequences (128). The role of the parents is crucial, for the parents are the most important reinforcing agents. Sears does not recognize socioeconomic classes or other social clusters *per se*—as discriminating variables for child-rearing practices. For him, the critical criterion is: What access do the parents have to the most relevant understanding of the best child-rearing practices? Sears strongly suggests that differences in child-rearing practices between various socioeconomic groups will diminish with an increase in access to the same information and the immediate communication of new learning to all socioeconomic layers of society. Therefore, the relationship between culture and personality development rests upon social learning.

SEARS' CONCEPTION OF DEVELOPMENT

Sears' research and writings imply two different stances on child development. His writings and analysis of his research findings suggest that he sees development as a continuous chain of events adding to and, in part, replacing previous acquisitions. He states:

> Child-rearing is a continuous process. Every moment of a child's life that he spends in contact with his parents has some effect on both his present behavior and his potentialities for future action.
>
> A child's development seems to be a fairly orderly process. He gives up modes of behavior that are no longer suitable, and acquires new actions appropriate for his age and his life conditions (130, 314, 466).

At the same time his research approach and presentation of data imply that he intends to deal with developmental phases. We therefore infer Sears' concept of development as follows: Development may be considered as a continuous, orderly sequence of conditions which creates actions, new motives for actions and eventual patterns of behavior. As long as everyday social life proceeds as if developmental phases were a reality, all social learning will tend to proceed in comparable patterns. To amplify, early training of the infant such as weaning, feeding, toilet training, sexual training, as well as the child's age-linked dependence, distinctly implies an expectancy of different levels of readiness. Therefore, social conditions dictate the existence of developmental phases, regardless of whether they are based upon independent fact.

We will consequently present Sears' view in three developmental phases.[2]

I. The phase of rudimentary behavior, which is based upon native needs and learning in early infancy.
II. The phase of secondary motivational systems which is based upon family-centered learning.
III. The phase of secondary motivational systems which is based upon learning beyond the family.

The first phase involves primarily the first few months of a child's life, when his environmental experience has not yet directed his learning; the second phase covers most of the impact of socialization on early childhood; and the third phase introduces questions of development beyond early childhood. This last phase, however, does not include sufficient material to suggest an exclusive-Searsian phase in itself; it merely contains material which extends beyond the first two phases.

These three phases are consistent with Sears' theoretical assumptions. They can be described figuratively as three expanding circles on a pool of water into which a stone has been dropped. The first, innermost circle represents the child's most intimate parental environment. The next circle stands for the child's emergence into a larger family environment, while the outermost circle symbolizes the child's gradual social penetration into his neighborhood. Each circle, as it expands, blends into the next larger circle, thereby losing its original limited separateness. Similarly, the expansion of each developmental phase, like converging circles, encompasses a larger sphere of learning.

In considering each of these three developmental phases, Sears' material will be investigated as it relates to the following: the meaning of the particular phase; the place of primary needs; the place of secondary motivational systems; Sears' five major motivational systems (dependence, feeding, toileting, sex, and aggres-

---

[2] Responsibility for the articulation of these three developmental phases rests entirely upon the writer's own interpretation and method of organization.

sion); especially important processes in development (identification, play, motility, reasoning, and conscience); and social factors (the parent's own status, sex, ordinal position, class, education, and cultural heritage).

Phase I: Rudimentary Behavior—Native Needs and Early-Infancy Learning

Most of an infant's behavioral efforts in the first six months of his life involve his attempts to reduce inner tension originating from his inner drives. The infant's human needs to secure food, to eliminate, and to experience personal warmth along with his physical comfort create the sources for learning. Simultaneously, the way in which these innate needs are met introduces environmental learning experiences. These nurturing experiences are increasingly related to the physiological stimulations until social learning becomes the prime instigator of behavior. It is this period of presocialization, the period of rudimentary asocial behavior, which comprises the first phase.

In this early phase, innate needs produce the primary drives and cues for action. Hunger, fatigue, pain, etc., produce tensions which seek reduction through any gratifying response. Much of this initial gratification-seeking occurs by trial and error. Crying, struggling, and breathholding, for instance, are actions based upon cues of pain, and are responses which merely happen. The child is in a purely autistic state unrelated to any social world. Slowly, the infant *learns* that the reduction of pain is related to some of his actions. Then he strives to imitate these previously successful actions. For instance, the cue of hunger becomes associated with the action sequence: *crying* and breast (or bottle) with the hunger-reducing fluid. His actions become more and more learned behavior; that is, his actions become part of an action sequence with a learned, goal-directed response.

When the infant's behavior tends towards specific goal-directed behavior, each completed action sequence which brings about a reduction in tension is the one which is most likely to be repeated again, whenever the tension arises. Repeatedly satisfied responses and the attendant events which lead to the satisfaction are viewed together as rewarding experiences. In the case of the infant, the mother's promptness, dependability, regularity, and personal warmth (close body contacts, fondling, etc.) provide the essential reinforcement. For instance, a mother who devotes much appropriate attention to her child at the times he needs her is supportively reinforcing. The child, in turn, is more apt to adapt his behavior to those forms which will assure him mother's consistent attention. There is more common interaction and guidance from a truly loving one than from a less available, or less affectionate mother. Consequently, the child becomes tempted to select the responses his environment seems to expect from him. He tends to manipulate his environment in order to pursue gratifying responses, while his environment suggests to him the range of satisfactions it can supply. The key to control is embedded in this dyadic relationship. The infant learns both to control and to be controlled. Moreover, the infant wills his submission to control. As a quick learner, he develops early "his techniques of co-operating with those who care for him, and of controlling them and insuring their nurturance" (**130**, 138).

From this time on, socialization takes place. "Every child always has a repertory of actions that needs replacing" (**130**, 464). Successful development is characterized by a decrease in autism and innate need-centered actions and by an increase in dyadic, socially centered behavior. Failure to develop results in a lack of movement, or in a reversal of the trends mentioned above. Early-child development introduces three essential questions:

1. Under what conditions is a child's motivational system learned?
2. What are the circumstances in which parents and other environmental factors reinforce the child's learning?
3. What are the products of the child's learning, or what are his behavior patterns?

Sears' learning theory classifies dependency as a most essential component of learning (**114**, **121**). Rewarding reinforcement in all dyadic situations depends upon the child's having consistent contacts with one or more persons. This essential relationship has its beginning in the earliest child-mother contacts when the child shifts his processes of learning from those based upon trial and error to those based upon dyadic reinforcement. A dyadic relationship fosters dependency and thus, reinforces it. The infant reveals dependent tendencies from birth. He tends to respond to people as recurring environmental phenomena during the first two months of his life. He calls upon them when hungry, cold, or otherwise in a state of biological need. The dependency drive is nurtured through the dyadic relationship of feeding during the child's fourth to twelfth months (128). Once appropriate behavior assures dependency, a truly dyadic relationship exists. Both child and mother have their repertoire of significant actions which serve to stimulate responses from the other which will be compatible with their own expectancies.

Initially, dependency, like other motivational systems to be discussed, starts with the child participating passively, until he can later actively maintain his dependency. Dependency involves a role practice "by the need to regain control of the parental resources that provide the child with many forms of gratification, especially the expression of love" (114). The learning of active dependency, therefore, proceeds from a state of passive dependency, with help from the adult as the major reinforcing agent, to a state of dependency, in which the adult no longer plays such a major role. The latter does not occur until the next developmental phase. The child's dependency becomes a powerful need which can be neither eliminated nor ignored. In fact, the more the child increases his efforts to satisfy his frustrated dependency needs, the more insistent and all-absorbing become his demands for dependency. It is not surprising, therefore, that permissiveness toward dependency serves to meet its needs.

The child's native need for the reduction of his hunger drive becomes quickly associated with two essential and interrelated components of his food-intake sequence: to suck and to be near the nursing person. Because of its constant repetition and powerful association with the goal-directed response, the instrumental act of sucking rapidly becomes an ingrained habit and an independent drive which gets stronger with age as long as it remains the primary means for pacifying hunger. The mother is seen as an indispensable part of the activity of sucking and the intake of all food. Her image, smell, feel, etc., are closely associated with gratification. The child "not only learns to expect her to come when [he is] hungry, he also learns that he needs her" (**130**, 66). It is this link between the desire for food and the desire for the mother which is essential to this phase of development, but is a potential deterrent to development in later phases of socialization. The mother bringing food, then, fosters a dyadic relationship and simultaneously reinforces dependency on herself as the caring adult.

The child's natural desire to eliminate and to express himself sexually remains an asocial desire. The pressures upon him to maintain body hygiene and to cover up his sex organs with clothing are not, during the first phase, directly associated with elimination by the infant at this point in his development.

Aggression, already explained in a discussion of Sears' basic assumptions, is a natural consequence of frustration. Aggression readily becomes an early and vital aspect of learned behavior because frustration occurs from the very moment the infant experiences discomfort, or pain, and delay in finding relief from the unpleasant experience. Aggression, usually manifested through anger, in the form of rage or a display of temper, is primarily a response to this frustration. The young infant, or an older individual with an infant-like behavior reservoir, depends upon those processes of life communication most important for him. His aggression finds expression through a generalized vocal expression (crying), changes in rhythm of breathing or food intake, or his entire body posture. Permissiveness toward exhibitions of frustration has a different meaning for the child than does permissiveness toward dependency. Parental permissiveness toward displays of frustration fails to reinforce the behavior patterns, but it leaves the infant with unchanneled aggression. In contrast, permissive acceptance of dependency logically leads the child to further dependency on his caring adult. Simultaneously, permissive acceptance of dependency includes a readiness for doing for the child what he refuses to handle himself. The latter most likely includes both overcoming frustration and direct assistance with the expression of aggression. The adult's handling of dependency and control provides the beginning for the process of identification. During the first phase, the child's self-control comes from the control by his parents.

Much of the social environment into which the child is born has inherent implications for his eventual development. The child's sex, his position in the family constellation, his mother's basic happiness, and his family's social position and educational status provide important variables which will affect his development in one way or another. Basically, a mother sees her child in the light of her general disposition toward bringing up children. Secondarily, she reacts differently to her child, according to its sex. From birth, her "child is allocated to one sex or the other, and society begins to implant in his motives, interests, skills and attitudes appropriate to such membership" (129, 221). The sex of the child "provides an important stimulus to a mother. It places the child in a social category that has enormous implications for training" (130, 419).

Sears finds the ordinal position of the child important because of its implication for the span of control from above. Large families have an extended distance in the reach of the final control (the parent), the oldest child being exposed to the most direct parental training while the other siblings tend to have an additional intermediary with each older sibling. More important than ordinal position is the age spacing between children, and the mother's freedom to deal directly with each child without having to "water down" such contacts with older children who also compete for her attention. Furthermore, a mother tends to become less frustrated by her daily chores with her second-born child. An only child tends to receive more attention from the parent of his own sex, while the youngest child of a large family seems to be left predominantly under the mother's discipline regardless of its sex (130). The mother's education has some relevance, or at least her capacity to deal simultaneously in different ways with children at various points in their development.

Much of a child's earliest development reflects the mother's personality—her capacity to be a loving mother, to regulate her permissiveness, and her attitudes toward sex and toilet training. The mother's capacities are greatly associated with her own self-esteem, her evaluation of the father, and her feelings about her current life situation. A high rating in each of these three factors correlates with high enthusiasm and great warmth in child-caring.

Finally, the mother's social status, education, and her cultural background predetermine many child-caring practices. The child has a greater probability for healthy development if the mother does not yearn for another station in life. This observation holds true for the working mother as well as the housewife as long as either one considers her lot as the most appropriate one for her. The mother's over-all position on the socioeconomic scale seems to affect the child's development less than the extent of her education. It is the less-educated mother (usually the lower-class mother) who uses inappropriate measures toward permissiveness and control. Conversely, more education and access to contemporary understanding of child care prepares mothers for a more rational use of control and a greater permissiveness toward dependency. Sears implies that the commonly assumed socioeconomic class differences between persons do not exist. Differences are primarily related to the degree of access to the contemporary major matrix of communication, to current knowledge and to the application of such knowledge.

This first phase connects the biological endowment of the newborn child with the endowment of his social environment. This phase introduces the infant to the environment, and provides the foundation for ever increasing interactions with this environment.

Phase II: Secondary Motivational Systems: Family-Centered
Learning

One by one, aspects of the undisciplined life of the infant become subject to the rigors of parental training. Socialization begins to take place during this second phase, covering the early childhood period; the time between the second half of the child's first year and the age he enters school. During this period, his primary needs continue to motivate him. However, these are gradually incorporated into repeatedly reinforced social learning, or secondary drives. Henceforth, these secondary drives will be his main motives to action unless his social environment fails to provide the necessary reinforcement. To illustrate, the child's hunger no longer depends entirely upon the contraction of his stomach, but becomes associated with the sight of such symbolic cues as the bottle or his mother opening the refrigerator. The mother continues to be the major reinforcing agent during the early stages of this phase; she perceives behavior which should be changed and she establishes standards for more mature forms of actions. First, however, she must instill in the child a desire to become socialized. If she accomplishes this successfully, the child's learned drive toward accepted social behavior will lead him in the direction of more mature activity and response. The child becomes aware that his personal happiness depends upon his readiness to do as he is expected, and, eventually, his actions become self-motivated. He tends to incorporate actions which bring satisfaction to him and are significantly satisfying to his parents.

At this point it is important to consider punishment as a factor in the process of socialization. Thus far, only reward has been cited as a socializing agent, while punishment represents a clear absence of reward. Sears himself gives little consideration to punishment as an alternative to reward. In his major study (130), he sees punishment primarily as a behavior complex with no single reinforcing effect. Most important, punishment does not tend to extinguish behavior. Thus, contrary to its intent, punishment does not alter behavior; it merely serves as a clear sign of refusal (or failure) to support a behavioral event. This observation applies only to punishment administered for the purpose of stopping or redirecting general behavior. Punishment, however, does elicit a reaction, and creates a response to the agent administering the punishment. For instance, a child who has been punished by his mother experiences mother's punitive behavior as an expression of an angry person rather than relating her actions to his actions. In other words, genuine social learning depends upon replacing previous learning with newer experiences based upon more appropriate satisfactions rather than upon avoiding unpleasant experiences or upon a fear of consequence.

Early-childhood development is essentially anchored in the satisfaction gained from the learned dependency upon the mothering person. The child learns to initiate and to rely upon his dependency, as if it were native to him. Such dependency has taught the child that he can secure compliance to most of his wishes through a generalized state of dependency which is made visible by specific help-soliciting activities. Thumb-sucking, outstretched arms, or helpless sounds are powerful and persuasive instigators to force the mother into responding, and effective means for securing gratification.

As soon as dependency becomes a drive-equivalent, punishment or the frustration of dependency results in the persistence of this secondary drive, because neither one stills this socially acquired need. Only gratification and gradual modification can produce a reduction in the need for dependency. Noteworthy is the fact that mere permissiveness of dependency produces no developmental change because it reinforces the *status quo*.

As the child grows older, a mother looks upon excessive emotional dependency as behavior which should be altered; frequently, this shift in emphasis will come about with the mother's preparations for a new sibling or her return to work. She herself will need to withdraw some aspects of parental care for her own as well as her child's protection. In discussing the values and disadvantages of dependency, Sears claims:

It [dependency] has a little of the quality of something infantile, of something that must be put away in favor of more mature kinds of expressed affection. The child should love his mother, to be sure, but with a less embarrassing degree of openness. He should want her attention, but not hound her for it or insist on it as a complete gratuity. The ultimate aim of the socialization process, as it relates to dependency, is for the child to be fond of the mother rather than passionately attached to her, to be pleased by her attention and interest but not incessantly to demand it (**130, 140**).

Some of the successful withdrawal of care occurs at this time because the child has learned to fill his own needs to some extent. His spontaneous imitation of an action sequence previously carried out by his mother represents the child's attempts to secure for himself the satisfying goal response. Imitation occurs and is reinforced by the child's self-activated, goal-achieving responses. Slowly, the child learns to gratify his dependency drive by performing actions that he previously anticipated and demanded from his mother.

Dependency, and gradual weaning from dependency, are conveyed differently according to the sex of the child. Girls tend to be weaned a month or so later than boys (**130**), but more important is the fact that during the child's second, third, and fourth years of life, mothers tend to require girls to relinquish their dependency in a greater variety of areas than boys. Yet, on the basis of Sears' empirical data, preschool-age girls tend to remain more persistent in their overall dependency behavior than do boys. Generally, however, dependency decreases with age, as the child learns to rely on an increasing number of adults, and eventually peers. The dependent state of the child gradually modifies into one of affection and esteem for those on whom he relies for care, as his mother increasingly teaches him to ask for signs of love, attention, and reassurance in a fashion which is less demanding, more subtle, and in accord with the propriety and dignity of adult behavior (i.e. a kiss, verbal recognition, a gift, etc.). Simultaneously, however, a universal, motivational drive of competition develops.

With less dependence upon a caring person, the child becomes freer to compete with others. When previously the sole object was dependency gratification, he now tends to experience others as competitors for goals which cannot be fully shared. He learns that nothing is his sole monopoly and he has to compete for his desired goal. The motivational drive of competition is in the making. His desire for his mother's continued attention is an important example. He learns to compete with others for such a goal, and his eventual gratification by gaining mother's good will fosters both his shared dependency and the experience he had with others in competing for mother's attention. He then behaves as if his goal is unshareable, while actually the experience of competing, the means—the competitively sharing of the goal—becomes as relevant for him as the goal itself.

As long as dependence upon the mothering person is still essential for the child, the threat, or the actual withdrawal, of dependency-maintaining activities becomes a powerful weapon in the child-rearing effort. For the child, a sudden or untimely withdrawal of support of his dependency means: I don't care for you any longer. It involves a withdrawal of personal care, love, and warmth. A child will instantly react to such a threat with behavior that will, in his estimation, secure for him the desired and needed range of dependency support. In other words, Sears considers a withdrawal or threat of withdrawal of personal care, love, or warmth as the alternative to reinforcement. The threat of the loss of dependency support can then serve as the facet of punishment. A child will tend to change his behavior in order to assure himself continued support. This latter remains true as long as the child finds sufficient satisfaction in his dependency. If, on the other hand, his dependency upon an adult is associated with nonsatisfying experiences, a threat, or actual withdrawal, of dependency will hardly motivate him to change, because continued dependency has equally little promise for him.

During the early-childhood years, actual feeding and the nurturing of dependency needs are intimately woven together. If the mother tries to change feeding habits, she not only interferes with strong habits of obtaining food, but also disrupts the dependent relationship. Consequently, change in feeding practices involves modification of recently entrenched motivational systems. For instance, sucking methods of feeding reward sucking activities and strengthen the oral mode of behavior for the child. The child's degree of sensitivity toward weaning is clearly related to his age when weaning begins and to the preparation for the final step of weaning. If weaning is started before the child is 6 to 12 months old, the completion of his weaning will take longer than if it is started later, but it will proceed with fewer setbacks than will occur during a subsequent period, when dependency has become a reinforced, learned drive. On the other hand, at the point when dependency is a well established drive—roughly at age 20 months—weaning is less a threat to its existence. Further-more, the mother's mode of behavior, the degree of decisiveness she conveys in her new feeding techniques, determines equally the child's response. In essence, it is the mother who proposes, while the baby disposes. For the young child, weaning involves five aspects: (1) learning to acquire food by other means than sucking; (2) learning to like this new method of food intake; (3) learning to want solid food; (4) learning how to handle solid foods orally; and, (5) learning to eat without being held (130). Girls, Sears' findings suggest, seem to take longer to be weaned, which again coincides with their prolonged dependency needs during this age period.

Toilet training, unlike weaning, requires socialized control over previously uncontrolled spontaneous behavior. Usually elimination control is demanded after weaning is completed, and, when the child-mother relationship has become more entrenched. In toilet training, the mother is not supporting or fulfilling a drive. The mother does nothing *for* the child, only *to* him (128). In toilet training, more than weaning, the surrounding circumstances of rewarding acceptance and punishment become important. The child is faced with the question of accepting a set of entirely new motivational systems which, at the time of their introduction, are irrelevant, as far as the child is concerned. Only gradually does the child himself learn to want bodily cleanliness and approved toilet habits. Toilet training introduces other new behavioral learning, such as bodily regularity, modesty, and cleanliness.

As long as toilet training is primarily an introduction of the mother's motivational system, reward and punishment continue to be interpreted by the child as acceptance or rejection by his mother. Intially, the child does not connect them with his elimi-native activities. Toilet training, consequently, must be related to the child's dependency and handled similarly to his dependency needs.

Sexual modesty is one of the first behavioral motivational sys-tems and an integral part of the socialization of children. The proper use of anything related to sex is treated as an inhibiting activity, even more so than in the case of toilet training. Acquired behavior related to sex finds its basis in the mother's wishes rather than in the support and control of the child's needs and specific actions. Potential sexual expressions are curbed before the child has any notion that these social amenities have anything to do with sex. Getting dressed, for instance, serves as the first step for "covering up" and denying the existence of sex organs. Furthermore, sexual organs are hardly ever directly mentioned, in contrast to ready and direct references to other organs. We frequently hear a request: "Do not play with your nose," while a similar request in relation to the sex organ becomes circumvented by common statements as follows: "Do not play with *it!*" or, "Do not play with *yourself!*" The child has to guess what is meant by "it" or "yourself." Boys and girls must deal with undefined concerns which have little meaning for them but much for their elders. Sex training, in general, involves primarily prohibitive instructions. Socialization in regard to sex then tends to proceed differently than in the case of dependency, feeding, and toilet training. Sex training rests upon implication and affect-laden terms. The lack of specific training does not seem to hinder the process of training as long as there are no misleading designations, such as: "Do not touch your genitals or you will need to wash your hands right away."

Aggressiveness emerges as part of socialization as much by accident as by design. Aggression develops as a consequence of action or from lack of it. First, aggression arises as a consequence of frustration which inherently is a part of growing up. Aggression in the form of anger or rage must be viewed as a sequence to frustration, for it occurs as part of a strong but futile attempt to achieve a goal which the individual experiences as unaccessible to him. When the frustrated infant cries out in rage, he accidentally learns that this behavior becomes associated with responses to his needs. He learns that he can utilize this very aggression to secure compliance with his wishes. By hurting the frustrator, he can get what he angrily feels is withheld. The child learns that his aggression causes discomfort to others and that his aggression instigates responses which will try to reduce others' discomfort by mitigating the child's cause for aggression. For example, when an adult retrieves a toy in response to a child's screams, the act becomes associated with the screams. Not unlike his dependency acts, the child learns to initiate aggressive acts in order to have his needs met. Social learning slowly introduces a refinement and more goal-directed aggression. Simultaneously, the child learns to estimate his parent's aggressiveness by the degree of counter-aggression which his parent exercises against his own. Sears suggests that parents of the same sex as the child provide the greater frustration by more rigid control and consequently, are the instigators and recipients of greater aggression.[3] Social learning also introduces the possibility of indirect and fantasy aggression (e.g., in play). Through fantasy, the child releases his aggression uninhibitedly against a substitute for the real instigator of his frustration (128). The child's use of aggression as a means of controlling his environment is a motivational system repeatedly confronted by parents. The mother, in attempting to control her child's actions, is actually aiming toward socialization of her child, and sees to it that his future actions will fall within an acceptable range. The handling of aggression is intimately tied to the development of standards and values within the child; the child learns when, how much, and what modes of aggression will be tolerated in various areas of his life.

Learning to inhibit or to redirect aggression as appropriate to the given circumstances depends upon a delicate balance of permissiveness and restraint during the child's early developmental years. Undue permissiveness of aggression leads the child to place a positive value on aggressive behavior. On the other hand, too much restraint of aggression can be just as harmful. The child then is asked to endure his frustration and to live with his anger, which lead to added frustration and feelings of aggression. Therefore, both extensive permissiveness and extensive restraint foster aggressive feelings.

[3] This observation parallels the concept of the Oedipus-complex (129).

Punishment of aggressive behavior occurs after the aggressive act has taken place, and thus, after the child has already found a reduction in tension and has undergone a reinforcement of his aggressive action. The result is that punishment competes with the satisfaction obtained by aggression. Severe punishment, therefore, introduces new frustration and increases aggression without providing an outlet for it. In many instances, this leads to negative attention-seeking and to continued, but devisive, aggression. This condition, in turn, creates a state of anxiety and discomfort about not only the commission of an aggressive act, but also the aggressive impulses themselves. Anxiety becomes intensified due to the fact that the child can remove neither the frustrating conditions through aggression nor control his mother's aggression through his own. The child will seek deviant techniques for avoiding punishment without successful reduction of aggression except by displacement. Sears' findings on aggression can be presented schematically by a curvilinear graph with minimal punishment or extreme premissiveness at one end and extreme punishment or minimal permissiveness at the other; either extremes foster intensified aggressive feelings. As far as coordinating aggressive feelings and actions are concerned, Sears states that "permissive child-rearing should be helpful in preventing emotional tension, explosion of uncontrollable aggression, and the socially disruptive forms of indirect expression of strong motives" (**130**, 487).

Around a child's third year of life, his behavior tends to resemble much of the behavior of his parent; he has started to identify. Identification as a process can be traced to the quality of the mother-child relationship, to the mother's efforts in providing gratifying experiences in infancy, and, conversely, in the infant's need for his mother:

By the time a child is a year old, he has become related to his mother in such a way that not only do many of his satisfying actions require her presence and cooperation, but her very orientation toward him—indeed, her simple existence near him—is a source of pleasure. He *loves* his mother; he is emotionally dependent on her (**130**, 377).

Thus, when mother cannot be with the young child, he seeks to recover what he has lost by her absence. He repeats certain action sequences as if his mother were present, in order to recapture, as far as possible, the satisfactions he had associated with these experiences. His own activities, including the pleasure that he can reproduce mother's caring activities, gratify his needs, reduce his frustration over mother's temporary removal, and simultaneously, his successful imitation of mother's behavior reinforces this behavior sequence and his desire to behave like mother without and later with mother present. In short, the child rewards himself for imitating dependent behavior without being dependent. He discovers a new source of gratification in the very process of self-initiated imitations which eventually lead from imitation of behavioral sequences to acting like another person. He acts as if he possesses the psychological properties and skills of another person —usually one of his parents (118). A nonmotivational system, that is, identification, emerges and becomes a goal response.

Identification differs from previously cited forms of learning. It rests neither upon trial and error nor from explicit child-rearing efforts. Identification evolves from the child's own role playing, his unsolicited behavior, of a desired, depended-upon but absent parent. Notably, neither nurturing of dependency alone nor withdrawal of love and/or care by itself produce identifying behavior. Learning to identify occurs without any specific teaching from the parents. Furthermore, identification does not necessarily produce desirable behavior. The child is apt to adopt everything in his elder's behavior which he perceives as appropriate to the person's role, which may involve any member of his family, but preeminently either or both parents. As identification, in part at least, depends upon a warm identificand, so does this person's warmth becomes the "warmth" of a new generation: "The more identification there is in any one generation, the greater will be the absorption of those qualities that induces identification in the next" (130, 392).

Sears stresses that sex-typing—the stimulating of "development of social behavior appropriate to the child's own sex" (130, 369)—

is perhaps the most pervasive aspect of the identification process. Boys, for instance, are encouraged to switch their major identification around the age of four. The father's interest encourages an eventual father identification in the boy child. Girls continue their major identification with their mother, and progress more rapidly to more mature forms of behavior than do boys because their identification is uninterruptedly fortified; they tend therefore to become more strongly identified at a decisively earlier point in their life with adult roles, standards, and values. Girls, consequently, remain more sensitive to mother's approval and disapproval. In contrast, boys' identification is complicated not only by the fact that they have to relinquish considerably their identification with mother, but also because they depend upon father's capacity and availability to exhibit a combination of warmth and love-oriented discipline. Father identification in boys is enhanced if the father can be a clear and unequivocal model, acknowledged and esteemed by the mother (119). We may assume that the same holds true for girls when father fortifies the girl's esteem by conveying respect and appreciation for mother through his own behavior towards her. As the child nears school age, he tends to live out the characteristics of the person he identifies with most strongly.

Play provides an opportunity for the child to explore, by trial and error, the make-up of his immediate universe. Play opens the door for exploring, relatively unhampered, physical properties and causality. Play occurs without promise or threat of much reinforcement by extrinsic rewards, and remains the child's territory, essentially free from the intrusion of an elder. At the same time, the child can incorporate his parents' behavior at his leisure, and he can express his joy or frustration and anger through acceptable play activity.

Socialization in early childhood requires the child to discard the autistic style of life of his early infancy. Socialization involves learning to communicate—above all to relate verbally to others. Socialization also teaches the child behavior which can serve as nonverbal communication in his interpersonal relationships. He learns a large variety of body movements and postures which can serve as body language, as influence techniques for trying to direct others' behavior toward a desired end. The child's style and speed of his movements define his motility and his mode of relating to others. Success, in general, increases motility and the capacity to relate to others, while failure may sustain a dogged attempt to continue to try. But with each additional failure, body language and general motility tends to become more and more ineffective as a means of interpersonal communication. Simultaneously, the child himself tends to limit his reliance upon others' body language. Failure, therefore, not only inhibits his own reliance upon wider ranges of influence techniques, it also inhibits learning.

Reasoning with a young child is not as important as the process of *labeling* which is an essential prerequisite to reasoning. Reasoning, in general, involves primarily the explanation and justification of a total behavioral system (i.e., the adherence to a certain value by means of carrying out certain behavioral activities, while labeling deals with specifying certain specific actions for their intent and outcome.) In labeling, a mother will "explain to a child exactly what it is she does and does not want him to do. . . . Its main purpose is *directing* behavior rather than *sanctioning*" (130, 351). When reward or punishment are involved in relation to labeling, a new complication arises. Labeling then tends to occur after behavior has taken place—a backward sequence. It connects the parents' action with the labeled event.

At the beginning of this phase, the child progresses from parental control to partial self-control supported by parental guidance. Around age 2, the child gains more and more control over his impulses. Self-control is a process in which the child gradually adopts his parents' wishes and standards as his own and develops a conscience. More and more of the parents' qualities of behavior and standards of conduct are incorporated in the child's own repertory of action (130). The child tends to imitate those qualities in his parents which are most sensitive and are apt to be censored by withdrawal of parental love. Therefore, conscience comprises those demands most strongly established by identification. A sense of conscience usually revolves around two aspects of each behavioral act: First, the task to be done, and second, the idea of obeying whatever is demanded, that is, obedience for its own sake. In each instance, the child will be motivated by his expectancy of reciprocal affection for behaving according to the expectations of others.

Increase in identification and conscience lead a child to behave more in keeping with his sex, but, at the same time, children of each sex must learn how the other behaves and what such behavior expects of him in return. The mother and father, observed by the child in a social context, gain added importance to the child. Their very capacity to be available, to use praise and withdrawal of affection appropriately, is intimately correlated with their own personal satisfaction and comfort in life as social beings (130). The parents' sense of well-being is closely linked with their sense of oneness with their social setting and the larger community. The parents must find their behavior in agreement with that expected by the larger environment, transcending existing class, ethnic, and educational differences. The parents' sense of self-esteem depends upon their ready access to the latest information, to the latest emphasis in child care, available.

Essentially, during the second phase the child develops his own personality as directed by his elders through their child-rearing efforts. The success of each method of child-rearing depends upon finding a middle ground; either too much or too little dependency, or too strong or too little identification and conscience will thwart the normal progress of development.

Phase III: Secondary Motivational Systems: Extrafamilial Learning

By the time the young child is chronologically and developmentally ready for school, he is ready to absorb from a world which lies beyond that of his family. By this time, he has acquired a system of behavior which will guide him for limited periods in this new outside world. His wider social environment now assumes a major share in further socializing him. At approximately age 5, the child's dependency becomes reduced to specific areas of family living and the mutual exchange of symbolic family trans-actions which include a potential or former condition of depend-ency. To illustrate, the child depends upon eating within the family circle, although he is no longer spoon fed by any member of the family. His dependency has been widened from sole re-liance upon one person to relying upon two or more individuals. This enlargement of the base of dependency continues. Usually, the teacher becomes one of these new resources of dependency. At first, the child tends to relate to each new adult he meets according to his earlier childhood patterns, rather than according to the more realistic demands of the particular situation (128). However, his dependency upon other children (in and outside of the family) will be more in line with the level of his current learning. Dependency on members of his family is modified both in manner and intensity, and is gradually replaced by his depend-ency on his peer group. As before, the manner and quality of this dependency rests upon his previous experience. Patterns of posi-tive attention-seeking—such as compliance with expectation—are perpetuated in his cooperative efforts with his peers. Negative patterns of attention-seeking also continue—through such be-haviors as teasing, exhibitionism, or practical joking. If negative patterns are not checked, they can remain an integral part of the adult personality. Sears describes one such example in his analysis of Samuel Clemens' dependency when he hid and stayed out all night. "Shame, terror and the loss of love were the prices he paid for the glories of attention sought and gained" (121, 28).

The young school-age child's desire for independence needs to be balanced by his acceptance of control and his awareness of his range of freedom. He will try to control other people in such a way that he can satisfy his wants. His new skills in controlling others are met by an increase in the controls demanded of him. More and more areas of life become defined to him. At the same time the range of permissiveness in borderline areas becomes narrower. Controlled areas remain strictly controlled not only by his parents, but also by his teachers, his neighbors, and by other adults in contact with him. In other words, controls become more rigorously defined and more inclusively reinforced.

By the age of 5, usually, the child will become most strongly identified with the parent of the same sex. Identification continues with models which are desirable at least in terms of the child's needs. If desirable models cannot be located in the world of adults, other children who happen to provide him with some gratification, will serve as identificands. As the child expands beyond the world of his home, he must exhibit strong indication of a conscience. His new and wider environment helps him to achieve more comprehensive, internal values as well as to achieve social, religious, and eventually political and economic values. All acquisitions of later value judgments are based on his earlier incorporations of his parents' behavior, and what he has learned from his parents' teaching. Ordinarily, the child wants to be like his parents in order to receive and to maintain their gratifying acceptance.

SUMMARY OF SEARS'
DEVELOPMENTAL THEORY

This chapter is an interpretive introduction to the work of a contemporary learning theorist. Sears' own efforts have been devoted to empirical research and theoretical speculations, yet his material can appropriately be submitted to theory construction. His theory reveals a number of unidirectional trends of development. There is constant change in the degree of precision, efficiency, and speed with which the developing child can manipulate his own actions and can communicate with others. More and more he relates himself to his social environment, while securing the very gratification he desires. These social gratifications invariably become his incentives and goals for actions. His development depends upon the dyadic interaction between his caring adults, usually his parents, and himself. Consequently, Sears surveys child development primarily as a mirror of child-rearing practices built upon innate drives which are modified by his socializing environment, and become the secondary motivational drives. They are potentially stronger than innate drives. The secondary motivational drives determine ultimately the individual's behavioral patterns. They become the behavioral systems of feeding, toilet training, dependency, aggression, competition, and identification. They become the critical variables of child-rearing practices, and consequently, of child development.

Sears' findings emphasize that child-rearing practices in these critical areas do not follow an accumulative linear pattern, but rather a curvilinear one. Child-rearing depends upon finding a proper balance between providing too much and too little in any one area. In the case of dependency or aggression, proper development depends upon furnishing an appropriate permissiveness and opportunity to depend or to aggress as well as upon appropriate limits in order to foster gradually more and more independent actions and control. In other words, curvilinear development implies that too much permission and opportunity intensifies the behavior under question while at the same time, too many limiting or controlling actions inhibit behavior.

Altogether, the socially acquired motivational systems determine the development of internal desires for action and the control of it. The young infant starts behaving in the direction toward which parental control steers him. Later on, he enacts this parental control; he identifies. Identification becomes another motivational system which "drives" him to behave as expected, as learned by means of identification.

To conclude, child development can be summarized as the totality of a child's behavior. As the child behaves, he develops. In turn, his behavior is the product of his immediate social experiences of being brought up. Child development, consequently, is the visible product of the parental child-rearing efforts.

5

A Comparison of the Three
Developmental Theories

EACH OF THE three theories presented in the preceding chapters embodies a dynamic system of its own. At the same time, each supplements the others and together they are essentially congruent. In providing a conceptual reference system on the different dimensions of human development for the professional, the parent, or for anyone who works with children and youth, the critical similarities and differences among the theories deserve special attention. We need to ask ourselves: Does the combined knowledge of any two, or of all three, theories suggest similar or conflicting points of view about the most appropriate way of understanding, caring, and treating a child or youth under a given set of circumstances? and, if researchable hypotheses were to be established, would the findings from any one agree with those from either of the other two? We shall consider the similarities and differences among these theories with the following subtopics in mind: terminology; basic assumptions (theory construction, the nature of human life, the etiology of human behavior, the core determinant of human behavior, environmental influences); basic balancing factors of life; the developmental continuum; the course of individual development; and questions of structure.

TERMINOLOGY

At first glance, differences in the terminology employed by the three theorists serve to accentuate the essential differences which exist in the theories, and to raise problems beyond those of pure semantics. Each theorist's strict adherence to his own technical language places serious obstacles before anyone wishing to apply directly the terminology of one theory to the others. Yet, if we look beyond the different usage of different terms or labels, and consider the contexts in which they are employed, we get a glimpse of similar concepts. Whenever we deal with different terminologies, we can either hold ourselves narrowly to the particular context in which technical terms are used, or, we can adapt the terms to fit broader definitions without necessarily adapting each of the original variables associated with the terms. In the latter event, we are primarily concerned with the learning and communication of ideas. To illustrate, the word *unconscious* is used by Erikson to encompass the psychoanalytic id-ego-superego developmental structure. Piaget means by *unconscious* the mental and active processes in an individual which operate outside of that individual's conscious awareness. Sears employs the term to refer simply to that which is beyond a person's immediate recall. Despite these differences, however, there is a common basis underlying all three usages. Each is referring essentially to those processes within an individual which are outside the realm of that individual's conscious understanding and control.

Another complication exists when each theorist introduces his own terminology for essentially the same range of observations and concepts. For instance, we find that each theorist refers to what is essentially the same stage of development. Piaget labels the first stage of life the *sensori-motor phase*. Erikson would call this period the *phase of basic trust*. Sears simply refers to the *infancy period* of learning. The important thing to recognize, then, is that each theory accounts for comparable stages in the sequence of human development.

Thus, it remains for us to search beneath the semantical variations among the theorists and to arrive at the essential ideas each theorist's semantic symbols intended to convey. It is within these essential ideas that a combined guiding reference system on human development lies. This is particularly true for the scope of this book, which is intended to explain the theories as a bridge of understanding rather than to expound and to establish any one theory for itself.

BASIC ASSUMPTIONS

In addition to reconciling semantic differences, it is of paramount importance to inspect and to compare the basic premises upon which each theory is founded. In this discussion, the selected theories are reviewed together in terms of their basic construction and in light of the assumptions they make concerning the nature of human life, the etiology of human behavior, the core of human behavior, and the environmental factors which influence development.

Theory Construction and Methodology

As scientists, the three child developmentalists commonly aim for increased understanding of human growth and behavior through specific investigations into specialized areas. Jean Piaget strives to establish a universal system of individual development which is consistent with the collective intellectual development of mankind. Differences among individuals or cultural groups of individuals are secondary to his theory. Erik H. Erikson, by contrast, endeavors to understand each individual in his uniquely complex situation in life. From their respective frames of reference, Piaget's and Erikson's theoretical considerations serve to balance one another in an appraisal of a given individual's developmental situation. Sears contributes further to this understanding through his study of man within his social learning matrix.

In their approaches to the formulation of theory, Piaget and Erikson operate deductively, Sears inductively. The first two agree that all research on human development has to proceed within the boundaries of a unified theory. Their separate approaches might be compared to the explorer who insists upon mapping the complete course of a river, including its springs and its final delta, before he can satisfactorily locate and investigate any one whirlpool within the path of the river. Piaget first constructs his theoretical model, then proceeds to test each of its parts, and finally considers his research findings valid only if they are first, theoretically consistent, and second, empirically substantiated. Erikson relies upon the psychoanalytic model with specific emphasis upon sociocultural factors as codeterminants. Sears adheres primarily to the edict of Clark L. Hull that theory building is a laborious process which requires systematic organization of empirically valid findings. Curiously, although Sears' approach to theory formulation is inductive, in the presentation of his findings—particularly in his most recent writings (69, 114, 118, 121, 130)—Sears proceeds much as do the other two, with his generalizations venturing far beyond the spheres of his data and their statistical significance.

Although all agree that the natural environment provides the most favorable laboratory conditions for measuring personality development, each differs with respect to *methodology* of investigation and to the developmental aspect to be investigated. Piaget structures his research in order to isolate variables of *thought processes*, aiming to learn precisely how one individual thinks about any one problem. Having gathered all the information he can from one individual, he relates his findings to his theoretical structure. Sears relies upon quantitative data which reveal the typical *behavioral* responses to certain stimuli under given (and controlled) sets of circumstances. Erikson dispenses with controls in the accepted scientific sense. He attempts to analyze all variables operating in a single individual within his social situation and focuses upon the complex *interrelationships* of these variables and their effect upon the total personality.

Yet despite these markedly different research procedures, the findings of each theorist are strikingly noncontradictory, and they become remarkably complementary when superimposed upon one another.

The Nature of Human Life

All three theorists believe in the regularity of human growth and development as well as in the potential predictability of human behavior. Piaget goes so far as to hypothesize that *all* physical, biological, and psychological laws can be integrated into a single universal formula. The prediction of human behavior, he stresses, relies upon a predictable universal order. He sees in the ultimate understanding of the order and nature of life processes a key to an understanding of universal laws, and conversely, in the discovery of universal laws, an ultimate explanation of everyday life events. Erikson, too, assumes a cosmic order, but considers it beyond his reach; it is thus not of immediate or primary concern to him. Sears—with his reliance upon the laws of probability—assumes with Piaget the predictability of human behavior; in his work, however, he limits his studies to those fractions of the universe which can be controlled, empirically measured, and comprehended. To summarize, Piaget, Erikson and Sears all assume that human life unfolds in an orderly process in an orderly world, and each ventures to investigate for himself and his contemporaries those facets of human life experience which are of particular interest to him.

Etiology of Human Behavior

Piaget, Erikson, and Sears all build upon an evolutionary view of the development of human behavior, but in dissimilar ways. Sears considers human behavior to be the product of stimulus-response learning—more advanced but essentially like animal motivational conditioning. This perspective somewhat mitigates man's exalted evolutionary level, explaining human behavior more mechanistically. In contrast, Piaget and Erikson devote their primary attention to those human functions which lift man above the animal level. All three suggest that human behavior arises out of the interplay of opposing forces; Erikson ascribes this polarity entirely to the struggle between opposing *internal* pulls, Piaget allocates the polarity to an encounter between an individual's in-

ternal understanding and the reality conveyed to him by the outside world, and Sears essentially considers the interplay of stimulus-response functioning between two individuals.

The greatest difficulty lies in reconciling Eriksonian views with
those of Sears and Piaget. If the three were to join in a roundtable
discussion, Piaget and Sears might take issue with Erikson's psychoanalytic assumption that human behavior results from needs
and motivation consistently internally nurtured. Piaget explains
needs as nurtured by metamorphic development—the change of a
reflex system into a rhythmic cycle of human functioning; Sears
prefers his more causal explanation of needs as a product of man's
own environmental and social-learning history. Erikson stresses
that the conflicting pulls which exist internally in man serve to
control his nature and his mastery of his behavior.

In a study of the origin of human behavior, these obvious
differences would appear starkly divergent. It is possible, however, that the three perspectives represent different levels within
any individual's development and can be reconciled on that basis.
The essential work of these three theorists concerns itself primarily with the *socialization* of man—with behavior as it unfolds
within the social milieu—and, in spite of their divergence, the
three theorists describe corresponding developmental patterns
with similar behavioral demands and consequences.

The Core Determinant of Human Behavior

Each of the theorists depends upon a different assumption in
his definition of the determinants of human behavior. Piaget's
emphasis upon *cognitive* comprehension as the decisive factor in
all human behavior is countered by Erikson's contention that
affective (emotional) processes furnish the basic motivations for
all human behavior. Sears suggests that a person's behavior is in
itself of overriding importance, past behavior being the foundation for new behavior.

Sears introduces a rapid shift from innate (or impulsive) to
learned (or socialized) behavior. For Sears, outward behavior
soon reflects the product of the social environment; the infant eats

when and what he has been taught, and not as his digestive tract urges. Piaget delineates the learning progression as the developing personality requires all of the childhood years and more to discard *egocentric* reasoning in favor of *socialized* thought. Erikson perceives of an individual's emotional makeup in terms of a life-long struggle between native desire and the internalization of social realities. Each of the three theories provides by itself only a partial understanding of personality development. The developing child can no longer be viewed as an individual who learns primarily to define his experience (Piaget), or a unique organism who strives primarily to establish his own style and sphere of living (Erikson), or a subject whose motivations are patterned primarily on the basis of his past satisfying experience (Sears). Instead, the developing child must be viewed as an individual who is subject to all three of these factors. The professional must recognize the child or youth as an individual who *thinks, feels,* and *acts* uniquely within the bounds of the laws of human development. Man's behavior must not be simplified when it is complex, nor defined as fully explainable and controllable when there is still much to be learned.

Environmental Influences

It is noteworthy that Piaget, Erikson, and Sears all unite in an unwavering faith in granting the individual the potential capacity to hurdle obstacles of his own or his environment's making, although each theorist does hold a different view of how environmental factors affect the individual. Piaget considers only those physical, social, or ideational components of a child's environment that are within the range of the child's conscious comprehension. Sears accounts for all the stimulating factors which have an immediate behavioral impact upon the child, regardless of whether or not they enter within an individual's cognitive threshold. Erikson would be likely to include all imaginable environmental factors—including those outside the range of direct influence upon the child—maintaining that all have relevance to the emotional development of the child. Each environmental factor within

or beyond an individual's immediate field of experience has bearing upon a child, or, upon the child's environment which eventually has its influence on the child. Figuratively, in each theory,
environmental factors feed into a different "dynamo" and generate separate dynamic currents affecting widely differing functions. It should be pointed out that Piaget and Erikson join in
viewing environmental factors as "feedback" points for internal
functions, while Sears depicts environmental symbols and events
as the essential *stimulators* for internally motivated overt behavior.

In viewing the means by which the individual hurdles the
obstacles of his environment, Piaget anchors his faith in the potential *cognitive* capacity of each developing person, while Erikson bases his trust in the *adaptive* power and creative capacity of
both the individual and the social environment. This adaptive
potential in each human being is rooted for Erikson in each individual's emotional makeup. He is willing to concede that intellectual potential does help, while for Piaget, it determines man's
course. Sears sees man as the creator and the recipient of his own
environment. Sears could readily subscribe to the old dictum:
Man can pull himself up by his own bootstraps. Sears' stress upon
the motivating factors in the present gives credence to his assumption that man can purposefully organize his and his children's
experiences in such a way that he can clearly shape their future
as desired by him and his contemporaries.

BALANCING FACTORS OF LIFE

Polarity, or the existence of opposing pulls, constitutes the
basis for the continuous dynamic conflict of life, according to
each theorist. From the cradle to grave, man strives to reconcile
these opposing pulls and to find a sense of manageable change in
a desirable direction. Piaget proposes a gradual but never complete equalization of the opposing pulls; to achieve mental maturity is to find a near equilibrium within the context of an
eternal need for change. Erikson, in contrast, sees a process in
which each new conquest in the mastery of the two-way pull

becomes the foundation for a new spurt of development. Sears comes close to Erikson's notions, stressing the importance of a momentary reduction of tension experienced by the individual, which is then the hypothetical condition for the motivation of new and more advanced achievements.

A difference among the theories, in this connection, becomes apparent if each is examined for an interpretation of the impact of the tension-reducing processes. Erikson stresses the accomplishment of a relatively tension-free state as a developmental goal, with the tension-reducing mechanisms serving as the means to obtain this all-important end. He teaches that attaining a sense of relaxation can compensate for all the energy invested in the effort to attain this sense. Piaget sees tension-reduction as an automatic psychological process, analogous to the metabolic process of exhaling. For Piaget, to find out, to know, is to open a new vista and to begin a new exploration. Sears treats the tension-reduction process as a necessary condition to behavioral functioning, and therefore, it is not the tension-free state, but the tension-reduction process itself which significantly stabilizes the individual and gives him a sense of well-being; finding satisfaction prompts a person to repeat the behavior which led to that satisfaction.

Thus, each theorist sees human development generated and stabilized in a different way through a basic polarity. Actually, however, there are no basic contradictions. The three theorists are analogous to the proverbial story of the blind men and the elephant; each is talking about a different aspect of the same animal. Each theorist's understanding as applied and confined to his particular area of investigation provides avenues to conceive of the various aspects of human development in greater depth as well as breadth.

THE DEVELOPMENTAL CONTINUUM

All three theorists equate development with dynamic, continuous change, focusing upon the orderly processes of this change. All three speak of the unfolding of developmental processes during which all new development finds its roots in previous acquisitions, and in which all new development provides additional opportunities for correcting or completing developmental acquisitions previously incomplete. Piaget shares Erikson's optimism that development is essentially a growing and rectifying process. Erikson suggests that, unlike Humpty Dumpty, the developing child, youth, or adult can put himself together again. Sears' scheme can more easily be described as an additive progression, in which each new acquisition significantly builds upon a previous one. This emphasis upon continuous change implies a progressive outlook in all three theories, and, simultaneously, all accept a strand of conservatism by recognizing the impact and inherent continuation of previous acquisitions. No learning, no emotional or social experience, is ever entirely new. Each experience becomes integrated within previously established modes of behavior in the history of personal traditions, and old experiences merely acquire new perspectives. Moreover, as Sears and Piaget stress, old experiences receive new labels.

The essential differences among the three theorists are to be found in the emphases they place upon the *analysis* of developmental change and upon the individual's disposition of previous acquisitions. Sears can be described as finding himself at both extremes of a continuum. In one sense, he considers only the latest social experiences as the major behavioral determinants which replace or reinforce previous behavior. Erikson is the most outspoken advocate of the lingering impact of early infancy and childhood experiences. Regardless of subsequent events, early experiences make a vital impact upon the child and continue to mold the direction of future behavior. Piaget challenges this interpretation as adultomorphic thinking so far as cognitive experience is concerned. He questions an individual's capacity to perceive and to remember specific events at a time when the infant was incapable of cognitively absorbing the events. Piaget's emphasis rests upon the *modification* of early experience, that is, the continuation of earlier learning in terms of the new level of understanding. Piaget and Sears implicitly arrive at similar conclusions in their recognition of the increasing relevance of ongoing experiences as the child matures. Piaget's research points out that, during early childhood, new events are perceived as they happen. Only as the child matures can he discern other than immediately causal factors through inference and abstraction. He then can perceive stimuli for their actual and inherent implications; he learns to deal consciously with his world for its patterns of relationship. For him, maturity means *understanding* patterns of relationship. For Sears, maturity means refinement in the selection of appropriate behavioral patterns.

Without denying the existing conflict, all three are closer in agreement than would first appear to be true. In a roundtable discussion, Piaget and Erikson acknowledged the compatability of their theoretical formulations concerning the impact and continuation, in one form or another, of earlier psychosocial developmental experiences in later life (**107c**, 154–160). Each approaches the question of change from a different angle. Piaget preoccupies himself with the etiology of the conceptual base of behavior and change in behavioral life experience, including habits, while Erikson (and perhaps Sears also if he had been present at this discussion) is concerned with the causative factors leading a person to choose one life experience (including habits) over another.

In reviewing the total stream of development, it is essential to note that only Erikson recognizes setbacks and reversals as essential ingredients of development which are explainable within the theory. This is not surprising, for Erikson is as much concerned with normal development as with deviant or pathological development. His concepts on regression are not in conflict with either Sears' or Piaget's theory, but he alone points up regression as a consistent and acceptable deviation within the progression of development. Regression as a developmental phenomenon is not mentioned in either Piaget's or Sears' theory. Both, however, recognize the occurrence of "plateaus."

Individual differences are accounted for by Piaget for differences in the rate and environmental circumstances of development. Erikson and Sears recognize individual differences, suggesting that external circumstances are probably the decisive factors which help to determine the rate of a child's development. Erikson gives special credence to cultural expectations, while Sears finds that the rate of development is primarily influenced by more immediate social settings. These differences suggest that the rate of intellectual development is an individual matter based upon particular genetic differences, while the rate of socioemotional development is influenced as much by external conditions, including cultural time tables, as by the individual's constitutional factors.

Piaget and Erikson are known for their explicit acknowledgment of developmental phases, while Sears' research and writing includes the existence of the phases only implicitly. Actually, however, Erikson is the only one of the three who conceives of development as the mastery of a series of prescribed developmental goals that are coincident with each phase, and the natural existence of developmental crises. Piaget prefers to focus upon the processes which produce the change, without emphasizing unduly the goals to be mastered. Sears acknowledges only the emergence of a new focus and has no desire to imply prescribed tasks or goals.

Charting the developmental phases which are implicit or explicit in each theory affirms a high degree of accord between them. By studying these theories in relation to each other, a single developmental continuum suggests itself. Table 5.1 delineates nearly identical developmental phases, highlighting the extensiveness of Erikson's developmental continuum as compared to Piaget's more limited explorations; for Piaget and Sears, development "ceases" at the most advanced age level they happened to have investigated.

There is a wide gulf between Piaget's and Erikson's approaches to the adolescent phase. Piaget expects personality integration during these years, at least as far as intellectual development is concerned—a factor which also exists in classical Freudian theory, but which is eliminated in Erikson's reformulation. Erikson conceives of a new crisis which both challenges and integrates anew

TABLE 5.1. *Comparison of the Three Theories' Developmental Phases.*

AGE (YEARS)	ERIKSON	PIAGET	SEARS	INTEGRATION
0	Phase I: A Sense of Basic Trust	Sensori-Motor Phase	Phase of Rudimentary Behavior	Phase I: Establishing Primary Dependency
1				
2			Phase of Secondary Motivational Systems: Family-Centered Learning	Phase II: Establishing Self-Care
3	Phase II: A Sense of Autonomy	Preconceptual Phase		
4				Phase III: Establishing Meaningful Secondary Relationships
5	Phase III: A Sense of Initiative	Phase of Intuitive Thought		
6				
7			Phase of Secondary Motivational Systems: Extra-familial Learning	
8				
9	Phase IV: A Sense of Industry	Phase of Concrete Operations		Phase IV: Establishing Secondary Dependency
10				
11				
12				
13	Phase V: A Sense of Identity	Phase of Formal Operations	(Little research done by Sears thus far)	Phase V: Achieving Balance Between Dependence and Independence
14				
15				
16				
17				
18				
19				
20	Phase VI: A Sense of Intimacy[a]	(Not yet investigated by Piaget)		
21				
etc.				

[a] Two more progressive phases of adulthood follow: Sense of Generativity and Sense of Integrity.

NOTE: No step-like pattern is intended here; rather, development is continuous through phases which merge into each other.

all previous conflicting pulls. At the same time, Piaget's view of the adolescent's cognitive struggle to comprehend his environment is essentially akin to Erikson's concept of the adolescent's psychosocial struggle to find his identity. With the completion of the adolescent phase, Piaget sees the individual as a mature and complete personality who has made the transition from adolescence to adulthood in a single step. Erikson strongly challenges such a position: He views the young adult as still forging his own place in his society. Genuine maturity (a sense of integrity) for Erikson, is still three stages ahead. In other words, for Piaget (and also for Sears), a growing person reaches adulthood the moment he surrenders his childish thinking and actions. For Erikson, adulthood means more than outgrowing one's childish and youthful ways, and psychological maturity—if it ever exists—depends upon continued development of one's self-awareness and understanding.

Maturity in a modern democratic society, unlike that in primitive culture, is not automatically bestowed with the traditional "rites of passage" that take place at puberty. Full adulthood is recognized when the individual is behaviorally mature enough to be accepted as an equal by other adults. It is interesting to note that it is Erikson, the clinician, who continues to see not only the adolescent, but also the adult as a developing individual. It is he who can go beyond the notion of equal citizenry. As a clinician, he can consider from a position of authority a differential maturity among social equals.[1]

In summary, Table 5.1 shows schematically that (1) each theory is consistent within itself in developing a concept of personality growth; (2) all three theorists show developmental phases similar to each other; and (3) the three theories are divergent when viewed horizontally because the developmental course of each theory deals with different spheres of personality functioning. Applicable generalizations for practice will arise out of the amalgamation of the three perspectives.

THE COURSE OF INDIVIDUAL DEVELOPMENT

In scanning an individual's development simultaneously through the observational screens of Piaget, Erikson, and Sears, both similar and conflicting concepts become apparent. Piaget and Erikson

---

[1] This observation was made by Edmund A. Smith, a political and economic social scientist, School of Social Work, University of Washington.

alike concentrate upon the very early patterning of native responses in emphasizing the concept that a basic rhythm of living, basic patterns of thinking, attitudes, and ordering of experience are predetermined during the early weeks of life. While Piaget and Erikson speak in terms of early *patterning*, Sears speaks of *conditioning*. In essence, however, Sears' interpretation of this early conditioning or "the establishment of secondary motivational systems" remains akin to Erikson's and Piaget's findings. Sears deals equally with whole complexes of behavior, which he describes as distinct clusters of behavioral sequences.

There are, nonetheless, noteworthy differences among the theorists' interpretations of the impact of previous experience upon the individual's current and subsequent experiences. Erikson hypothesizes a continuous thread of life events that starts from the very beginning of each individual's life history. Piaget satisfies himself that early life experiences establish the essential patterns for dealing with later life events. Sears sees earlier self-satisfying experiences impinging upon later ones until their aggregate begins to have a directional effect upon the individual. Moreover, Piaget and Erikson find different interpretations for a child's early self-centeredness: Piaget requires no explanation—for him, the child knows no alternative; from Erikson's viewpoint, childhood egocentricity constitutes a child's early effort to establish his own sphere and to locate himself as an independent being among others. Sears tends to side with Erikson; that is, he defines a child's self-centeredness as an expression of the central struggle between self-satisfaction and the acceptance of social controls. These theoretical differences bear directly upon everyday practice. They point to the necessity for differentiating clearly between intellectual and emotional self-awareness. They imply the continuous separation between the states of feeling and the knowledge of one's independence and identity. Yet, they actually operate very much as one in everyday experience.

A similar problem arises in regard to sex differences. Erikson alone sees the infant child as sexually differentiated; the infant's sex defines his specific genetic and sociocultural heritage. Sears recognizes sexual differences only to the extent that these differences affect the child's immediate environment since this environment will, in turn, affect the child. Piaget recognizes no essential sexual differences in his study of intellectual development. In other words, the three theorists combined teach us that male and female are *equal* intellectually but psychologically they are differently endowed. Socially they are as equal as cultural factors allow.

In another area of infancy development, Piaget challenges the analytical contention that unconscious processes are as potent within the first phase of pychological development as they are during subsequent phases. He questions—but does not fully negate—this analytical concept. In Piaget's theory, the infant does not yet possess the intellectual capacity to conceive of and to remember objects when he is in direct contact with them. Piaget argues that memory of experience and its conceptualization are prerequisite to unconscious memory and transference phenomena, and thus, recall—conscious or unconscious—cannot actually occur until a child has the capacity to symbolize, to retain, and to recall previous experiences—a capacity usually not achieved until the child is about 1 year old. Even then, memory of objects remains linked with the memory of the sequence of the total experience. Sears would not be apt to agree with this. Erikson maintains that unconscious processes as emotional states can be reexperienced with little or no accurate intellectual ideation. These differences are viewed for their impact upon the translation of theory into practice. In the actual application of theory, the practitioner does not deal directly with a child's infantile image of his parent—real or implied, conscious or unconscious—except as it might apply to the child's reactions to persons in his ongoing life experiences. The three theorists imply that individuals in the social surroundings of the child deal with him as if he knew and remembered his previous experiences. Consequently, whether a child can consciously or unconsciously recognize and remember his actual infancy, he reacts to the idea of adults' expectations. He tries to behave as if he knew.

There is a potential conflict in the three theorists' interpretation of unconscious processes. For Erikson, unconscious processes are a reality; for Piaget, beyond his questions about infantile unconscious retention, unconscious processes are a probability, and have been demonstrated to his satisfaction by others' investigations. Piaget places them outside his sphere of interest and range of research (100). Sears, like Erikson, accepts them as an implicit reality (69, 114, 121, 124, 127, 130)—an unmeasurable reality—because his studies focus upon the results of human motivations, conscious or otherwise (126).

All three theorists view the process of *perception* differently without inherent conflict. For Piaget, perception is a neurological experience with no psychological relevance until the individual intellectually incorporates his perceptual experience. In short, only as an individual cognizes his perceptions do they have any meaning to him, however realistic or distorted his awareness may be. Erikson, on the other hand, recognizes perception as part of a person's experience from birth. Sears describes perceptual processes only for their stimulation. All three theorists agree that selective perception is an essential human quality based upon a combination of differential developmental experiences and readiness. Each one proves his contentions from his own perspective. Each one relates his perspective to those aspects of personality development with which he is concerned. We may assume then, that theoretical differences are dependent upon perspective differences only. Perception and comprehension is one thing while a review of perception in relation to the circumvening stimuli directs us to a third range of variables which impinge upon an individual's perception. We may then conclude that each dimension adds to the total quality and range of each individual's perception of his ever changing experience.

Controversy exists around views of habit formation and the imitation of others' behavior. Both factors loom large in Sears' theoretical frame of reference, but, they receive little attention in the eventual application and analysis of his findings. Piaget implies that habit formation occurs mainly during a child's first twelve months. For Piaget, habit formation constitutes self-imitation; that is, persistency in behavioral patterns. The young child's ever-increasing capacity to perceive and to imitate outside models automatically destroys his inclination to live according to habits. More and more he conforms to the behavioral patterns of others in a manner which is increasingly adequate to him. Erikson never gives much attention to behavioral patterns as such; his interest remains with the underlying emotional theme of the individual. Again, an analysis of the three theorists' teachings leads us to disregard differences in their specific details and to recognize the similarities in their overall approaches. Curiously, all three actually by-pass earlier psychologists' and educators' concern about habit formation. Piaget rules out the possibility of the persistence of habits; for him, each new age level reached produces in the individual new forms of thinking and accompanying patterns of behavior. Erikson and Sears direct their attention to the circumstances which perpetuate habits; concerning themselves with the emotional overtone which either supports or negates habits. Thus, all three unite in focusing upon the context in which habits occur rather than upon the investigation of habits *per se*.

Piaget and Erikson recognize trial-and-error learning as an important factor in early childhood development, but in this they part ways with Sears by relegating this process of learning to a minor position in all later childhood development. Altogether, Erikson is the most willing to recognize a power within the infant which is knowingly exercised. Sears prefers to relegate the direction-giving power for most infant behavior to the stimuli outside the infant. Piaget, on the other hand, first counters Erikson's idea that early-life experiences become generalized by the child for all subsequent experiences, but he then submits a similar observation—albeit with a different rationale—by stating that the infant *does* build upon his own previous experiences because he knows no alternative.

In all three, the processes leading to identification are the central developmental processes. Imitative and trial-and-error behavior are merely minor and supplementary processes utilized to achieve identification. All three visualize the child as an individual who selects other beings as his models. They conceive of a two-part process: (1) the selection of others as models, and (2) living up to the behavior, ideas, or values assumed to be mastered by the persons selected. Selection and makeup is a part of the concept of identification for all the theorists. Piaget conceives of identification as the process of choosing models according to existing patterns of the child's understanding. Sears conceptualizes a process of fitting *available* models to the satisfactions associated with them on the basis of similar and previously pleasing experiences. Erikson pictures the selection of models as a natural, need-fulfilling process in which each developmental phase demands the development of different qualities and a different range of models. Altogether, the selection of the identificand is a child-oriented process, and is based upon each child's unique perspective as circumscribed by the range of available and appropriate models. Identification, as depicted by all three can be described in terms of Bronfenbrenner's three levels (14): (1) Identification as a *behavioral* activity, with emphasis on absorbing a model's overt action; (2) identification as a *motivational* activity, with emphasis on the disposition to act like the selected models; and (3) identification as a *psychological* process, with the emphasis on mechanisms involved in emulating a person of special psychic relevance. Significantly, identification bestows symbolic significance upon the model apart from and beyond the previous ongoing relationship to the model, and creates additional significant persons in a child's life which may be within or beyond his immediate social matrix.

In their respective developmental schemes, each theorist maps a varying course for transfer of behavior. Erikson stresses two factors. The first of these is the transfer of the symbolic significance of a previously important experience with one model and continuing it with a contemporary model. Secondly, a fanning-out process takes place, moving the identification with one to differential identification with two (of opposite sex) and eventually with several persons or even with groups of individuals. Piaget charts only the ongoing changes occurring in the use of different models without defining specific patterns in the progress of relationships. In contrast, Sears cites development of identification as an additive process. Each successful identification results in the potential for renewed and improved identification on a higher social level. All three, then, unite in specifying identification as a central process of development. They seem to be close in analyzing the process of identification, while each of the three theorists gives a special emphasis which tends to support and to supplement the others' contentions.

It becomes apparent that Piaget, Erikson, and Sears share the conviction that whatever occurs during the early developmental years is basic to the child's later adjustment. All three see this period as the beginning of socialization; each recognizes that the social implications of new experiences are more important than the actual mastery of the tasks accomplished. The actual processes of social learning, however, are described by each differently. Piaget considers social learning to be a process of personal adaptation between what is known and mastered previously and what is perceived as new and appropriate to be mastered. Erikson interprets social learning or adjustment as primarily a question of "psychological digestibility." For him, social learning takes place concomitant with psychological accessibility. Sears counts on the relationship between past experiences and the rewards that socialization has in store. Piaget, then, sees social learning as an ongoing and balancing process between internal and external impressions. Erikson modifies this contention by maintaining that this balancing process is primarily influenced by the child's psychological effort to make his social adaptation psychologically "safe" *for him*. Sears adds that the selection of the eventual "balancing factors" and the psychological mechanisms depend ultimately upon the satisfaction that the child intuitively tries to find in keeping with his past experiences. When viewed together, each theorist alters the other's emphasis without actually negating the others' teachings; yet for purposes of working with children, all three create a dilemma of choice and one must ask: Which shift of emphasis is appropriate at any given instance?

The three theorists recognize spoken language as the conveyor of meaning as symbolized by words and sentences, and the conveyor of a message as words and sentences imply it. In addition, Piaget attributes to language a second essential function; an auxiliary operation of the thinking process. As the child learns to use language, Sears and Piaget alike suddenly view the child as a new and different person, an organism with a unique personality attribute. For Erikson, language is merely an additional but most significant resource for transmitting—as well as for camouflaging—feelings, thinking and actions. For Piaget and Sears, spoken language constitutes the major avenue of investigation for all major inquiries conducted by the child. Erikson alone continues to attribute equal importance to nonverbal communication even as the child resorts to verbal communication. In giving equal attention to verbal and nonverbal language, Erikson alone is interested in both, and the inner consistency or divergence between these two forms of communication. (Naturally, Erikson as a student of pathological behavior, wants to know when a person's communicative systems are at one with each other and when they lack integration.) Language for Sears reflects symbolized learned behavior while for Piaget it is the key to deciphering behavior. For Erikson, it is a revelation to be analyzed together with action. For all three, the use of communicative language, combined with differential identification with more than one model, symbolizes the operation of a conscience, or superego, although it is Erikson alone who discerns the mechanism of superego processes without departing from Piaget's and Sears' concepts. In fact, Charles Odier maintains that Piagetian and analytical thinking come closer together in the sphere of superego development than any other aspects of their respective theories (84, 20). Yet, all three agree that the parent's conscience serves as the child's until the time that the child can locate and incorporate his parent's conscience as his own. Piaget also stresses the importance of the peer group as an alternate superego which, for him, becomes operational at an earlier developmental level than for the other two. Similarly, each acknowledges the emergence of the child's own conscience at a somewhat different point in development, but not more than a year more or less apart in each theorist's developmental continuum.

Piaget finds that conflicting feelings cannot be labeled as guilt until the child has attained the intellectual capacity to appraise adult prestige and authority, and thus, Piaget finds no place for the sense of guilt or the desire for punishment on any level prior to the child's conscious awareness of the seat of authority. Erikson and Sears, on the other hand, define guilt as the product of conscious or unconscious experience at any age level, even prior to the conscious awareness of taboos. Here Piaget and Erikson again present a dichotomy. Cognitive conscience does not exist until an individual *knows* of its existence. The affective conscience, or superego, emerges years before an individual senses and is consciously influenced by its effect.

In viewing further the developing child, Piaget considers periods of transition between phases as developmental opportunities for advancement to new levels. Erikson and Sears concur with Piaget's optimism, but they also point to the dangers of uncertainty and confusion inherent in these transitory periods. At this point, it seems advisable to look into one of the most perplexing and potentially controversial concepts, the Oedipal conflict.

The Oedipal conflict as a decisive psychological phenomenon receives no mention in Piaget's or Sears' theory, but in Erikson's psychoanalytic theory, it has been presented as both a phase of shifting, as well as conflicting, loyalties in varying attachments toward key elders of the opposite sex. Piaget and Sears observe in their findings similar shifts and conflicting alignments in regard to imitative learning and the establishment of a single model as the source of primary identification. Both observe an increase in the child's awareness of and interest in behaving like the parent model of the same sex. Simultaneously, the child endeavors to maintain and to insure close ties with the model of the opposite sex. It is interesting to note that Piaget unwittingly defines an intellectual conflict in a child's apparent sexual identification during his nursery-school years. Much of a child's role confusion and conflict in his understanding of the meaning of this conflict for him is parallel to the emotional conflicting loyalties in the Oedipal situation. Sears stresses that during this same age span the parent of the same sex as the child is apt to be the instigator as well as the recipient of greater aggression, while the opposite parent tends to be more lenient, and consequently more approachable (129). Erikson would summarize these observations as symptomatic of the Oedipal situation. Actually, a possible, though primary, theoretical difference exists when Erikson explains the Oedipal situation as a period when the child strives particularly to relate closely to the parent of the opposite sex; therefore, the relationship to the parent of his own sex becomes altered and more complicated. Piaget's and Sears' findings imply that, in this same period, the child attempts particularly painstaking behavioral approaches to the parent of the same sex, which, in turn, suggest of the child a more urgent attachment and new complications with the parent of the opposite sex. Thus, there is little fundamental conflict as long as the concept of an Oedipal situation is not limited to the earlier Freudian interpretation of a biologically triggered complex and is dealt with as a perplexing problem in the shifting of interpersonal attachments and the creation of new differentiated relationships.

Erikson sees the Oedipal situation in puberty as a developmental crisis, a struggle between gaining a sense of identity and being left with a sense of role diffusion. Piaget alludes to similar complications as the adolescent attempts in his own mind to define his social relationships within a new and larger social matrix. Sears' work does not sufficiently extend into this age period to commit his thinking in one way or other. Piaget conceives of a more advanced cognition of patterns of relationship as the solution to this period of stress. Erikson attributes the successful integration of this period to the mastery of conflicting *affective* processes. Both recognize this time of confusion and conflict as an essential ingredient of growth. Erikson again suggests that developmental processes differ according to sex. Piaget does not seem to deem sex differences as significant. The eventual synthesis

of Erikson's concept of the second Oedipal conflict during adolescence, and Piaget's allusion to a confusion about symbolic
relationship is open to future investigation.

In the subsequent pages only essential agreements and differences between Piaget's and Erikson's material will be covered.
Sears' work limits itself essentially to the preschool-age child.
Piaget and Erikson assume distinctly different positions in regard
to the fantasy life of young children. For Piaget, fantasy remains
a continuation of the egocentric phase of a child's life. He defines
it as a compartmentalized continuation of a young child's one-
dimensional life of which the child is the center, free from all
conflicting boundaries. Erikson, in contrast, attributes to the child
both an awareness of his fantasies and a conflict over such an
awareness. Yet, both stress that the caring adult deals with the
child as the adult perceives or wants to perceive the child's world.
(The child's elder deals with him independent of the child's
fantasy, on whatever level it might have occurred.) Erikson adds
that the parent, too, deals unconsciously with the child's fantasy
which has also been both communicated to and sensed by the
parent unconsciously. The parent tends to deal with these fantasies because he, in part, unconsciously relives his own childhood and strives to forestall mobilization of long forgotten
feelings.

Piaget and Erikson see the young school-age child as pushing
forward incessantly, creating for himself new horizons of skills,
knowledge, and emotional maturity. Piaget and Erikson both
recognize the child himself to be the driving force. The adults in
his environment, especially those who care for him, can substantially help or hinder his progress, but by this age they no longer
simply "bend the twig," for the child now has a life sphere in
which he can operate relatively unchallenged. In other words,
Piaget and Erikson both acknowledge the school-age child's
intense concentration to improve his understanding and his techniques of living which result in a gradual shift from home dependency to dependency upon peers and new adult influences.
Both recognize a change in the style of living which does not

result in a substantial alteration in the child's basic personality structure.

Piaget's approach to adolescent development as a finite process, the culmination of all previous development, is in conflict with Erikson's central theme that this period constitutes the second formative period of life—the years of youth and of becoming an adult. The differing positions center around two major points: (1) Piaget depicts adolescence as a period in which the youth finds unity with the world, a period in which the outside social world "falls into place" and can be fully comprehended for its division of roles, its interrelated laws, and its permeation with unity. Erikson, in contrast, defines adolescence as a period in which a relevant social position is sought with the full implication of this position yet to be established in the ensuing years of adulthood; and (2) Piaget's approach to adolescence as a period of tying together loose-ends, as a period of completion, is contradicted by Erikson's stress upon defining adolescence both as a period of reasonable delay in development and as a period of commencement. These apparently conflicting positions can be reconciled in part by the fact that Piaget and Erikson deal with different elements of personality: the cognitive and affective ones. In addition, these differences might be further bridged by Piaget's findings that comprehension always precedes the capacity to explain that which is understood. Knowing and substantiating what is known are logically prior to achieving the capacity to translate such comprehension into action. Piaget and Erikson both suggest that their developmental progressions incorporate age norms only as points of reference. Their developmental charts stress developmental sequences which occur upon the achievements of previous developmental goals. Both stress that any advanced phase of development, such as adolescence, can occur at any time in a person's life, even at that point when an individual, so far as his chronological age is concerned, has been accepted as an adult in his society. The apparent differences, therefore, are not necessarily contradictory; they merely apply to two different aspects of personality. In the absence of essential research on the interrelationship between these aspects, the two systems might be paralleled as long as matching and corresponding, developmental achievements are focused upon.

There remains, however, a significant difference as long as one theory depicts total personality development as a life-long process and the other defines cognitive development as circumscribed and finite, similar to physiological maturation. These complications rest primarily with the expectations demanded of the *developing* individual. One theory implies that a person's range of mature comprehension should be complete and at its highest achievable level when the youth becomes a young adult. The other advocates that emotional and social development are not completed within any circumscribed age period. In fact, Erikson stresses that, whatever development cannot be fully accomplished within one age level, can be later developed independent of other developmental aspects which occur during subsequent phases.

QUESTIONS OF STRUCTURE

In turning to a review of structure, we must ask ourselves: What functional purpose does each theorist's structural framework serve? what relevance does each have to the others? To recapitulate, for Piaget, all cognitive processes are related to the schematic structure of assimilation and accommodation—between the structural reference points of inside (egocentric assimilation) and outside reality (accommodation or reality adaptation). In contrast, Erikson operates with the analytic structural trio of id-ego-superego. Sears specifies two chains of dynamically interrelated structural determinants—the action-sequence and its motivational-reinforcement sequence.

Piaget and Erikson overtly, and Sears implicitly, create a secondary structural framework—namely, developmental phases. In one sense, developmental phases serve as criteria of developmental achievements. In another sense, developmental phases for Piaget and for Erikson serve as organizational (*structural*) matrices within which developmental achievements take place. Actually, these phases become basic to an understanding of each theory and handy new tools in the study, evaluation and interpretation of human behavior. It is not surprising, therefore, that Erikson's or Piaget's phases tend to be more commonly known as handy points of reference rather than as descriptive terms for variant constellations of processes.

All three authors apply structure as a theoretical entity in the absence of any specific spatial (topological) reference points. While Erikson departs from this when he relates psychosexual development to man's physical and physiological makeup, associating psychological development with the sexual topological characteristics of male and female, his departure is not significant. It is the id-ego-superego structure which counts while sex differences and sexual behavior define the modality of development.

In the final analysis, structure serves in each theory as a convenient conceptual construct, while the dynamic processes stand in the foreground. Structure holds for these theorists what Roy Grinker suggested in his book: *Toward a Unified Theory of Human Behavior*, that contemporary theories on human behavior reflect little concern for structure and constitutional determinants of behavior (58, 137–139). Consequently, in this comparative study, differences in structure remain irrelevant because development and behavior is determined by the interplay of processes rather than the projection of structural characteristics.

If a parent or practitioner was required to choose the major theme of either Erikson's or Sears' theory, he would need to understand and to deal with the child in relation to a *central caring person (or persons) within a social matrix*. In the case of Erikson, the stress is upon the successful solution of conflicting pulls which results in a more independent trust and interpersonal relationship between the child and his parent figure. With Sears, the emphasis is upon establishing behavioral experiences which permit and lead to the incorporation of patterns of identification with the parent figure. And, both deal with a proper balance of *support* and *limitation*. Both themes focus upon the attitudes reflected by the parent as the most decisive variable in influencing the process of identification, and both feel that it is the quality of interpersonal relationships—both attitudinal and physical—between parent and child which is more important than the child's behavior, *per se.* In other words, though only Sears utilizes the word, both concentrate on *dyadic* situations within a larger social context. Piaget, in contrast, never investigated child-parent interpersonal relationships. Erikson and Sears also both stress the process of identification that arises from interpersonal relationships as a central developmental theme. For Erikson, identification involves the transference of unconscious attitudes plus an array of social expectations. Sears, on the other hand, shows identification as a process evolving from a delicate balance between the experience of support or frustration, love or the denial of love.

Interestingly, Sears' descriptive explanation of identification could readily be interpreted in terms of Erikson's analytical schema. Thus, the degree of the parent figure's love and his desire to guide the child without willfully pushing or letting the child flounder haphazardly, can successfully be inferred by the helping professional through adhering to Sears' or Erikson's concepts.

Piaget's major theme of the replacement of old forms of comprehension with new and deeper understanding is not in conflict with Erikson or Sears; he adds another dimension.

SUMMARY

In the foregoing discussion of similarities and differences inherent in the three theories, one point emerges as particularly significant. As Stock and Thelen concluded in a different context, logical rather than empirical means promise the greatest opportunity for reconciling differences (132). To review these differences, then:

1. The differences in terminology are the most troublesome, but they can partially be overcome by absorbing technical terms for their intent rather than for their pure definition. After all,

technical language serves as a vehicle of communication rather than as a tool for substantiation.

2. Each theory is grounded in a different cluster of assumptions. Most striking, each theorist attempts to obtain his facts by starkly separate methodologies, and each pursues a different purpose. Yet, the mutual compatibility of their findings remains more convincing than the stance each theorist assumes in embarking upon his research.

3. Each theorist explains the origins of human behavior differently, Erikson being the only theorist among the three who actually deals with this question explicitly. All three theorists concentrate upon behavior as it unfolds.

4. A more complicated situation arises as each theory introduces different assumptions, data, and conclusions about the stabilizing factors in each child's development, and especially on the child's own efforts to find a sense of balance as the foundation for more advanced development. Each theory introduces its own set of "basic ingredients" for its chosen core behavior. They are nontransferable and remain applicable only within each theory's main teachings.

5. In a review of the development continuum, the major difference rests with the question: When is a mature person "mature"? Erikson alone recognizes a clearly open-ended continuum. We find a glaring difference between Piaget's tendency to grant the adolescent near-adult maturity, while Erikson sees the adolescent in his emotional development still very much below the threshold of psychological maturity. Altogether, we can conclude that Piaget and Sears, having dealt far less with adulthood, yield to Erikson by default. Erikson's work continues where the other two leave off in their investigations of development, and their developmental continuum.

6. Only Erikson considers sex differences as an essential variable. For Sears, it is the environmental reaction to maleness and femaleness which defines differences in the developmental path of a boy or girl. Cognitive development, for Piaget, remains asexual.

7. Each theorist creates a perplexing problem with his approach

to the processes of identification. Each theorist introduces a different emphasis which cannot be integrated with the other. They remain parallel developmental phenomena.

Thus, together, the three theories provide in some aspects of the developmental continuum, a three-dimensional approach and in other aspects each theory adds a new dimension to the other. For the practitioner, each theory adds understanding and lends direction to the helping activities of the professional. Jean Piaget's consideration of cognitive functions is certainly vital to one who works with children, but to consider only the intellectual functions would be highly inappropriate. Erik H. Erikson's concern for affective and interpersonal processes, conscious and unconscious, is needed to supplement Piaget's contribution. Both of these processes must be considered in all efforts in the care and treatment of children. Robert R. Sears' stress upon the effects of immediate activities becomes particularly applicable to the solution of immediate and ongoing problem situations, especially in defining a child's and his family's prevailing level of operation.

Each theory obtains a partial, and consequently, varying answer concerning the child's development, but the child, if he is to be helped toward successful and social development, must be viewed in light of his *total* development. The pursuit of helping activities based upon any single theory would thus be incomplete as an approach. The tendency, therefore, of one theory to supplement the other by far outweighs all existing and residual conflicts noted in this chapter.

6

The Helping Process

To UNDERSTAND FULLY how the three theories of child
development presented in this book can be used in the helping
professions—singly and together—a clear understanding of the
helping process itself is needed. In practice, the helping activities
bring together the processes of diagnosis and treatment, observation and relationship, and empathy and rational judgment, all
aimed at enabling the client to alter a portion of his personal
situation. The unfolding developmental processes of life involve
continuous individual growth, and include periodic self-corrective alterations of the personality. It is only when "normal" development—and especially when spontaneous recovery from a
particular problem—is no longer probable that the intervention
known as professional help is indicated.

THE HELPING PROCESS DEFINED

Our definition of the helping process is: *A process of socially
engineered intervention in which the practitioner deliberately
introduces into the experience of an individual specifically structured means of preventing or treating deviant development.*
Whether treatment serves to rehabilitate or to prevent, the practitioner needs to regard the helping situation as supplementary to
the myriad of experiences every individual encounters in his
daily life.

Viewing the professional helping process as a supplementary one does not deny the existence of other ordinary enabling processes. Deliberate helpful intervention occurs daily in a child's life. For example, it is common for a mother to discuss appropriate "curfew" hours with her teen-age daughter. The mother is thereby helping her daughter to incorporate appropriate limits into her daily life. It could happen, however, that mother and daughter have come to such an impasse that an evening hour suggested by one would bring about the wrath of the other. When such a conflict cannot be solved by mother, daughter, family, and/or friend, a third, uninvolved and professionally equipped, party might have to furnish the needed help.

In both these instances a helping process occurs, but the two differ significantly. In the first situation, the actual process is of mother helping daughter and daughter helping mother in working out together a developmental task. Daughter and mother mutually attempt to find and to grant one another limits of independence and dependence acceptable within their shared social sphere. Helping here occurs as a part of the give-and-take of everyday living.

The second situation requires a special helping process of intervention by a third party. This supplementary helping includes study and appraisal of the fundamental problem causing the difficulty, and the introduction of a method of treatment which will most adequately reduce the problem by promoting daughter's and mother's healthy and autonomous adjustment.

As has just been said, the helping process in its wider sense is not, of course, limited to the professional function. Helping may occur intuitively in the give-and-take of everyday relationships, as a spontaneous process, and as an intrinsic feature of man's adaptive processes and his socialization. When this spontaneous help fails, it is the diagnostic appraisal and subsequent deliberate effort required to alter the deviant trend that constitutes the professional helping process.

In a professional context the helping process, as Helen H. Perlman describes it, constitutes a scientifically based "systematic procedure" (88). Such a systematic procedure of intervention builds upon two basic assumptions which have been fully developed in preceding chapters: first, that ordinary or "normal" development is understandable and predictable, and second, that ordinary development can spontaneously take its course after gross complications have been reduced or altered. Professional intervention, therefore, occurs with the knowledge that once the deviating circumstances have been corrected, "normal" development can resume.

CHOICE OF HELPER

Help can be introduced either to prevent or to correct deviant development. Whether he be the person in distress, a concerned family member, or one of society's "trouble spotters" such as teacher, nurse, policeman, or clergyman, the person first to note or to suspect the complication is also apt to label it as a social, psychological, psychiatric, legal, spiritual, or educational deviation. His assessment of the nature of the deviation leads him to seek out the helping professional deemed most likely able to help with the complications as initially defined by him. The helping person selected most likely is also the representative of the professional group socially sanctioned to solve the particular range of deviations in question.

To illustrate, let us consider a 10-year-old boy's inattention and consequent slow progress in school. The boy's mother might confer with his teacher about this problem. If parent and teacher considered the problem to be physically caused, a medical examination by a health specialist would be in order. Parent or teacher might infer that the same complication was a problem in learning, in which case special educational intervention would be considered appropriate, and the parent might explore the advisability of remedial work with an educational specialist. The same problem might be interpreted to be emotional: if the child had fewer psychological stresses, he could learn more freely. Therapeutic help in this case might come from one of several helping professionals; namely, a social worker, a psychiatrist, or a clinical psychologist. The selection of one of these potential helping professionals would depend upon the parents' estimate of the nature of the child's problem and upon their knowledge of the professionals most closely associated with "curing" such problems. Finally, the cause of this same situation might be considered a psychosocial problem, and a parent or teacher might conclude that the best therapy would consist in strengthening the child's healthy interpersonal relationships with peers and adults. This could be achieved by the parent's seeking the help of a social worker with special qualifications for helping individuals within a specially structured group situation.

In each of the foregoing possibilities the fact that the child's educational progress in school is in jeopardy remains constant. It is the definition of the nature of the deviation and the corresponding effort to correct it which vary. Therefore, we can conclude that *the selection of the helping agent and the associated helping efforts depend largely upon the interpretation of the problematic situation.*

It is important to keep in mind, however, that the decision to ask for professional intervention remains a sociocultural one when a deviation is noted. For example, in contemporary America, for some social groupings, an illegitimate child requires the services of specialized helping professionals to alleviate problems which mother and child are apt to encounter. In other social groupings, an illegitimate birth is accepted as part of everyday life and no specialized intervention is required.

THE HELPER'S PROFESSIONAL ROLE

Following the client's or his mentor's request for help, a professional reviews the lay assessment and tends to withhold his commitment until he has established his own definition of the situation. It is for him to decide whether his service (his method of help) would be the most appropriate form of intervention.

Even the acceptance of a referral from one professional to another hinges on the second professional's own assessment of the problem in light of his estimated ability to help.

Inherent in the helping process is the mutual compatibility of roles of client and helping professional. The person seeking help is expected to commit himself, however tentatively, to be a recipient of help as client, patient, or charge. The professional practitioner, likewise, commits his energies toward helping the client to change. For the client he becomes his change agent or helper. Together, helper and client create a system of interaction based upon mutual dependence, each contributing his share so that the helper is able to intervene and the client to profit from the intervention. The nature of the helping situation however, destroys the very sense of parity which it attempts to induce. The individual as a client is never fully on a par with his helper because to be helped, the client must first accept the social and psychological consequences of accepting the promise of help, namely, a sense of dependence, and the psychological relationship of master and tutor. Society likewise assigns client status as a dependent role. The social consequence of seeking help is a stigma for having failed to be independent when independence is expected. Altogether, the acceptance of client role is often very difficult; yet, as Werner Boehm states, "it is a necessary condition for the helping process, one goal of which is to eliminate or reduce the degree of dependence" (13, 42).

The material on the preceding pages suggests that the helping process can be analyzed in detail from any of three perspectives: the role behavior of client and helper, the essence of professional functions, and the dynamics of the interaction process within the helping situation. For instance, in a definition of the mutual expectations of client and helper, one might consider the function of role perception, behavioral role expectations, and the associated norms.[1] In addition, one might make a study of helper functions,

---

[1] See Nathan Ackerman (1, 2); Werner W. Boehm (13); Roy R. Grinker (58, 59); Neal Gross, Warren S. Mason and W. W. McEachern (60); E. Gartley Jaco (63); Florence Kluckhohn and John P. Spiegel (66); Henry S.

including an analysis of functions of the helping activities themselves and their relationship to the purposes and goals of each respective professional effort, which would lead to a consideration of the relationship between structure, function, and value systems of each of the professional disciplines.[2] Unfortunately, time and space do not permit fuller treatment here, and the reader is referred to the numerous excellent works on the subject covered by others. It is the third consideration—the dynamic process of interaction between client and helper—which will be dealt with in the remainder of this chapter.

THE HELPING SYSTEMS

In working with children and youth, the helping process can be introduced and fostered by four different helping systems. First, the individual child may be assisted through a one-to-one relationship. This helping effort is the most traditional and is most frequently denoted as the "individual-interview system." Second, the child's family or another appropriate social group could be selected as the most advisable system within which to apply the helping process. This method, dealing with the individual within a group which includes the helper, might be called "the system of the group." Third, parents, teachers, youth leaders, etc. can be selected as those with whom the professional will deal. This system, which depends upon cooperation between parents, child, and helper, can be called the "auxiliary system." Fourth, the important programs, services, or policies directly relating to the child's life can be brought to the foreground; here the helping process could

Maas and Richard E. Engler (74); L. J. Neuman and J. W. Hughes (83); Talcott Parsons (86, 87); Otto Pollak (108); Theodore R. Sarbin (70a, 223–258); John P. Spiegel (131); and Edwin Thomas, Norman Polansky and Jacob Kounin (133). Each of these references deals with one or several aspects of the role concept within the context of a helping situation.

[2] See George W. Albee (4); Harriett M. Bartlett (7, 8, 9); Werner W. Boehm (12, 13); Joseph W. Eaton (18); E. Gartley Jaco (63); Giesla Konopka (67); Ronald Lippitt, Jeanne Watson and Bruce Wesley (71); Henry S. Maas and Richard E. Engler (74); William Schwartz (112); and Robert D. Vinter (134a).

assume the task of altering pertinent aspects of a program, service or policy for the child in a way which would enable the child to develop more effectively.

Once the helping professional has agreed to work with a client and his problem-to-be-affected, he assumes the responsibility for defining the system in which the helping effort is to be introduced. He needs to clarify for himself: What deviating circumstances require change? which helping system will best faciliate such a change? what are the everyday life experiences—which will be affected by the newly structured helping system? From answering such questions he decides on the appropriate helping system to be used. Most important, the helper has to remain aware of the fact that he and his client(s) operate within two interlocking systems. They can be graphically presented as follows (see Figure 6.1).

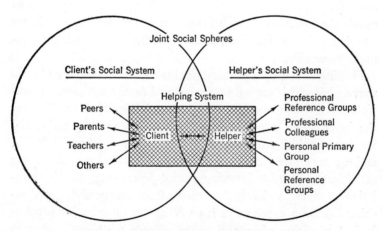

FIGURE 6.1. *Bordering Social Systems.*

The Individual-Interview System

The individual child and his professional helper comprise the most commonly thought of helping system. Here a one-to-one relationship exists. The client (the child) is perceived as the one to be changed, the one to reflect, and the one to perpetuate change. The helping person in his role as the change-agent, introduces conditions to facilitate the helping process; simultaneously, he brings into the child's life a new multifaceted personal relationship. Although the child might have temporarily gained a new key person in his helping professional—social worker, therapist, or special counselor—the child's everyday associations with his immediate physical and social world continues. Regardless of the quality of the child's therapeutic relationship to his helper, he continues to depend fundamentally upon contacts with his parents, siblings, peers, and other significant associates for most of his daily experience.

The individual-interview system can operate on two levels: (1) the *associate* level and (2) the *primary* level. Working with individuals on an associate level occurs in social casework, clinical counseling and psychotherapy; the helping process is intended to enable the individual client to function and to develop within his ongoing primary (family), social (peer), and extended (community) worlds.

Helping clients on a primary level takes place when the child is removed from his natural or accustomed family environment and placed in a foster home or other residential situation. In this case, the foster parent or child-care worker (cottage parent, residential worker, etc.) becomes the key change agent in the child's life, and a parent surrogate, as well. Both the nurturing and helping activities are aimed at fostering mutual dependence—that is, simulating as far as advisable the tenor of the parent-child relationship. The term *dependence* is used here to refer to the psychological condition of mutual trust: reliance upon each other in areas in which activities, guidance, or support of a primary figure is needed. *Caring* depends upon the mutual accepting of care when it is offered and offering of care when it is needed. Childhood always involves a state of dependence: The child is judged to be dependent in those spheres of his life in which his culture cannot yet justify granting him independence. If the child's natural family cannot provide him with the minimum nurturing ingredients of dependence, society then engineers a substitute. Here too, the practitioner must deal with a dual involvement; despite the fact that both the helping and the living situation are merged, the child's previous primary surroundings will continue to linger in his mind and in his behavior, and will provide him with residual experiences, fantasied perceptions, and hopes for the future.

Helping individuals on either an associate or on a primary level includes working with each individual's past *and* his ongoing relationships. This is true even in the most intimately cloistered interview room or the most remote institutional child-caring setting. In working at an associate level, a client may act toward his helper as if his "significant others" (his past relationships) were right there watching him over his shoulder. Consequently, the client is apt to weigh the implications of change both in terms of his relationship to his helper and those personally significant to him in the past. The helper, therefore, must deal with his client's omnipresent circle of "others" as if they were literally with the client. Working with a client on a primary level involves a similar dual focus. One part of the helper's approach involves steering the helping process toward providing a new primary, nurturing relationship for the child in the absence of his own; the other part requires a recognition of the influence upon the child's development of factors outside the helping situation.

The System of the Group

When helping occurs within the context of a group, the helping process can either be aimed at changing the behavior of the group as a whole, or it can be designed to affect each individual member through the medium of the group. In the first case, the group members are dealt with as parts of a larger whole; the emphasis is upon the *group's* adaptation to a larger social system. Although individual differences and needs are not negated, the individuality of each member is deemphasized in favor of group cohesion and group integration within the society at large. It is assumed that individual adaptation occurs spontaneously as the group's tasks, goals, and values change. Naturally, spontaneous individual adjustment presupposes that each individual has the capacity to share competently in the group's adaptation to outside demands. This approach is most pertinent in work with children and youth with an adequate range of "normal" development, because expectations set for their group experience involve individual challenges for socialization. This approach may occur in summer camp, for instance, when a cabin group fails to fit into the overall program and organization of the camp. Then, the cooperation of the group as a whole may be sought in order to assure its members and the camp a positive camp experience. In such an approach, the frequently applied expression "working with a group" is appropriate.

A second approach is commonly referred to as social group work, group therapy, or group counseling. The primary objective here is to aid *individuals* with their particular developmental difficulties, rather than to achieve a harmonious and cohesive group. Changing the behavior and value system of the group as a whole is considered to be relevant only to the extent that group members are individually helped.

Like the individual-interview system, helping the individual can take place on an associate or on a primary level. At the associate level, the group may be comprised of various unrelated members (i.e., a group of teen-agers with similar personal complications), or the group may be made up of the individual members of a single family. In the latter, work is with the family unit as a "group."[3] In any case the helping process is geared toward effecting therapeutic change in each individual through guided association with other members of his group and the helping agent. The group interaction becomes the arena wherein each member's everyday reality—including his past and ongoing family relationships, etc.—is tested for credibility and revision. Regardless of the composition of the group, whether family or nonfamily members, the helping process relies upon the system of the group. The treatment effort is directed toward changing interpersonal rela-

---

[3] The reader's attention is called to the numerous recent articles, monographs, and other publications written on this rapidly expanding field, frequently specified as "family therapy" (1, 2, 10, 16, 59, 108, 131).

tionships within the group, and individual self-concepts, in order that each client's patterns of relating and behaving will eventually be altered satisfactorily for meeting his usual life experiences. To assure this system's success, the helper must associate himself with the group and must perceive himself as a part of the group in order to serve as an instrumental group member who facilitates and tests relationships with any one of the group members.

At a primary level, the group provides the arena for everyday life experiences. The helping agent introduces and pursues parent-like activities; the group members' relationships are sibling-like. The same framework applies as outlined in the discussion of the primary individual interview system.[4]

The Auxiliary System

In the previously mentioned helping systems, the child has been the pivotal figure in the helping activities; that is, the practitioner has dealt *directly* with the child or a group of children. Each of the next two helping systems aims at helping the child *indirectly*, by affecting one or more key environmental influences upon the child. In the case of the auxiliary system, the professional works with the appropriate key adults involved in the child's problem. For example, a school social worker or psychologist might work with the teacher in arriving at some solution of a child's—or a class's—educational difficulties. But the most frequent occurrence of auxiliary help is when the helping professional works with the parents or foster-parents rather than with the child himself. Although the concern is still basically the child's development, the pivotal figures are the parents or their surrogates. Such a shift should not be too surprising; child development is also, in a sense, parent development.

It is worth mentioning at this point that even when the practitioner has only one parental figure to deal with, he should bear firmly in mind the existence of the other parent's role, however

[4] The author has dealt with this approach in a separate publication, "Child-care as a Method of Social Work," in: Child Welfare League of America, *Training for Child-Care Staff*, New York, Child Welfare League of America, Inc., 1963, pp. 62–81.

hypothetical that role might be in the child's actual everyday life situation. In cases in which there is only one parent in the child's life, this single parent assumes in reality dual parental functions. The helping person, then, deals with this parent as a representative of both parents. This observation, however, does not imply that the remaining parent can fully compensate for the gap and deviation in the parent system.

Whether the helper is working with a single parent or both, he attempts to assist these key persons in the child's life to alter their relationship patterns—behavioral, ideational, and attitudinal—to the child. Work with parents requires full recognition of the parents' needs and responsibilities, their mutually dependent relationship with their child, and the position the parents assume in relation to other parents and in the community. The helping process involves a system of parents with helper, while the service to be rendered continues to be directed at altering the child's developmental process. If the focus were to be placed upon the parent or parents themselves, quite a different helping system would be involved. The parents in such instances, would become clients in their own right and their child-caring efforts would be dealt with in terms of their own personal requirements.

The helping professional, when working with parents, forms a distinct but interdependent (auxiliary) system; the parents stand as the natural and instrumental partners in the child's development, and the helping person as the facilitator of this natural partnership. Work with other key persons in the child's life introduces a similar auxiliary system with the focus upon helping the key person to adjust and enrich this special interpersonal relationship to the child's best advantage.

The System of Program Alteration

Like the auxiliary system, the system or program alteration does not touch the child directly. Further, this system introduces a shift from intervention in an interpersonal relationship to intervention in a program, service, or policy which have a direct influence upon the child's development. Thus, the helping professional involved directs his efforts to the alteration of a program, a service or a policy as it affects the child's total life situation. The helping process, then, undoubtedly becomes associated with questions of social standards and control. To illustrate with a previous example: the boy's learning difficulties could be viewed and dealt with as a curriculum problem (program), a question of organizational placement (structure of service), or a matter related to the school's educational philosophy (policy). Change, then, would have to be directed towards a condition more conducive to learning, with the assumption that an alteration would create conditions favorable to the child's learning. This illustration takes into account the obvious middle class bias in which adaptation to contemporary programs of education is equated with "most appropriate learning" and continuation of school as an appropriate goal for all.

There has been no reference to any of the parties responsible for program, service, or policy. In the system of program alteration the child's development is kept as the basic consideration; content, policy, or structural alterations become second in importance to the system, and interpersonal dealings are tertiary and directed toward influencing the first two.

Helping within the context of a program alteration system involves the processes of joint planning and policy deliberation. Helping could also take place in the form of consultation. Yet, in all consultation, whether it occurs between two professionals or between a professional and lay person, the consultative process is markedly different from the other forms of helping. In consultation, consultant and consultee join for a temporary state of interdependence with full acknowledgment of their professional independence. They join as quasi-equals. Each engages the other, and has a desire to create a common frame of reference. However, they do not join in action to apply this knowledge. The foregoing distinctions are important in order to avoid the fallacy of viewing and treating the teacher as if he were the object of the helping process when, actually, questions of program, service, or policy are here of primary concern. In this system, help is structured so that helper and other persons in the system devote themselves jointly to the task of altering content, structure, or decisions. In each event, interpersonal relationships are only relevant insofar as they facilitate the pursuit of a particular task.

Helpful intervention for the purpose of program, service, or policy alteration is sometimes viewed as "working with a community" and analogous to working with individuals or groups. This author finds it inaccurate to consider working with a community as a system parallel to working with individuals as clients singly or in groups. Undoubtedly, there are illustrations in which a neighborhood, a community, or an organization enter with the worker into a quasiclient and worker relationship. For example, Clarence King's analysis of *Working with People in Small Communities* (64) illustrates clearly community organization work in which the community became "the client." Apart from these isolated instances, especially in our primary urban and vastly more complex society, the helping process can only deal with distinct aspects of community life. A neighborhood might solicit the aid of a community organization expert to work out voluntary curfew rules for its teen-age population. We perceive such a situation as the helping agent dealing with issues of curfew policies rather than intervening within a system of clients. The helping agent, as outlined above, concerns himself with one or the other aspect of program alteration.

THE HELPING RELATIONSHIP

The helping process has been portrayed thus far as a continuous process of interaction between helper and client. Every such relationship finds its beginning the moment a first contact is made, whether in person, by phone or by letter. The person in search of help begins to establish his part in the relationship, while simultaneously evaluating his prospective helper's share in the relationship. At the same time, the helper evaluates the applicant's potential involvement in the relationship. The actual meeting between client and helper to begin the diagnostic appraisal, marks the client's achievement of client status. From this point, both parties need each other in varying degrees. This is demonstrated by a helping professional's comment, upon discovering a minimal readiness on the part of his client: "I once worked with a schizophrenic boy who was very lonely. I discovered that I also was very lonely because he gave me a little opportunity to relate to him."

Helper and client reach a tacit and mutual understanding of their joint state of contractual dependence and its inherent boundaries. The term dependence is applied here to mean a dynamic relationship in which certain aspects of one's personal individuality are entrusted to the care and direction of the person depended upon, who in turn needs the trust of his client in order to initiate and effect helpful intervention. Most important is the inherent mandate for the client which grants as well as demands, in varying degrees, a sense of personal dependence. Certain aspects of this kind of dependence foster psychological processes in the client (imperative for "helping") which include imitating, caring, identification, transference, and, above all, free communication of feelings and understanding.

A helping relationship is never an end in itself. This assumption holds whether the helping relationship is a product of or the means for the helping process to take form, and it can be considered a basic boundary which offers structure to helper and client. The relationship serves as the vehicle for assessing the client's situation and altering it so that finally the relationship can be terminated in the client's resumption of independence from such a relationship.

THE DIAGNOSIS AND TREATMENT PROCESSES

The helping process has thus far been conceived of as a unification of relationship, diagnosis, and treatment with each part lending meaning to the others. Table 6.1 offers a dynamic model of diagnosis and treatment, with a systematic presentation of its various components and subprocesses.

TABLE 6.1 *Schematic Diagram of the Diagnosis and Treatment Process*

HELPING PROCESS

→

DIAGNOSIS AND TREATMENT
Eight Steps of the Helping Process:

1. Observing situation
2. Ordering and assessing observation
3. Predicting course of development *without* intervention
4. Predicting course of development *with* intervention
5. Formulating tentative hypothesis and alternate
6. Purposeful intervention, including acknowledged noninterference
7. Observing anew after intervention
8. Reassessing the previous appraisal and formulating new hypothesis

SUBDIVISIONS OF THE HELPING PROCESSES

STUDY PROCESSES	APPRAISAL PROCESSES	TREATMENT PROCESSES
Observation (1)	Prediction *without* intervention (3)	Purposeful intervention (6)
Ordering & assessing the observations (2)	Prediction *with* intervention (4)	
Observing anew after intervention (7)	Formulation of a hypothesis (5)	
	Reassessing the previous appraisal and formulation of new hypothesis (8)	

Traditionally, diagnosis has been thought of as a prelude and prerequisite to treatment. Diagnosis is defined as "the art of recognizing a condition for its symptoms, deciding as to its character and establishing a classification." Such a definition serves to limit location, description, and classification of deviating conditions. Medical science has relied upon these kinds of quasimechanistic models for diagnosis for centuries. Psychological counseling, psychiatry, social work, and others have been prone to adopt this model by viewing diagnosis and treatment as interrelated but separate phases of a single continuum.

In a dynamic interpretation of diagnosis and treatment, diagnostic activities must be conceptualized and defined as an integral part of the helping process. René Dubos in *Mirage of Health* (15), develops eloquently the theme that the doctrine of the specific etiology of disease, matching a single cause and effect, has been a most constructive force in medical research. Yet, all studies of cause and effect and the application of the model of causality in the treatment of disease have failed to combat the great medical problems of our time. Medical sciences, Dubos continues, must now proceed with a new and different approach. Dubos challenges the field of medical research and medical health sciences to search for a more dynamic approach. He requests a fuller attention to the concepts of multiple causality as well as the recognition of the fact that purposeful change creates both a removal of the undesirable condition and a new condition which again is vested, like all novel situations, with perplexing problems. Multiple causality allows for the artistic component of diagnosis and denies the earlier assumption that diagnosis is primarily limited to the helping person's establishment of an initial clinical evaluation to guide him in his treatment effort. The process of diagnosis is inherently in conflict with the notion of multiple causation. It delineates the number of relevant factors when theoretically and in essence, multiple causation implies that all factors are important.

Diagnosis and treatment, as they are perceived by this writer, involve associated and continuously interwoven processes. Diagnostic activities are intimately intertwined with all transactions of helping. Diagnostic activities are always complemented by a sense of urgency to initiate activities which may change the undesirable conditions which have been discerned (13). Diagnosis means initiating intervention, and intervention means a shift, however temporary, from diagnosis to treatment. Discovery and the utilization of one's findings occur simultaneously!

The author submits that diagnosis and treatment must be conceived of as interdependent activities which simultaneously permeate all spheres of the helping situation. Each process depends upon a continuous system of mutual feedback. Each minute or overall effort to effect change depends upon a previous appraisal, a set of predictions and a selection of a momentary hypothesis. It might be said that first a hypothesis must be made. Action will follow with the understanding that the hypothesis is conceived of as momentary and subject to immediate revision as a new hypothesis is formulated for still further action. The multiplicity of such an approach is infinite because there is a new situation created by every activity. At the same time that the helper recognizes this duality, he must clarify for himself his immediate professional activity, be it diagnosis or treatment.

In actual practice, assessing and doing occur throughout both the processes of diagnosis and treatment. The labels become convenient when one effort tends to be more relevant than the other. The diagnostic process highlights what can be learned while the treatment process focuses upon what needs to be done on the basis of what had been learned. To illustrate, in a diagnostic interview, the helper might appropriately convey a sense of empathy to his client in order to foster a trusting dependence so that the client can confide in him, because empathy and support are prerequisite to obtaining essential observations. At the same time, empathy and support can produce change, the latter being related to the fact that a client's complications are frequently connected to a need for these human relationship elements. At one and the same time, the helper may be diagnosing and treating. Conversely, the development of the treatment relationship—of dependence—permits further significant and intimate revelations on the part of the client. This very personal information is useful diagnostically to direct the helper in his job of promoting change. We might say that diagnosis is essentially both a precursor to and a partner in treatment. Conversely, only treatment can confirm or refute the initial diagnosis.

The diagnostic process is equivalent to the research process of fact finding and hypothesis testing. It includes (1) an effort to establish the ongoing levels of behavior in each appropriate dimension of functioning; (2) a prediction of the implications of such behavior for future functioning; (3) determination of the degree of divergence of the conditions (functioning) from "normal"; and (4) an estimation of possible avenues available to correct predicted deviations. In contrast to research, however, diagnostic activities always carry with them an inherent commitment to utilize what has been discovered and to help to amend what has proven to be significantly at variance and unsatisfactory to the client.

The Study Process

In the following analysis of the study process, study techniques such as direct observation, interviews, the study of records, the use of questionnaires, tests or other factfinding devices will not be specifically reviewed. The study process itself will be considered.

Observing, and ordering what is observed, are on one end of the diagnostic continuum, while renewed observations and reordering of new and previous observations are on the other. The act of observing within the study process denotes the empirical activities of the diagnostic process; the observable is noticed for its recognizable facts. But here reliance on inductive thinking comes to a quick end. In all diagnostic thinking, it is deductive reasoning which is employed, because one must select pertinent information in order to think diagnostically, and one cannot know what is pertinent or relevant without a deductive appraisal.

Study activities proceed simultaneously within three separate spheres. First, there is the dual focus upon the problematic situation *per se* and upon the circumstances which surround the problematic situation. The dual focus forms the client's world. Second, there are two time dimensions: the horizontal, the ongoing contemporary life situation, and the ever-present vertical antecedents, the "living past" which involves the dynamics of development, personal history, and social heritage. Ongoing observations gain added significance when they are associated with relevant past events. In turn, past experiences give added relevance to ongoing behavior. Third, observations extend from a study of overt to covert behavior. This involves the directly observable and inferential or hidden data. The latter is primarily secured through sensed observations. It is spontaneously registered through the intuitive or felt reactions of the helper. These personal reactions provide telling information without benefit of a known ordering and classification system.

The helping person, in using the three spheres conceptually, must set about to order the observations he makes. Conscious observations must include the cognitive process of ordering and classifying what is observed. He names what he sees; that is, he labels. Ordering becomes more overt when the professional person or client sorts his observations for relevant material, until finally whatever material is ordered and designated as "relevant" is subsequently labeled the *findings* of the study process. Actually, all ordering incorporates a miniature diagnostic process. The most minute observational data is studied, appraised, and screened in relation to a set frame of reference. Since the process of observing occurs within the context of the observer's frame of reference, it is the observer's role to note an event for its behavioral content, its psychological relevance, its cultural implications, and its social significance. He orders the selected data within the context of the theoretical framework which *he* considers applicable. In short, the observer denotes, with the assistance of his client, what he as the helper considers to be pertinent data. Therefore, the findings actually represent the helping person's estimate of the material he has labeled, and therefore rendered significant, rather than the thinking, feeling, or general behavior of the client *per se*. Fundamentally, the study process involves an evaluation based upon deductive thinking. Contrary to the previous assertion that gathering of data involves inductive reasoning, a valid case could be made that all observing requires exclusively deductive reasoning. The mind always projects and directs observations into the scope of deductible general knowledge.

In one respect, social distance and personal noninvolvement enhances objective judgment. In another, intimate material, such as the essence of a person's real feelings and personal beliefs, can only be discovered and estimated when client and helper perceive and feel themselves very much involved in the same working situation. Only at the point where the helper can perceive himself to be part of his client's world can his client communicate his feelings and the most vital details of his life situation. To cite an example. We learn in a group recording: ". . . Leo walked somewhat aloof about three steps behind the other boys crowding around me, [the group worker]." "Leo walked somewhat aloof" connotes Leo's physical and emotional distance from the other boys. Part of this can be accounted for in a study of the spatial relationships between the persons within the situation. But, at the same time, there is a *sensed* (inferred) observation in: "Leo walked *somewhat* aloof." He is described as walking emotionally apart from the others. Such an observation requires projection into the situation. The observer must see and feel himself as a participant. (134, 139).

Benjamin Wright, in his study on the relationship between emotional involvement and professional development, calls special attention to the mode of *participant observation* in contrast to such modes as mere *observation* and *intrusive participation* (139). An emphasis upon, and preoccupation with, observation denies opportunities for sensing more subtle communication of affect, because the observer maintains too much of an emotional distance to allow himself to be receptive to observable material. In addition, as an observer he may tend to exclude himself, in spite of his presence, from the observational field. He is then apt to overlook the impact of his own intrusion as a participant observer. Actually, any observation brings about a participation. The question is also related to the degree of intrusive participation. If the emphasis shifts from intrusive observation to intrusive participation, the attention shifts from observing the actions of the client to a preoccupation with the participant's own actions and the client's reactions to him. Participant observation, in contrast to mere observation or intrusive participation, allows the observer sufficient freedom to observe and to participate, to utilize what he has observed, and to evaluate the ongoing impact of his participant observational role (139).

The Appraisal Process

The appraisal process involves the conversion of ordered observational material into a series of applicable propositions. From these propositions, a selection is made of the most promising operational predictions. Appraisal, on the one hand constitutes an assessment and disposition of findings; on the other, a preparation for action. Basically, the mode of reasoning is oriented towards future actions. Previous observations are viewed as data for planning rather than as an account of findings. In fact, previous ordering and assessing of relevant material has probably already been undertaken with the aim of formulating a pertinent course of action. It is this emphasis upon prediction which assists helper and client alike to focus upon future activities. Both are concerned with the promise of the future, as they "read" it from their findings of the client's ongoing and past life experiences. For example, a client might be described as anxious. Such a discovery is important to appraise the helper's activities and the client's potential behavior in the immediate future rather than to establish a mere descriptive account of the client.

Again, appraisal processes occur at two different loci in the diagnostic continuum: first, appraisal processes emerge into the foreground when observations are fitted together and plans for action are derived from them; secondly, appraisal processes come again into play when past actions are appraised to predict subsequent actions. In any event, three interrelated predictions must be formulated in order that a proper appraisal may be made:

1. Ordered observations must be applied to predict subsequent development or events under prevailing circumstances. The client's immediate development can be forecast, even if he were to receive no further help. In other words, his subsequent development is predicted *without* purposeful intervention.

2. Observational material, including the prediction of subsequent development without purposeful intervention, must be utilized for an alternate prediction, a prediction of subsequent development in light of introducing projected intervening treatment activities.

3. The two alternate forms of predictions, development with and without purposeful intervention, lead to the formulation of a unified momentary hypothesis. A review of these two predictions hints at the most desirable outcome and the likely course to accomplish it. A third and guiding hypothesis is then formulated.

Although appraisal relies on the predictions of the helping person, the appraisal process must be viewed as the joint enterprise of client and helper. For example, Leo's worker may conclude from knowledge of Leo's past and present behavior that he has difficulty relating to his peers. Correspondingly, Leo himself may want to convey to the worker his own findings that he feels apart from his peers and wishes the world would sense his state of detachment. Following a review of the client's situation, the first of the three essential diagnostic predictions may be ventured. *If, on the basis of preceding observations, no intervening activities are initiated, then the situation is expected to continue to develop as appraised.* In short, the proposition is: No purposeful intervention is necessary if the natural course of development is either considered within the range of desirable behavior, or if it is known that no potentially available intervention would be of significance (see Level IV, below).

Werner W. Boehm's proposed typology of four levels of role performance functioning for diagnostic appraisal in social casework may have equal relevance to other helping professionals and should be listed here:

Level I. Role performance violates explicitly stated minimum standards enforced by society and may cause stress to individuals and groups in the role network.
Level II. Role performance meets minimum societal standards but causes stress to individuals and groups in the role network, leading to dysfunction.

Level III. Role performance meets minimum societal standards for members of the role network, but is not commensurate with role performance potential.

Level IV. Role performance meets minimum societal standards and is fully commensurate with role performance potential (13, 119).

A second prediction involves a logical alternate proposition: *On the basis of preceding observations the situation may be changed, as predicted, by means of purposeful intervening activities.* The helper appraises the child's development with the projected intervening activities in mind. The helper's understanding of the ongoing situation is combined with his knowledge of the impact of purposeful intervention and his assessment of his client's potential capacity for change.

A third alternate prediction then is derived from the second. *If, on the basis of preceding alternate predictions, the following intervening activities were to be introduced . . .* (state nature of intervening treatment activities) *the situation would be changed to the one predicted . . .* (state predicted outcome) *as a more desirable course of development within the visible circumstances.* This third prediction includes a plan for action. This plan will determine which of the observational information and subsequent predicted propositions will emerge as the most direction-giving material. Material leading to and substantiating such a plan is culled out as diagnostic findings. Earlier, it was surmised that Leo would be unable to bring himself into any close association with the group members unless some intervention occurred. Furthermore, the implication has been made that some form of closer association is desirable and potentially possible. The worker has to decide upon the nature of the desired change. He might decide that Leo either needs to be brought into closer association with the other boys or with the worker. Each of these two alternatives is based upon a different appraisal of available observational material, and in turn, each set of diagnostic findings suggests a different form of intervention.

We see that the diagnostic process involves a series of fact-finding and predictive activities where detailed and composite observations are weighed: (1) for their relevance and promise of establishing patterns of behavior, thinking, and feeling; (2) for their utility in making diagnostic pronouncement. The helper must decide which factors require immediate attention and separate them from the less important facts.

Beyond the ordering of findings, the overall diagnostic appraisal is also influenced by the actual availability of additional professional skills and resources, and the helper's awareness of their existence. The breadth and depth of every diagnostic appraisal is markedly determined by the helper's professional competence, the accessibility of additional resources, the auspices of his professional efforts, and the value system of his professional reference groups. Prediction for change, therefore, is directly related to the helper's (and client's) notion of how much change can be accomplished within the available time and resources, and how much of the available time and resources are actually considered by helper (and client) as *potentially* available and worthwhile. In the helping process, diagnostic material only has meaning as long as it leads to a design for action, but such material also provides boundaries to the helper's efforts.

Fritz Redl speaks of "hunch skills" as a vital quality in feeling momentary diagnostic decisions in order to enhance spontaneous reactions and inquisitive probing for more comprehensive understanding (111c, 88). Once a diagnostic appraisal has been hunched or pronounced, it must still be verified by subsequent events. A renewed assessment is in order, in light of actual intervention (or nonintervention). Such a reassessment, as a second installment of the process of appraisal, can then verify or cancel previous appraisals. This latter process becomes analogous to the meaning of Norbert Wiener's aphorism: "I don't know what I have said until I have heard the response to it."

The Treatment Processes

In treatment, as in diagnosis, all activities are ultimately related to the particular value system, knowledge base, and specialized techniques of each professional discipline. Each discipline has its chosen theoretical reference system which defines the treatment theories to be utilized. Moreover, each discipline relies upon its unique set of treatment methods, which "translate" the professional treatment theories into practice. Treatment as a process, therefore, is closely associated with the chosen therapeutic methods of each helping discipline.

Treatment can be analyzed for its mobilization of interpersonal relationships and the skillful application of specific techniques. Furthermore, interpersonal relationships are enhanced by these techniques and in turn make the techniques accessible to the client. Although interpersonal relations are the essential vehicle for treatment, it is the content and context of the interpersonal relationship which determines the nature of treatment. Techniques applied must be considered for their impact upon the interpersonal relationship *per se* and its purpose. A technique may foster interpersonal relationship at one moment, or its purpose at another. To illustrate, a helper's attentive listening to a client's comments may serve to foster a relationship, because the helper wants to convey his interest and his ready availability. Mutual listening builds a relationship. It also provides an opportunity for both client and helper to share the client's thoughts and feelings and gain a better comprehension of the client's situation. We must be mindful, however, that neither a relationship nor relationship techniques provide treatment. Treatment embodies the purposeful creation and utilization of a relationship which serves as the means and the context for the introduction of activities geared toward desired changes.

Relationship becomes the means (or "vehicle") when, for instance, it furthers communication. Relationship also serves as the context when its ingredients, such as support, identification, transference, etc., become salient features of treatment. In the preceding analysis of the diagnostic process, the concept of prediction on the basis of momentary hypothesis construction was introduced. Treatment involves the testing of the hypothesis—the execution of a course hypothesized to be corrective.

In spite of the danger of being too mechanistic, we suggest that treatment be perceived as an activity which incorporates the following proposition: If action x is introduced, then the predicted outcome o will occur (if x then o). In each step of treatment, minute or global, such a proposition is in order. Let us return to a previously cited illustration. If Leo should become more integrated in the group and should feel less aloof than in the past, he has to experience a sense of closeness with at least one other group member. Let us assume that none of the group members seem ready for this. The helping agent may be the first link to provide such a sense of closeness for Leo. If a sense of closeness is desirable in this instance, the worker must provide an opportunity for it. We may assume that the worker might turn to Leo and engage him in conversation. His prediction and expectation would be to find a common experience through conversation. In terms of the above formula, if conversation with Leo is undertaken (action — x), then greater closeness with worker may ensue (outcome — o).

In brief, all treatment activities comprise an aggregation of many minute steps of treatment, executed from previously established or intuitive predictions. Each step is a developmental step towards the diagnostically derived treatment goal. Each treatment activity is introduced as the most efficient means to bring about the desired change. It follows then, that each treatment step must be evaluated for its outcome, to determine if the predicted outcome (o_1) coincides with the actual outcome (o_2). For instance, a conversation with Leo about his model cars, based on the assumption that Leo's hobby is a subject of intimate interest to him, might potentially result in introducing ideas which Leo could likewise find in common with some of the other boys. In the event that Leo failed to respond, the worker would be faced with a new diagnostic situation, since reference to Leo's hobby ($x =$ planned action) did not produce the desired and predicted outcome ($o_1 =$ conversation). Rather it produced no overt response ($o_2 =$ no conversation). This single episode in a treatment process illustrates that the helper *selects* appropriate actions, based on his *appraisal* of the existing circumstances and based on his prediction of which ones out of a potential range of treatment activities most likely will bring about the desired treatment objectives. His skillful performance in applying his understanding of the client and the available treatment techniques shifts attention from the helper's proper understanding and scientific selection of techniques,—the science of helping,—to the qualitative, personal skills and artful application of such knowledge,—the art of helping (13a).

Each treatment activity must be clearly defined for its structural and dynamic components. Structural factors such as a specified and protected appointment period, reliance upon the worker's position in his role as the helper, etc., serve merely to facilitate dynamic functional processes. Dynamics must be relevant to the structural circumstances (the reality) of the helping situation. For example, to set a definite appointment introduces a combination of structure ("this is your time with me.") and dynamics ("I want to be with you and you can count on me."). Such a practice is based upon the following predictions: if the client knows he has a definite appointment time, he knows it *is* his time and he is more likely to *feel* that he will be welcome. Therefore, making a point about a definite appointment time becomes essential when such an activity will facilitate the desired outcome. On the other hand, it may be unnecessary; such a structural arrangement would rest upon a mutual tacit understanding, and perhaps the client can relate more effectively without such a definite structure.

The importance of differentiating between structural and dynamic components in treatment can be further elaborated upon by the following situation. Client and helper may be engaged in discussing a particular topic, the selection of which is a structural phenomenon. The dynamic consideration is how client and helper use the topic and how their relationship is manifested by the topic. Focus upon a particular topic can serve as a structural aid to be utilized therapeutically with the client.

Dimensions of Psychosocial Intervention

The three developmental theories in the foregoing chapters provided a framework of knowledge for child development. Treatment builds upon such knowledge in order to select appropriate intervention which may introduce conditions that, in turn, will help the child to salutory developmental patterns. Most important, treatment can only be predicted, initiated, and pursued within known patterns of development. Moreover, we introduced throughout this book three major dimensions of psychosocial functioning: understanding (cognition), feeling (affect), and doing (experience). Each dimension relies upon a different constellation of factors in developmental process. We submit, therefore, that treatment as dynamic intervention requires an intimate understanding of these dimensions and their developmental processes. Let us examine each of these.

Change in cognition refers to efforts directed primarily towards effecting a client's understanding of a situation. Frequently, the helping process is focused upon working with a client to expand his sphere of understanding. Client and helper attempt to clarify the client's understanding of relevant aspects of his life. On other occasions, efforts are directed towards introducing new perspectives, hitherto unknown. When circumstances are perceived and understood in a new perspective, a client is apt to feel and act differently. For example, let us assume that if Leo knew the other boys' bantering behavior and exaggerated talk were merely for their entertainment and were appropriate to their age, he might become freer to feel part of the group and to join the other group members' experiences fully. The extension in understanding may be relative to long forgotten and past experiences, or it may be related to more recent learning. Knowing differently means feeling and acting differently.

Change in affect opens up another dimension of personality development. Such a dimension encompasses a person's emotional involvement in past and ongoing experiences and those of the future. The helping person frequently gives the client better insight into his feelings and previous relationship patterns. The mode of interaction in the helping situation centers in the client's feelings. Moreover, the helping effort is then directed toward introducing a relationship which will enable the client to correct his feelings about himself, those significant to him, and the social, ideational, and physical world around him. In Leo's case, the focus would then be upon his need to feel aloof from others. Leo's feelings could be handled by reflecting upon his past experiences, by supplementing his relationships, or changing his environmental experiences. In any case, the mode of interaction depends upon the understanding that if Leo could feel differently about himself, he would then perceive and behave differently.

Change in experience, as the primary target of the treatment effort, shifts the emphasis to the experiential content of the helping situation. Rehabilitation and development proceed on the basis of appropriate experiences. Experiencing properly how and what to do enables the client to build salutary facets into his repertoire of behavior whenever they apply to situations in his everyday life. His experience may relate to interpersonal relationships, to meeting problem situations, or to the acquisition of knowledge and skills. For Leo it may mean, as he experiences successful social interaction with his worker and/or other group members, that he can also react more effectively in his contacts with those in the group, and eventually with participants in other life experiences. Experiencing new and variously different life situations, then, leads to understanding and feeling more adequate in dealing with them.

Depth of Treatment

Intermittently, all three treatment modes come into play, and the helper's efforts with his client must be thought of in terms of depth as well as breadth. The traditional distinctions between "going deep" or dealing with "surface material," and among environmental, supportive, or insight treatment will be our concern in this section. We suggest the following differentiations as guiding concepts for treatment. The nature of treatment should reflect at what experiential level treatment will occur: (a) rehabilitation of a past experience, (b) supplementation of past experiences in the present, or (c) controlled ongoing experiences.

If rehabilitation of past experiences (which linger out of proportion to intrude into the present) is a treatment goal, the client must understand and experience differently in order that he may consider his past as a prologue to the present rather than the essence of his presently ongoing life. How deep and how much the helper should deal with past material depends upon both the helper's diagnostic evaluation of the change required within the client's life experience and his ability to achieve a corrective understanding. This focus is appropriately used when ordinary developmental processes, for some reason or other have failed to be self-corrective.

The goal of supplementing past experiences in the present calls for quite a different level of work. The helping situation serves to build on past experience by relating to unusual aspects of "unfinished business" in the client's life. The helping situation serves to introduce additional experiences in order to supplement past ones. Such treatment may employ environmental manipulation because a client's developmental age may dictate a different milieu than his chronological age has allowed him in his ongoing life situation. Treatment may substantially consist of support in order to meet formerly unfulfilled dependence needs.

Controlled ongoing experience, in contrast, begins with the past and builds upon it with the expressed understanding that the living past is controlled and enriched in the living present. The provision, then, for controlled ongoing experiences is closely tied to the client's former developmental acquisitions. In short, helping activities are designed to complement and enhance the past. Treatment utilizes ongoing experiences within the helping situation to control, and to assure that appropriate developmental opportunities become accessible to the client. Treatment may deal with insight, when insight into the client's own functioning assures him more reliable accessibility to his immediate ongoing experience. Treatment may deal specifically with support, when the ordinary client-helper situation is not supportive enough to encourage ongoing developmental change in itself. Treatment may deal with environmental manipulation, when different environmental experiences are more likely to assure the client a clearer effective use of his ongoing life experiences.

The foregoing material, in a sense, stresses a rather mechanistic separation between techniques and interpersonal relationships, structures and functions, scientific knowledge and the art of applying such knowledge, as well as between levels of intervention and the approaches by which such interventions may be executed. Such a conceptual separation is a necessary step to clarify and to focus the treatment effort. Furthermore, such a systematic understanding may serve as a fundamental preliminary step to purposeful and creative coalition of these considerations in an integrated effort. The preceding pages likewise make repeated reference to the interdependence of these various facets of treatment. They reaffirm our emphasis upon a multidimensional approach in dealing with multicausal human situations. The implications of such an approach mean that in treatment, as was true in diagnosis, the effort is toward mobilizing changes within varying constellations and processes of interrelationship.

A DYNAMIC MODEL OF DIAGNOSIS AND TREATMENT

We have considered the components of the process of diagnosis and treatment. One may view this process as a unit—a dynamic model.

Diagnosis and treatment occur through the interaction of a helper and his client as they create change and interaction within a dynamic situation. Helper and client project their past experiences and relationship patterns into their joint situation. The helper contributes his backlog of professional knowledge and experience, in addition to his personal self-awareness. His past professional experiences are projected into the current milieu where they are verified, altered, and expanded. The client brings his living past, which becomes part of his client-helper situation. This latter distinction is important for it sorts out what constitutes the client's reactions to his past in relation to these interpersonal relationships *per se* and what has been mobilized by the social context in which these interpersonal relationships are transacted.

Moreover, the reality of the ongoing relationship as its exists within the interview or the group situation is brought into play. This "working situation," as it is sometimes called, becomes a temporary social arena for ongoing experiences and social learning, whether that learning concerns knowledge, behavior, or attitudes. Diagnostic appraisals and change efforts occur within this complex of multiple systems. No one relationship system can be studied or dealt with apart from the others. Diagnostic or treatment activities within one system are enmeshed with experiences in others. Interactions in the helping situation allow one to sense and discern the course of events in other systems. Concurrently, the course of events (the change efforts within the helping situation) reach into other spheres of the parties involved. Change occurs beyond the context of the interview, group meeting, or consultation conference.

Diagnostic pronouncements and treatment activities reflect the helper's attempts to understand rather than to classify people and their situations. Within the helping system, the helper uses diagnostic labeling as mental shorthand which enables him to abbreviate complex descriptive observations. As observations are ordered and totaled under one descriptive label or another, they become fully clarified in the helper's thinking process and he is able to communicate them to others. In addition, the helper has access to observations communicated from his own unconscious as well as unconscious communications which occur between himself and his client. The combination of conscious and unconscious communications is one of the most critical dynamic aspects of the diagnostic and treatment process. As the helper gains awareness of the impact of such material, it becomes workable for him even if its nature remains a mystery.

All diagnostic efforts, including diagnostic labels and hunches, must be viewed as dynamic and transitory. The client's effort to change has specificity, but the ongoing situation and the desired outcome do not. There is no clear and discernible cause-and-effect relationship. Diagnostic and treatment efforts represent a constant search for underlying circumstances—for as yet undiscovered causal factors. Working hypotheses are formulated out of a tentatively assumed cause-and-effect relationship, but the hypothesis is always tentative until tested and then must be immediately appraised in light of a subsequent change. Like the god Janus, the helper must at the same time, look backward and forward to understand the client's living past as it takes form in the present relationship system.

The theme of this chapter has been to bring diagnostic and treatment considerations into *one* field as interdependent, intertwined processes. We have seen how factfinding always involves intervening change. Intervention, in turn, instantly creates a new condition of which the helper and the client are a part, and from which they cannot divorce themselves. Diagnosis and treatment are interchangeably linked. Although such interchangeable links would threaten a research effort, they constitute the life line for the helping activities. The helping process is furthered by the lack of clear demarcation between diagnostic and treatment activities within the helping situation. The boundaries of diagnosis, treatment, and relationship do not exist except for the purpose of rational thought and action.

Professional disciplines define their working spheres from the onset, but beyond this definition, the helping process has no boundaries *a priori* except those which emerge out of the helping process itself. As client and helper join together to effect change, it is, in fact, their joint investment rather than the professional mores, agency policies, and structural arrangements which determine the ultimate nature and outcome of the helping process. If one accepts this emphasis, the essence of the helping situation makes the helping agent a person contracted to perform professional functions and tasks set for a particular setting, rather than an employee of an agency, hospital, or institution. Above all, it is the client's situation which defined the nature of the helping process and the helping system to be utilized. Moreover, the helping relationship must be such that it frees both the client and the helper to study what needs to be assessed and to act upon what must be changed.

7

The Three Theories

in Practice

OUR ATTENTION in this chapter turns from theory to practice, from viewing child development and the helping process conceptually to actually applying our knowledge. We shall sketch in broad strokes some of the implications of the foregoing theoretical considerations for the professional helper's work with children. In no way do we intend to provide a handbook for practice or a how-to-do-it kit; rather, we plan to demonstrate our conviction that professional helping requires a theoretical frame of reference encompassing human development and an intent to apply such theoretical understanding to all aspects of the helping activities.

DEVELOPMENTAL PHASES

In an earlier chapter it was mentioned that every individual is in a constant state of developmental change. Despite widely varying individual patterns, this change becomes increasingly complex as it progresses. Any effort to bring about changes in a child's observable behavior and personality, therefore, must be aimed at the developmental processes themselves, instead of at an individual's behavior *per se*.

Each of the theories heretofore presented makes use of developmental phases rather than exact age norms. Chronological ages may suffice as general guides, but they should not be employed as exacting criteria for judging a child's developmental progress. When development does not proceed as "normally" expected, the fault may lie either with a real developmental problem or with unrealistic expectations of the child's behavior based on what is thought to be "right" for his age.

To illustrate, an 11-year-old is usually capable of adjusting to temporary separation from his parents without behavioral repercussions. Nevertheless, he may solve some of his separation fears by a socially acceptable device; for example, he may put through several phone calls to his parents to compensate for their absence. If a child of this age is unable to cope with a temporary separation lasting no more than a few weeks, it should not be concluded immediately that he is emotionally unstable, retarded, or in any serious way "abnormal." As was implied in each theorist's findings, the child's behavior may, for him, be quite in keeping with his particular developmental rate. The alternative factors which might be at work in situations of this sort constitute a major challenge to the helping professional, whose task is to relate to the child in terms of the child's own developmental schedule, while recognizing symptoms of real deviant development. A practitioner may realize that his 11-year-old client has difficulties in being separated from him. He may be too old to cling to his helper's hand; he can be allowed, however, to continue to hold on to a note from his helper showing the time and place of his next session with him. We submit that an understanding of the loosely defined phases proposed by these theorists provides a valuable aid in assessing each client's immediate developmental needs.

Making investigations with reference to general developmental phases permits the practitioner to review more realistically a child's behavior in terms of past developmental patterns, present manifestations, and future ramifications. In addition, actually to help the child, his past, present, and future experiences must be dealt with as they are viewed by the child himself. Any individual recalls past events somewhat differently than they actually occurred, and his remembrance of the past tends to color present experiences. Similarly, his future—to the extent that he can sense it—is comprehended in terms of the past and present. Thus, while constructive intervention takes place within the individual's living present, it must also change the child's feelings about, and perceptions of, the past and future.

The three theories also suggest that in the continuum of development, whatever the individual does, thinks, or feels in any one area of his life at any given point in time is intrinsically linked to the person's image of himself, his family (and immediate peers), and his key reference groups. Each individual is inwardly dealing with his own inner experiences, his primary environment, and his secondary environment. He can only relate to these three spheres in the way they are integrated by him; regardless of the image others may hold of him. Consequently, a client cannot be helped toward desirable adaptive behavior unless his perceptions, feelings, and behavioral expectations about these three spheres are altered realistically.

Bearing this in mind, the author has chosen to deal with the three theories' implications for the work of helping professionals by offering a five-phase spectrum of development with which to study the theorists' findings in an integrated way. The five general phases into which we propose that the spectrum be divided are: (1) establishing primary dependence, (2) establishing self-care, (3) establishing meaningful secondary relationships, (4) establishing secondary dependence, and (5) achieving balance between dependence and independence. These phases constitute what we consider observable levels of dependence; their differences denote substantial variations in the nature of dependence. Every acquisition of independence frees an individual to establish a more advanced dependence in a new area; and, in turn, each new base of dependence assures the individual a greater autonomy in previously acquired spheres of independence. We hold that secure dependence points to freedom to act independently, because energies can be invested competently as long as dependence is assured. Basic developmental shifts in dependence have been selected because of their appropriateness in diagnosis and treatment of developmental problems.

DIAGNOSIS

What implications do the theories of Erikson, Piaget, and Sears hold for helping a professional to use in diagnosis within the content of the four helping systems outlined in the previous chapter? Each of the three theories directs him to assess explicitly what he wants to know, because any initial observation can, at best, only be an invitation to further study and appraisal. Moreover, each aspect of human functioning—physical, cognitive, emotional, or behavioral—requires a separate assessment; each must be evaluated in terms of the others.

It is important to recall Piaget's observation that an individual first experiences a situation *affectively* before he can comprehend it or explain and utilize his understanding of it. This suggests that separate assessments of a situation should be made which differentiate a client's first feelings about it, his later understanding of it, and his realistic plans for coping with it. To demonstrate, when an infant first senses a situation, he responds emotionally to it; only much later (usually more than a year) does he "discover" that situation behaviorally. More time is needed for him to comprehend, describe, and explain his behavior appropriately. A similar progression of learning occurs with each new chain of experiences at any point in his life.

Assessing an individual's developmental status and readiness, then, requires an evaluation of (1) his individual capacity to *perceive* (to see, to hear, to feel, etc.), (2) his awareness of his sensory experiences, and (3) his comprehension of these experiences. The child must at least be aware of his sensory experiences in order to incorporate their content knowingly into his behavior.

Thus, diagnostic appraisals must similarly differentiate among the client's own understanding of the situation, his acceptance of new modes of dealing with it, and his capacity for incorporating this understanding into his behavior.

These steps in the learning process have significant relevance to the assessment of the child's communication. Even when the words the child uses express just what he intends to say (which frequently is not the case), they may also carry a message which the child is not able to articulate. The helper wants to know what the child *means*, not what he says. Moreover, he wants to know what the child's communications mean to the *child*. Piaget suggests that, in diagnosis, attention should focus upon the child's comments rather than on the questions put to the child. Very often a child will try to provide the "right" answer to the professional's question, rather than to respond to it as he truly thinks and feels. Piaget's techniques for inquiring into the child's understanding of his own communication become significant to the helper in this connection.

The foregoing points call to our attention that customary "why" questions may yield little genuine information in work with young children. A question such as "why do you think it happened?" or a mere "why" may be a senseless probe, because it implies that there must be a clear and discernible explanation where most likely there is none. At best the child is unable to establish the relevant causative factors. Furthermore, the author's stress upon the concept of multi-causation implies also that any one event has more than one explanation.

Study of early childhood development, in many ways, is an inquiry into the mother-child relationship. The modality of mothering—that is, a mother's readiness to include her child through bodily posture and movements while holding him, and into her thoughts, social life, and daily routine while caring for him—furnishes helpful hints on the child's potential developmental progress within this first phase. The infant's own modality, as well, holds relevant clues to his developmental achievements or retardation. Erikson's material on the child's modality in associa-

tion with each developmental phase suggests that his play behavior and his general approach to his body, space, and time may
reveal to an observer his own inner developmental preoccupation.
A child's shift from an all-incorporative mode to one of incorpo-
rative-holding, for example, can serve as such a developmental
index. Moreover, Piaget, as fully described in an earlier chapter
under the six stages of a child's first developmental phase, adds
another possible dimension to the study and testing of early
infancy development.

The degree of primary dependence that has been solidified
during the early months of the child's life, or how much early
deprivation has been compensated later—these are essential considerations which can be assessed by a study of the symptoms of
primary dependence. One guide to the level of the child's dependence can be inferred from the interactive behavior between
mother and child, from the latitude of the mother's permissive
acceptance of the child's dependence, and from her efforts to
avoid frustrating experiences for the child. Another hint at his
degree of dependence can be observed in the responses of mother
and child in separation situations.

The extent of generalized behavior as opposed to specific responses is another clue to the child's developmental level. Gross
emotional, intellectual, and behavioral responses to specific situations can indicate that the child has not successfully completed the
first developmental phase, for as the child formulates a sense of
trust in his primary experiences, he begins to expand his spheres
of attention in terms of a more specific interest in the separate
aspects of his environment. Diagnostic questions can center upon
the delineation and the variety of boundaries the child has learned
to recognize and to incorporate into his behavior.

A valuable medium for assessing the child's acquired abilities is
the play situation, in which the child reveals not only the aspects
of development which preoccupy him at the moment, but also his
unresolved conflicts. For in playing the child plays life over. He
is what he plays in fantasy and in life. The professional observer
can also gain much from what the child leaves out of his play, as

well as what he includes. For example, if the child displays more autism than confident autonomy, it may be assumed that there are aspects, at least, of the second developmental phase which have not been reconciled or solved within the child. Erikson's contributions concerning grasping and releasing can be of help in this connection, for a tendency to hoard, to hold, or to retain can also reveal his attempts at control typical in the second phase. The ability to hold and to release would indicate a relatively developed self-control.

All of the foregoing factors are prerequisite to successful sociality. We may add that some degree of sibling rivalry, such as moderate competitive rivalry, is part of "normal" development. In contrast, rivalrous possessiveness may imply that important aspects of the first two phases—perhaps cumulatively—have been left unresolved.

The child who displays an excessive interest in his sex, or curiosity in the other sex, may well still be grappling with this typically third-phase developmental concern. The practitioner can detect the possibility of inadequate sex-acceptance from the child's interpersonal relationships, particularly with people of the opposite sex, and from assessing the client's behavior in terms of that which is appropriate to his sex.

In the fourth phase the child is primarily concerned with improving the *quality* of his social relationships, and with understanding his social objective and environments in terms of highly specific and complex situations that are involved.

In diagnostic explorations, a practitioner will be most interested in assessing the quality of a child's efforts in mastering life at home and away from home. A child's competence in relating to various persons within a wide range of circumstances can serve as one index of his developmental accomplishments or the lack thereof. Another aspect could be his readiness to see himself as part of a larger group and this group's relationship to society in general. A child's explanation about his activities, especially descriptive accounts of his work on projects, experiments, or his planning for these, provides an accessible view to his mode of thinking. Attention could be directed toward discerning his ability to gather facts or to employ objective measuring devices (i.e., use of a tape measure) in preference to mere subjective guesses. Children within this developmental span are preoccupied with rules. The way the client deals with rules and the degree of relativity he can grant these rules may convey to the observer considerable insight into the actual progress within this developmental phase.

On the social plane the child's sense of relativity is demonstrated by his capacity to respond differentially to people in different roles and his own readiness to assume intermittently tasks with varied role demands. For example, a child's capacity to act temporarily as baby sitter for another child depends on whether he is able appropriately to put aside some of his own needs as he plays with his charge.

The child can be studied for his progress in discerning relationships and in applying what he has learned from one situation to another. An observation of his play and leisure pursuits is perhaps most revealing, because in play or leisure activities he will toy with task and ideas with which he is wrestling in real life.

A client whose adolescent development we wish to assess—in the fifth phase—can be appraised for his readiness and capacity to relate himself to the world of his peers and his elders. The practitioner may want to evaluate to what extent are the adolescent's activities tied in with his attempts to discern his own standards of living and to what degree do his activities reflect a resistance to standards *per se*. Furthermore, the helper may want to reflect upon the youth's progress in finding his identity in the several spheres of adolescent development, because an adolescent has to face simultaneously many challenges associated with movements towards adulthood. A closer look at these would include: (1) a sense of certainty as a person in his own right, (2) a sense of appropriate timing, (3) a sense of sexual adequacy, (4) a sense of social competence, (5) a sense of workmanship, (6) a sense of authority integration, and (7) a sense of forming an ideology. Any one or several of these social challenges and promises of potential adulthood could be discerned as a source for an acute crisis in the youth's total personality development.

In the previous phase we were concerned with the child's capacity to differentiate between variant social roles and his general adaptation to them. In this fifth phase, the focus would have to be on the youth's own role playing—the versatility and themes of the many roles he pursues readily and, hopefully, happily. We suggest that a review of the range and variation of the social roles he assumes within any one day adds a more comprehensive picture than an intensive inquiry into any one of the youth's role preoccupations.

Earlier, sibling rivalry was reviewed for the clues it holds to a child's wish to be close to and fully possessed by the person for whom he competes with his contemporaries. Sibling rivalry in adolescence may reveal similar dynamics. Or we suggest that it may indicate, to the contrary, a different and more advanced phenomena. Sibling rivalry in adolescence may revolve around status—a striving for authority; that is, to be the person closest to the one in the authority position. Consequently, in work with adolescents or adults the helper may want to appraise if the rivalrous person strives for secure dependency (a vestige of an earlier developmental struggle) or competes for a position of status and greater independence (a factor more intimately tied in with movements towards adult development).

Many of the youth's temporary and "trying-out" activities hold valuable clues for his actual integration of age-bound social demands and emotional readiness. The youth's play activities—his tom-foolery—may readily reveal that the youth is preoccupied with "playing small" while he tries to recover what he feels he missed earlier in his life. "Playing big," on the other hand, hints at his ambitious thrust toward greater maturity.

In the cognitive area the helper may want to ask himself: To what extent does the youth search for explanations in order to comprehend his social or physical surroundings, and ideational world and his lot within it? These may be questions which have plagued him for many years.

A good number of the preceding points can be applied in working with adults so long as they are adapted to the adult's particular social situation. In particular, a worker may want to be mindful of the fact that an adult experiences developmental phases as an adult, who normally is presumed to have coped successfully with such questions in his past.

Thus, the practitioner may find it useful to diagnose his client's problems in terms of the developmental phase or phases which are particularly significant to the client, and may want to proceed to treat and to intervene in terms of those phases.

THE INDIVIDUAL-INTERVIEW SYSTEM

The implications of the three theories for professional intervention will be reviewed within the combined framework of the sequential developmental phases; further, we shall apply these developmental phases to each of the four helping systems outlined in Chapter 6.

Phase I: Establishing Primary Dependence

In his earliest years, a child has no social perspective. He depends indiscriminately upon the adult who happens to be with him, while the adult senses concurrently an immediate and full responsibility for a totally dependent child. In essence, helping of this kind becomes child-caring. Helping in this sense implies that nurturing care is as desirable as food, clothing, or shelter—and consequently, is another essential ingredient of human survival.

This kind of helping encourages activities leading towards dependence and discourages activities which would frustrate the child. Of course, momentary frustrations are natural and inevitable. But a child's attempt to relieve his frustrations through aggression, as we learned from Sears, often requires careful handling. Such aggression may be a last-resort measure in which the child tries to bail himself out of a difficult situation or it may be directly associated with the child's personal reaction to the caring person, as in a case in which a child attempts to blackmail a caring adult into removing the frustrating conditions.

A helper who is fostering dependence must keep in mind the vulnerability of that dependence when it is in the making. A child who starts to depend on an adult reacts very sensitively to the adult's causing any variation in the dependence relationship, so any such alteration should be undertaken cautiously in order that it may foster rather than hinder the relationship. Sibling rivalry in this connection should be recognized as evidence that dependence seems worthwhile enough to the participants to compete or contend for, and the caring adult should welcome it as such.

Phase II: Establishing Self-Care

Developmental problems which appear during the time when a child begins to help himself and to desert his earlier total dependence are frequently related to the availability, or the withdrawal, of the helping person's care. During this time, helping continues exclusively on a primary level with an emphasis upon encouraging the child to carry out more and more activities on his own. Helping in this way involves finding safe alternatives for actions as well as prohibiting actions. Permissiveness now entails both letting the child try on his own, and providing a safe harbor in which he may find refuge before and after making such attempts. Frustration, internally or externally provoked, is now permitted to exist in a controlled way for purposes of challenge.

Language as a tool of communication and an advanced form of dealing with one's dependence deserves attention here. A single phrase can convey a whole series of activities in which the child perceives himself as the central actor. The language he uses is that of his elders; his communication, the helper may note, still reflects only his own impressionistic understanding. Therefore, as we learned from Piaget, the depth of comprehension of one's own use of language varies according to one's level of development. The significance to the child of words such as "good" or "bad," is linked to the dependence upon the adult who says these words rather than to their actual meaning. Erikson's consideration of the influence of the adult's *unconscious* affects should also be a part of the helper's understanding.

Helping at this point in a child's life also means working within

the confines of his comprehension at a time when his understanding of his experiences is determined through reasoning by proximity, judging by external appearances, and locating action by
visually perceiving motion. The child is taught to label each
experience, action, or feeling for what it is, and his efforts to
separate them are encouraged. He is shown that he can be angry
without necessarily expressing his anger in the full-body language
of kicking and screaming. This understanding holds also direct
implications for helping with aggression. It is not the adult's
explanation of the child's aggression which is apt to be communicated but rather the adult's own mode of aggressiveness (even his
merely verbal explanation) which serves to act upon the child's
aggression. The child himself experiences control: *how much* and
when aggression will be tolerated, rather than the essence of his
aggression.

Both play in the child's life and play in the helping situation can
be used as a reflection of the child's everyday experiences at this
time in his development. The use of play yields pertinent information which neither the child nor the adult could provide if it were
verbalized or fully acted out in the office interview, at home, or
within the ward of a children's institution.

Phase III: Establishing Meaningful Secondary Relationships

As the child becomes old enough to venture beyond the physical and interpersonal confines of his home, he himself begins
searching for new kinds of relationships. In a helping situation,
likewise, he is now capable of proceeding either on an associate or
a primary level. On either level, in contrast to the earlier stress
upon the helper's fostering satisfaction in dependence, a new
emphasis should be placed upon the helper's promoting modifica-
tions in the child's sense of dependence. Efforts are now directed
toward helping the child to feel counted *among* others and toward
preparing him to live in a way that others can count on him so
that he can become an individual secure among, and dependent
upon, others.

As the child gains more experience, he becomes particularly attuned to the supporting and controlling functions of the adults around him. For the helping professional, it becomes important to communicate clearly and firmly to the child what constitutes acceptable attitudes and forms of behavior. To illustrate, in a treatment situation a client can learn to differentiate between expressing himself freely during the interview and maintaining greater controls in the waiting room or hallway while meeting his worker. Similarly, boundaries are explored and established when client and helper discuss the problems of the client's everyday life.

Both speech and actions serve as tools of reasoning. What a child does or says, while relating to his helping person, may represent as much a process of reasoning out ideas in the presence of another as a communication of ideas. He deals with one problem at a time. Analogies are out of the question for him. Judgments are made by end results as he experiences them at the moment. Experiences, things or persons, are either "good" or "bad." A friend is "a friend" or "no friend" at all. Shadings or degrees have yet to emerge.

The helping professional should keep in mind the sex of his client. In applying Sears' research data we note that, for a girl, dependence can be dealt with best through a direct, one-to-one relationship. For a boy, symbolic signs of dependence as well as remnants of an earlier independence can be effectively employed by greater reliance upon a boy's interpersonal dependence upon peers.

Workers with children of this age (or at this point in their development) should remember that much of a child's energies are devoted to becoming his own parent—that is, in developing his own superego (Erikson). To become his own parent requires that the child devote his energies to doing something himself the way the parent of the same sex presumably would do it. The child's preoccupation is with himself, his everyday world, and attempting to master every problem set before him.

In combining the three theories, we learned that, in "becoming his own parent," a boy or girl prepares for his respective societal and parental role. Consequently, the nature of either's sex activities deserves special attention. A boy requires opportunities to be masculine (intrusion), to dare on his own, to master himself, to control, and to be on top of a situation, while a girl must be allowed to develop a capacity for making herself attractive to others (inception), for getting others to include her socially, and for caring for others. Moreover, a child's failure in these efforts requires equal consideration. Commendation may be given to the child's courage for trying, because the desire to move ahead and to succeed is as deserving as eventual mastery.

It is not only for practitioner and client to discern the client's relationship to his parents as his prototypes of maleness and femaleness; but both client and worker have to deal with the same questions in their own unique helping relationship. In general, beginning with this phase, the client will be acutely aware of his helper as an adult—and as a male or female, whatever the case may be. Conversely, the helper himself will be preoccupied with the task of not only helping his client to find his appropriate developmental path, but also to progress to the one most appropriate for his or her sex.

Ample time and opportunities for play in the form of indulging in fantasies of accomplishment now become of utmost importance in care on a primary level. Play has to afford the child opportunities to become that which everyday life does not yet allow him to be.

Piaget's material highlights the implications of spoken communication for various stages in a child's development. When language becomes the major tool of the helping process in working with individuals, his findings are particularly relevant. As we learned from Piaget, early in a child's development, speech stands for action. "You said so," means readily for the child, "You did so." An event described may easily become (in the child's mind) an event which occurred. More complexly, he may use language appropriately without realizing the meaning of the words. For instance, a child may speak of walking on the left side of the street without having much of a notion of what constitutes "left" or "right." Professional attention should be devoted, therefore, to a child's actual range of language comprehension.

Phase IV: Establishing Secondary Dependence

In working with individuals during this phase, helping efforts are directed toward using previously acquired "safety zones" of dependence. New experiences beyond those of primary dependence can be sorted out with the cooperation of the primary caring person. Helping is then directed towards mobilizing the child's trust in his own initiative and towards encouraging his autonomous strivings. Helping here means enabling the client to see how his individual creative industry can gain for him an important position in his world. To succeed means for an individual in this phase to do better than *he* did before, and competitive feelings and activities should be recognized by the helper as the individual's desire to come out "all right" *himself*.

Play remains an important resource for communication and common explorations; but in child-care or play therapy it becomes important to know that play, in this phase, is losing some of its equalizing quality. Roles and role expectations become relevant now, as do a concern for rules and the working out of mutual regulations in order to sort out and better understand relationships. The one-to-one method is employed to good advantage at this time to clarify relationship and new centers of authority. In short, the interview serves as a means for disclosing new measuring sticks for concerns far beyond those of the immediate helping situation.

At no time in the child's life is his insistence upon equality as important. For him fairness and justice exist when equality is assured. Consequently, the helper's role is constantly shifting from caring adult to guiding elder, to social educator, to representative of the adult world, to adult identifying and playing with a child, etc. The child knows these various roles and the helper can, therefore, draw upon whichever of his own varying role expectations he considers relevant.

Phase V: Achieving Balance Between Dependence and Independence

A one-to-one relationship between client and helping adult on either level presents a perplexing situation for a youth who is developing and solidifying his own balance between dependence and independence. In a primary situation, the focus is upon resolving the personal need for dependence and/or independence in everyday living. It involves the gradual shift of the child's conception of the caring person as a parent-surrogate to considering him as a supportive trustee. In an interview situation on the associate level, the aim is to help the client to become an independently contributing member of his interdependent society. A helper may have to see himself both as a counseling specialist who contributes one half of a personal relationship and as a representative of the larger society of which both client and helper are parts. The client has to deal simultaneously with questions involving both his personal and his societal relationships.

It is important, in this connection, for the practitioner to realize that the youth is shifting his value system from that appropriate to a child to one utilized by adults. The youth compares his own set of values to those evidenced by the adults in his sphere; therefore, any difference between those espoused by the practitioner as values for the youth to adhere to and those actually exercised by the practitioner himself is likely to be challenged—overtly or covertly—by the client. Assuming there is a valid situational difference behind the disparate value systems in question, this factor needs to be explored with the youth. Frequently it is a case of individual differences and capacities, and these differences are relevant for the youth's understanding of differential standards.

In a one-to-one helping situation, speech serves as the major vehicle for problem solution. Language now is employed to test, to think through, to dare oneself or to dare others, to boast or to confess, to examine or to discard varying life experiences—until finally talking about one or another form of living becomes a commitment to it. Language therefore facilitates role experimentation. Thinking aloud together serves as a major relationship matrix. The client plays with thoughts and words in place of behavioral experimentation. We learned from Piaget that the youth starts to comprehend through abstractions. Yet, reasoning, which involves abstract thinking, does not spring into being automatically as an extension of concrete learning. It has to be engendered anew on this level, and all concrete learning contributes to its generation.

THE SYSTEM OF THE GROUP

The question, What does group membership mean to the client developmentally? has to be answered along with, In what way does the client use his helping agent as the central person in the group situation? each time a client is considered for treatment by the "group system." The individual's respective investments in the following four major facets of group membership must be determined:

1. Dependence upon individual group members, including the helping agent as the central person;
2. Utilization of the group situation as a social arena for trying out old or new relationships, skills, ideas, values and behavioral patterns;
3. Use of the group situation for becoming part of a social unit;
4. Dependence upon the group as a social reference system which will influence his thoughts, feelings, beliefs, and behavior in future associations outside the group.

Phases I and II: Establishing Primary Dependence and Self-Care

Working with individuals within a group who are functioning within developmental Phases I or II calls for individual work with each. Relationships have to be on a one-to-one basis. It is questionable, therefore, if children in either of these elementary developmental phases can be effectively served by the group system because development at this time depends fundamentally upon a concentrated relationship with a single adult.

In the author's opinion there are occasions when children in a very early developmental level might find potential help within a group situation. This might hold true for work with autistic children or children who need to develop and acknowledge a sense of need for a caring person. For this type of child, it is desirable to stimulate a sense and expression of rivalry; the latter will afford opportunity to deal with their desire for care. Their struggle with others for such care is not the dynamic conflict.

Phase III: Establishing Meaningful Secondary Relationships

A successful group experience takes place in a group which is sufficiently small to guarantee ample personal contacts—specifically, child-adult contacts within a sibling (a peer) situation. Two or more individuals' demand for unobstructed adult attention gives rise to rivalry, which becomes apparent in (1) striving for a favored position near the central adult, and in (2) the maintaining of a safe distance between his own position and those of others who might threaten its security. In this phase, the cause of primary competition among peers is the desire to win and maintain the support of the central person: competition among peers for other reasons remains a by-product. On this basis a helping professional should take into account that it is *his* relationship to each client which needs to be considered first, even when events force him to deal with interpersonal strife among two or more clients. In this phase, there is neither awareness nor understanding of competitive hierarchical relationships; so the helping person could suitably award "first prize" to many contestants. In fact, every one of his clients can be an individual winner so long as winning means to the winner, "I am really recognized."

In work with individuals in a group system during this phase, toys, pets, equipment, or group members (including the central adult) serve as important accessories for living and for acting out personal problems through play. Language of play, physical motion, or verbal utterances are all means of communication with others and should be employed as efforts in communication rather than for their content of speech. Within this phase much of a group's play is nominally the same as the play of developmentally more advanced children (i.e., playing cowboys, playing house, etc.). However, between these age phases there is a notable difference in the content of the play behavior. In the younger phase, a single reference point might encompass a whole play episode; for instance, a sheriff's badge pinned to the shirt might signify "I am playing cowboy," or sudsing doll clothing might stand for the notion that "I am playing house." Play develops into an increasingly more meaningful group experience as the child grows older. "Let's build a hide-out!" becomes "Let's do something together!"

The helping agent has to keep in mind that the child in this phase still sees group norms and rules in the present, which means that group discussions and activities need to relate to the individual group member's current needs and to the planning of effective activities in the immediate future.

Phase IV: Establishing Secondary Dependence

Group workers presume validly that children with the developmental achievements of this fourth phase are able to perceive and assume differential roles. The meaning of group membership here shifts from a preoccupation with social contacts and activities with others to an actual desire for more deeply established personal relationships. A sense of dependence upon a few key persons gives way to a desire for security within the group. The child can now simultaneously be a member of his family, his school class, and his play group without one group experience necessarily obliterating the others.

Primary group care, which from this point on may substitute as an alternative to family living, provides a basic nurturing environment supported by the activities of group living. A client's change to dependence upon peers and upon the group as a whole permits the helping person to use such new forms of dependence for therapeutic purposes. He may now deal with relationships other than those between each client and himself because he no longer has to act as the coordinating figure in the group.

Whereas previously the group was visualized and labeled by

the child as the helper's group, from this point on, the individual members' activities, encouraged by the helper, will strongly influence the group's character. Play, talk, and work gain increasing importance as social catalysts, and personal relationships continue to be valuable for the immediate social satisfactions they can yield. Each member wants to see himself succeed and measure up to the others; much of one's association with peers is carried on to measure, improve, and maintain self-esteem. Problem solving is still a common motivation for building relationships.

In group deliberations during this phase, much attention is devoted to questions of group-shared rules and regulations and fit retribution for their violation, a consciousness that the seat of authority tends to be more and more found in his friendship groups than in the world of his elders. Such awareness has particular relevance in helping group members with their group deliberations. Fairness for a group at this point means planning of and sticking to standards which they developed.

To sum up, working with the group system on either the associate or primary level means enabling each client to feel that he genuinely counts in the eyes of the other group members, and through such experiences to feel that such a group is *his* group. A group experience during this phase has to assure ample opportunities for talk and play, for much ado about what to the adult world may seem minor differences, for intermingling work and play, and for experimentation. Here the group provides a second testing ground of dependence following that in the second developmental phase. Group games and competitive or individual activities are employed for the development of plans, rules, and regulations. As we were shown by Piaget, learning now focuses upon questions of "universality": in this phase the group acts as a handy laboratory for thinking through experiences and ideas which might bear on the creation of social rules and standards. Helping by means of the group system entails encouraging group experiences for the mutual benefits to be derived from them rather than putting undue emphasis upon the productions of the group as a whole.

Phase V: Achieving Balance Between Dependence and Independence

The group plays a vital role in the way of life of our contemporary youth. Adult participation, from the youth's perspective, implies an intrusion. A central adult may have to learn a group's norms and culture before he can effectively communicate with the group members, and, as the intruder, it is up to him to adjust. The group, if skillfully manipulated, can be a useful tool with which to influence developmental lags or to avert developmental complications.

On a primary level, group living such as that provided by a unit within an institutional program may offer a starting point and a retreat to which a child may return when life in the outside world becomes too stormy. The group provides a social and psychological base for belonging. The helping person is a part of that base and he should be available when the youth needs the sort of adult guidance and support which cannot be furnished by the group alone.

On the associate level, it is essential to determine which aspects of existing or predicted developmental lags or complications the group experience is intended to help. Within this phase, the group takes over more and more adult prerogatives, but at the same time (regardless of the youth's and his friends' outward behavior) adult authority continues to stand without question in certain well-defined areas. It is not surprising, therefore, that problems involving a division of authority are frequently encountered. Both authorities (the old and the new) must at this stage begin to blend.

An important consideration is the size of the group. For youths who are primarily preoccupied with self-integration and its myriad aspects, a small, intimate, and closed circle of members is desirable. On the other hand, youths who are moving ahead to societal integration and who need to experiment with their newly integrated selves in terms of the society at large can be helped significantly within a larger group of diverse but similarly focused individuals. For these adolescents, productive involvement in organizational functioning, social structure, and a wide range of role experimentation become essential facets of their group experience and provide a useful means for gaining experience in becoming full members of their society.

The abundance of talk and random activities of youths, in this developmental phase show that they are endlessly thinking about and experimenting with the many alternatives before them. The helper must refrain from too quickly labeling these explorations as actual commitments. Such trials reflect the youth's efforts to apply newly acquired abilities and to test conflicting feelings about his developmental capacities.

In working with a group of adolescents, Erikson's and Piaget's material suggests, study of the youth's versatility and diffuseness of behavior is often more productive than study of such behavior's actual content. The behavior of several youths within the same group might give cause for anticipating a state of anarchy. This could alarm many adults who are concerned about the autonomous nature of many youth group members. The helping adult needs therefore, to delineate the group's structure with firmness and clarity, because a youth can only attain a proper degree of independence and a sense of identity within a context that is well defined.

Many of the youth's intragroup dealings at this time have to do with his own role expectations and developing ones that he can meet. In working with a family as a group this issue is often crucial. The family members need to be studied for both diffusion and possible incompatible duplication of their roles. Discerning what are compatible and attainable role expectations for the client is a major function of the helping person, and his aim is to gradually equalize the youth's and his society's expectations of the youth's role.

The youth himself is frequently preoccupied with procedures and rules and their applications as if he were the judiciary. This is his way of dealing with some of the problems which face him, and since such activities are often beneficial, they need to be fostered. Mental consideration of all possibilities and probabilities, ceaseless discussion of what constitutes fairness and justice, loud squabbles over contradictions, and trying out "ifs"—all of these are measures which reflect a youth's struggles to find his place and to mold a sense of equity. Such activities deserve attention and time in a group session. Much of a youth's verbalization is role experimentation or relationship testing within a familiar and protected social unit. Individual clashes and social conflicts may be most welcome for their value in casting private confusions and resentments into the open arena of the group, where they may be dealt with as problems common to all of the group members within this developmental phase.

To illustrate, a heated argument over the right of one group member to miss a group session without valid reasons may reflect all of the group members' inner conflict over being independent and dependent. A group discussion for the ostensible purpose of resolving this question might well simultaneously benefit each individual's strivings to balance dependence and independence by further identifying an acceptable set of role expectations for the group members.

We referred to a change in the youth's conception of authority and a consequent change in the helping agent's role. In addition to his intermediary role as the relevant society's representative and the enunciator of its expectations, the helping person must now modify his position within the group to accommodate the client's personal conflict with authority. Within a group such a struggle is two-fold; it consists of (1) the primary struggle of the individual against the majority as represented by the single member's reaction to the authority of the rest of the group, and (2) the struggle of an individual to win a position of authority within a group of other separate individuals. Opposition to the central adult, or competition for his attention, may be undertaken to secure a better position within the group rather than to improve the youth's relationship with the central adult. Rivalry in this phase, therefore, has a new meaning; it is no longer engaged in for the purpose of *receiving* (depending upon) care from the adult, but its purpose now is to win the right to *exercise* such care by mobilizing it, via the adult in authority. A shift occurs from a desire for care to a desire for authority, or at least a desire to be the second in command.

Basically, the group with its professional worker provides an atmosphere for experimentation, for dealing with that which perplexes the youth. The fact that group experiences vary so much from client to client within this developmental phase may be explained by the variety and velocity of expressions of personality among youths rather than by any appreciable differences in their developmental processes.

THE AUXILIARY SYSTEM

Work with significant persons in a child's (or youth's) life is done with the understanding that the child will remain in the center of this type of helping system, while the help-seeking adult (one or both parents, teacher, etc.) receives consultation in order to improve his contribution to the child's developmental progress. Work with parents should take into account each parent's age, his occupation, and his marital, social, ethnic, and economic status. His status and developmental readiness as delineated in terms of the three adulthood phases described by Erikson partly determine the adult's mode of responsiveness to his child and his potential modes of interaction with the child. This kind of helping system should also include the sharing of relevant knowledge about the client in order to broaden the parents' perspective and thereby affect child-parent relationships. Much of the helping effort should be concerned with assessing the child's situation as it is and interpreting his behavior in terms of his developmental readiness instead of (as parents often do) judging a child by his chronological age and its accompanying behavioral expectations. On the other hand, parents can be considerably relieved and encouraged in knowing that many of the "problem" situations that arise in child rearing are perfectly normal in the particular developmental phase in which they find their child.

In working with parents, two not always compatible ideas may need joint consideration: (1) the notion that a "good parent" is active, one who *does* something with a child, and (2) the realization that a child's ordinary development may sometimes be in a state of subtle balance where parental interference could at times circumscribe the child's range of enriching experiences. Therefore the counselor can make it clear that attentive parenthood should include selective periods of inactivity.

We learned from Sears that punishment does not tend to foster an alternative way of behaving; instead, it conveys personal disapproval and thereby impairs the closeness of a relationship. On the other hand, noninterference (or so-called "permissiveness") leaves the child directionless and, at times, at the mercy of his own guilt, which may make him feel as rejected and isolated as would punishment. Both approaches to child care—punishment and permissiveness—ought to be reviewed by the parent and the counselor for their bearing on the life of the child under study. Counseling of this kind means moving from an examination of techniques, themselves, to weighing the implications of such techniques.

Phase I: Establishing Primary Dependence

In working with parents of children in this first phase, it becomes the helping professional's responsibility to use his understanding of the pervasive nature of the formative years and of the child-parent relationship during those years. What baby does to mother, his family, and his family's place in the community requires as much attention as what mother, family, and community do to baby. Such understanding all but renders obsolete labels like "the rejecting mother," "the unwanted child," etc.

Piaget, Erikson, and Sears all agree that development's skeletal framework is constructed of experience patterns. In evaluating child-parent relationships, then, the parents' patterns of regularity (such as the extent to which a mother assures her child a sense of predictability by her outward behavior) play a vital part in the baby's responding to recurring experiences. Investigating child-caring patterns may help in discerning the effects of child-caring efforts. Weaning, toilet training, and the other cycles of separation should be considered in terms of their connection with previously established patterns of dependence; the child's main problem in each cycle may be to replace an old dependence pattern with a new one.

Child training is also parent training. In order to avoid a parental preoccupation with doing "the right thing," it may be helpful to remember the hypothesis that can be derived from all three theories—that child and parent learn best from each other. Above all, concurrent learning depends upon discovery through trial and error.

The vulnerability and innocence of infants create a powerful urge to which mother, family, and society respond with a desire to give all that is wanted and more. Parents must be assured that it is safe, desirable, and beneficial to be a giving parent, and that to instill a sense of trusting dependence is the first major parental task of child-rearing.

Phase II: Establishing Self-Care

In this phase, the gradual release of close parental control over the child demands that decisions be made about what, how, when, and where the child's self-care and independence can be encouraged and at what points the parent's direct care must continue. Again, we must be conscious of the specific considerations with which parents are dealing. Using the toilet, leaving books in the book-case, or staying in bed when told, are activities which might demonstrate a child's struggle in a world of many demands. The helping person, as an authority on human growth and development, may assure the parent that the ups and downs in child training are inherent developmental crises which in no way reflect an individual's quality of parenthood. It should also be stressed that evidence of a child's acceptance of parental care takes many forms, and unless he is careful, a parent may misread them. To illustrate, a mother's exasperation at her child's sudden insistence upon feeding himself may be clarified when she rightly interprets his crude attempts at self-feeding as strivings to do just as mother did and as positive signs of his dependence upon her and a desire to emulate her.

At the time the child starts on his own do-it-yourself developmental course, parents need to know that their withdrawal of care in any area without demonstrated readiness on the part of the child constitutes a general threat to his sense of dependence. Such withdrawals can serve as powerful and dangerous weapons of control. To be specific, a remark such as, "If you do not come right away I'll have to leave you," should be considered in light of its future effects as well as for its immediate handiness.

The professional helper should share theoretical information with the parent whenever it might promote better caring practices. For instance, a parent may discover with real bewilderment that his child no longer responds to him as he used to. Knowing that external pressures of a situational change such as a move or the birth of another child can decrease internal control while increasing the need for dependence may permit the parent to regard the condition as a new learning situation rather than as a child's or a parent's failure. In this regard, Sears' concept of labeling can be applied as a device for linking a preceding experience to a later related event. In these childhood phases, labeling serves primarily to establish a connection between related experiences rather than to explain their logical interrelationships. For example, a child burning his tongue because his cocoa was too hot may hear the experience labeled: "tongue hurts, hot cocoa." He becomes aware that there is some connection between "hurting his tongue" and "hot cocoa," but the logic of hot drinks burning tongues will remain for him a hidden mystery for some time.

The theoretical contention that play embodies a child's attempts to master developmental tasks holds the following message for parents: All of life may become play, but not all play may become life. A young child may get himself fully dressed in play; that does not necessarily mean, however, that henceforth he can dress himself. Piaget's and Erikson's recognition of play as one of the most essential developmental and autotherapeutic processes holds as much significance for the parent as it does for the professional helper. In fact, we may assume that if provided with ample opportunities for unhampered play, particularly in the early phases of development, the child may deal more precisely with his problems than the parent and helper could. Therefore, suggestions to a parent for providing play opportunities should concern the helping professional just as much as alerting that parent to the importance of a balanced diet, sufficient sleep, and other benefits for the child.

Phase III: Establishing Meaningful Secondary Relationships

In this phase, the immediate child-care (mother-child and father-child) relationships and differences between them require particular attention. Previously made judgments about what is safe to do for the child now must be augmented by decisions about interpreting the child's feelings and actions. Parents may take comfort, perhaps, in the knowledge that a child's true feelings need not always be expressed in actions which will require direct response from the parents. Unconscious communication is a normal part of life. A parent's comments such as: "I know she has really done nothing that should get me so upset that I feel like screaming at her," reflect typical reactions to the intermingling of the child's affective, cognitive, and behavioral processes.

In interpreting children's needs, the helping professional will likely have to stress for the parent the continuing importance of play with objects, pets, and peers, but now such play may take place as much outside the range of the parents' supervision as within. In playing with their children, parents should realize that they are introducing values for the children's future, since they will be instilling (often unconsciously) in the children their own identification with standards and ideas. Playing together, therefore, with an emphasis upon exploring, winning, having fun, or just being together, will breed later developmental consequences, and parents may have to decide which attitudes and aptitudes—such as those having to do with competition, pleasure seeking, sociability, or creativity—most need encouragement for the contribution they will make to each child's developing personality.

With a child's intuitive actions approaching more and more rational forms of behavior, it is hard for any adult to realize that despite some gains, a child's actual social competence is still in a most primitive state. Parents may have to differentiate between teaching behavioral practices and expecting a child's adherence to standards which those practices exemplify. Expectations of courtesy, order, responsibility, or good hygiene, for example, will probably not be fulfilled yet. The child's behavior, parent and helper should note, falls within the sphere of the adults' mores and understanding, while the child's comprehension of such practices' meaning does not—it is his alone, and may be easily misinterpreted by onlookers.

To sum up, in a phase noted for the child's independent explorations in thinking, feeling, and acting, parents need to be shown visibly that their boy or girl still fundamentally relies on them and wants his nurturing care both within the home and outside.

Phase IV: Establishing Secondary Dependence

In this phase, it may be necessary to deal with the child's parent(s), his teacher, or any other significant adult in the child's life. Each such individual becomes both a depended-upon person when the child needs the kind of nurturing benefit he can provide, and a societal representative when the child requires that type of contact. The helping professional, being aware of the child's increased comprehension of the world around him, should lead him to investigate such questions as: To what extent do the child's questioning parental authority and his comparing his family's ways of doing things with those of others represent a personal psychological conflict, and to what extent do they signify a cognitive crisis caused by the child's discovering two unlike but nevertheless acceptable kinds of behavior? The child's questioning may appear to be a personal challenging of the rights of parenthood when actually it is only a pondering of why there are so many alternatively acceptable ways of behaving.

It is noteworthy that in this phase we often pay more attention to a child's comments than to his actions. A reliance upon spoken communication as a major gauge of the child-parent relationship during this phase develops in working with parents, and a preoccupation with parents' activities is replaced by a new interest in verbal communication between child and parents. Thoughts and feelings are now often communicated through an expanding group of symbols, both verbal and nonverbal. The child is able to grasp a fuller meaning of a word such as "don't" or a gesture such as his mother shaking her finger in disapproval. Much of the effectiveness of this kind of helping effort may hinge upon parent and helping agent jointly attempting to acquire an accurate picture of the child's activities away from home. In the child's out-of-home behavior the agent can often help parents find a revealing indication of their child's relationship to them, for in spite of the child's apparent lack of interest in his family's activities and economy while at home, he cannot help but display often his parents' care, behavior, and values when he is away from home.

Phase V: *Achieving Balance Between Dependence and Independence*

This phase holds a special challenge to the helper and parent who are working jointly on an adolescent's problems because each finds himself in the position of having to prove himself a dependable person to the adolescent at a time when he is outgrowing dependence and his natural adolescent strivings are toward independence. Adolescence represents a distinct period of development between childhood and adulthood; but a period in which the adolescent is a dependent without childhood status. Parents often need to be reminded that adolescent behavior is not an isolated behavioral phenomenon and that it cannot be considered separately from the social context within which it is experienced.

Previous examinations of adolescent experimentation with words and actions have prepared us not to be satisfied with any single explanation of an adolescent episode which professes to portray a true developmental status. A helper may want to remember that adolescent behavior often includes experimentation with extremes, and it is important for the helping agent to bear in mind that adolescent behavior and thoughts are transitory.

In work with parents or other key persons, the helper should try to anticipate realistically the youth's immediate future; what tomorrow holds for, and requires of, the adolescent is at least as important as what has happened to him yesterday.

Erikson's material interprets adolescence in a highly civilized world as a prolonged conflict between the need for identity and temporary role diffusions. This prolonged conflict will entail a simultaneous prolonged dependence upon responsible caring elders. As we learned from both Piaget and Erikson, such caring adults continue to serve as sounding boards for the youth's feelings, thinking, and actions while the adults' authority remains undiminished.

An adolescent's development is continually affected by opportunities offered not only by the family but other social institutions beyond the parents' immediate personal control. To help parents to see themselves as sharing contributors to an adolescent's development rather than as those solely responsible for it may encourage them to proceed wisely in influencing the adolescent's life.

THE SYSTEM OF PROGRAM ALTERATION

In Chapter 6 we mentioned that helpful intervention may mean altering certain conditions which impinge upon an individual's life situation so that developmental complications may be prevented, controlled, or corrected.

All three theories—particularly those of Erikson and Sears—point out that the nurturing person can instill in the child a basic sense of security only as deep as his own. Therefore, it becomes important that parents themselves are assured emotional, social, and financial security. This premise becomes a *social* issue, because each individual, parent, and family can expand his potentialities only so far as his community supports and grants, and only so far as each one is prepared to invest in his community's development.

The importance of each parent and family finding himself as

a participating member of his community carries over also to the work of persons who assume parental functions. Nurses, child-care workers, homemakers, foster-home parents, or teachers like-wise need to feel and act as members of their respective communities in order to be able to pass on such a sense of continuity to those entrusted to them. Arrangements of working hours, pay scale, social prestige for their work, and the location of their place of work become important considerations in order to assure each of these professionals a potential place in their community.

The fact that healthy personality development is anchored in the family's sense of well-being stresses the importance of those services—Aid to Dependent Families, Family Counseling, Housing Developments, and numerous others—which intend to foster economic, psychosocial, and physical security of families.

Questions of peace or war, threat of contamination of vegetation due to nuclear fall-out, fear of unemployment or the staggering cost of living, second-class citizenship due to racial, religious, or ethnic discriminations, or other phenomena of advanced civilization—these become as much child developmental questions as the ones related to reading readiness, the Oedipus complex, or proper social motivations. In short, a helping professional needs to concern himself as much with the context—social, psychological, ideational, and physical—in which the child is to develop as with the child's own psychosocial functioning. To be specific, a boy or girl can only drink a glass of milk both as body-building food and as a symbolic expression of mother's goodwill so long as his mother's *personal* faith is anchored in her own deep conviction that the milk is *good*, uncontaminated, and she can afford it again the next day.

Sears' finding that differences in child-rearing practices are less related to the socioeconomic status of the parents *per se* than to the parents' access to more recent knowledge, stresses the importance of making all new understanding as accessible as possible to all groups and strata. Moreover, his findings that age differences and the age span of all the children in a family are correlated to the quality of mothering suggest pertinent arguments for the provision of homemaker services, for the evaluation of adoptive or foster-home placements and for graded supplementary support in such programs as the one for Aid to Dependent Families.

Although this book deals with his work in the field of child development, Erikson's perceptive observations on continued development throughout adulthood hint at the need for reform in social programs, services, and policies intended to affect adults. (Such reforms might hold particular import for the situations in which the older members of our society frequently find themselves.) Erikson also shows repeatedly that children need to grow up in an environment which fulfills the needs of the adults around them, because when parents cannot find satisfaction in life they tend to take their frustrations out in all of their life experience, including their relationships to their children.

Finally, the three theories under study here make us conscious both of the continuum of development and of intermittent critical periods in its progress. They have made us aware that there are particularly untimely periods for separating children from familiar surroundings. Such periods may be noted (1) during the first nine to twelve months of a child's life when he becomes cognizant of regularity in his own personal existence and recognizes the dependability of those caring for him, (2) around the time when he begins to leave his own family nest and establish new contacts, thereby endangering his sense of security in his basic family relationships, and (3) when he reaches adolescence and feels the need (and is urged) to relinquish more of his dependence upon his family in order to establish new social relationships. The potential separation crises of these periods should be heeded in arranging a foster home or institutional placement, or in changing a child's daily existence from institutional to family living.

Phase I: Establishing Primary Dependence

All three theories stress the significance of maternal care in producing whatever society wants the infant eventually to be. In our society food, clothing, and shelter seem to be virtually assured to everyone, regardless of his status. But food, clothing, and shelter serve as powerful symbols in the act of giving and in the giver's relationship to the receiver. Therefore, in infancy and early childhood, as we learned, giving should be deliberately structured so as to engender dependence as a healthy first step in the long progression of normal child development.

Just as early maternal care decisively offsets a normal developmental adaptation, continued foster care (within the same home and proceeding through a variety of experiences) has a vital influence on a child who may eventually have to be institutionalized. If the child is to achieve a trusting sense of dependency, his early experiences should provide him with a reliable security. Dependable consistency in his care at this age may insure in him a better adaptability if his later life should have to be varied. For this reason, the idea of an interdependence between mother and child broached by Erikson and Sears reemphasizes the value of early adoption and of such arrangements as those provided by lying-in hospitals, where parents stay with a child during the child's hospitalization.

To recapitulate, the three theorists' material on early childhood development pointedly suggests that maximally beneficial conditions are those which assure a mother time and resources to exercise her full capabilities as mother.

Phase II: Establishing Self-Care

This second phase encompasses a young child's continuing need for individual nurturing care. Unavoidable separation such as that caused by hospitalization of a child or parent necessitates substitute nurturing for the child; in the case of a child's hospitalization, a nurse or other hospital staff member is the person entrusted with the care of the child and the logical person to provide it. Most children within this phase who are separated from their parents are not ready for "day-care" unless it can assure sustained individual attention throughout the period they are away from home. Separations, then, have to be considered in light of the capabilities for self-care the individual child can master, as well as the amount of nurturing care he still requires when he finds himself in a hospital, at a detention center, with a baby-sitter, etc.

The percentage of this book which is devoted to discussions of play illustrates play's importance to child development, especially if it is unstructured and spontaneous. Budgeting and programming of children's aid services would do well to take this into account: A community must ask itself if its hospitals, foster homes, or Aid-to-Dependent-Families budgets guarantee sufficient funds and opportunities for children to grow and benefit through recreation and play. As our theorists frequently imply, play constitutes a child's most reliable device for self-help.

Phase III: Establishing Meaningful Secondary Relationships

In this phase the young child tends to relate to his caring adult according to sex. He begins to identify strongly with his own sex group and becomes conscious of differences between the parent of the opposite sex and himself. In regard to foster care, then, these questions arise: Do contemporary child-care services realize the importance of differentiating relationships between a child and a caring adult according to the sex of the child, and do they provide the youngsters in their care with ample opportunities for adequate social relationships with both men and women? Also, do such services offer the social status, and the educational and financial resources to make possible the employment of men and women who can act as wholesome carriers of traditions to the children they are helping? Modern emphasis upon the nurturing aspects of care, which assures an institutionalized child opportunities to associate with a readily available caring person, indicates that many services are trying to answer these questions positively and underscores two contemporary trends: (1) acceptance of the family mode of living as the most desirable form of living for all children regardless of their social or developmental complications, and (2) recognizing that nurturing child care is as essential to solving a child's problems as rehabilitative effort for the deviations which brought him to the institution in the first place.

Economic, social, functional (blindness or deafness), or mere psychological maladjustments (neurotic disturbances) are no longer accepted as valid reasons for separation from family living and as a justification for institutional placement. However, if medical or psychopathological conditions cause family living to be interrupted for either medical or psychosocial treatment, the agency involved must provide a quality of child care to fulfill a need as basic as those for food, clothing, and shelter. Understanding the importance of such care may call for a reevaluation of the policies, services, and programs of our children's hospitals, convalescent homes, detention centers, and other institutions for children of preschool age who still need either family care or a workable substitute.

A small group should form the basic living unit for proper care. A young child's sense of belonging is clearly related to his group living with caring adults, immediate peers, and any pets that are a part of the living unit, whether it is the family or an alternative.

Phase IV: Establishing Secondary Dependence

When we review our programs, services, and policies for children in this phase we discover reassuringly that our practices seem much better in tune with their developmental demands than with those in other phases. We seem to find real evidence for Erikson's observations that society accepts children best when the children consider themselves children and wholeheartedly devote their energies to being children. We should remember that the significant adults and the respected institutions serve as bearers of values to a child within this phase, and that our own political, economic, and social attitudes and behavior continually affect the values being instilled in our children. It is therefore important that educational, recreational, religious, and social-welfare programs be geared to serve all three major facets of the development of the child within their trust. As Piaget so well substantiated, a child perceives and operates as a child, and much differently from an adult. This may reveal a periodic need for reevaluating such programs as little-league baseball, boys' clubs, Junior Republic, and others primarily patterned after adult prototypes.

Currently, one frequently hears the concern expressed that our next generation—our children of today—should demonstrate more evidence of their pride in our American heritage. Our contemporary knowledge suggests that a child's capacity to identify with his elders and their joint heritage is directly related to the quality of his personal relationship with them. The more healthy and the more realistic one generation's social and national identification is, the more it will be assured and reflected in the next.

Phase V: Achieving Balance Between Dependence and Independence

Although there is only a limited lag between knowledge and practice in child development, a different and theoretically predictable situation exists in adolescent development. The adolescent's pattern of psychosocial dependence need not parallel that of his maturational development. Also, the span of adolescence carries a distinct and separate developmental status which fits neither the mores of childhood nor those of young adulthood and for which proper structural provisions have never been made in the institutions which deal with it. This state of adolescence is what Talcott Parsons chooses to allude to as "youth culture." The youth is neither a child nor an adult, and therefore he is intermittently treated as either, neither, or both.

We would like to propose that adolescence be regarded as a separate state with special needs. Perhaps it could be considered first and foremost as a time for exploration. Each adolescent needs to explore with his teachers their related ideas, and with his parents their joint needs for "belonging" to one another. The youth may require an indeterminate amount of time for vocational planning, for choosing a dating companion, or for accepting one out of many philosophies of life, and it may be necessary for guiding adults to grant it to him as well as to encourage his participation in a special program particularly suited to his individual needs. The Peace Corps, for instance, with its combination of adult sponsorship and well-defined spheres of action and opportunities for creative investment for the youth, might serve as such a means for certain adolescents' healthy development. A custom accepted by some communities in which curfew regulations are worked out by

adolescents for themselves is another example of a policy or program which can have a desirable influence upon individuals in
this phase. It seems that there is a need to encourage social institutions which will permit adolescents—in this exploratory time—
to work out ideas and to investigate interpersonal relationships,
while furthering their own preparation for adulthood and making
some useful contribution to society.

There is no justification discernible in Erikson's, Sears', or
Piaget's work for the current tendency to regard parents as cul-
prits who cause their children's failures or delinquent exploits. As
far as the three theories are concerned, delinquency, just as all
other social phenomena, cannot be explained away by or analyzed
in terms of any *one* factor. Delinquency must be understood in
all its ramifications—psychological and social, individual and institutional.

In working with adolescents, each youth should be dealt with
as an individual rather than as a representative of an age or sex
group, or as a person typed by any one aspect of his behavior.

SUMMARY

The foregoing material stresses that, in spite of vast gaps in our
contemporary knowledge of human development and behavior,
we know far more than we apply. A systematic understanding of
child development will, hopefully, free a practitioner to imple-
ment his helping tasks more knowingly and more creatively.

In examining the implications for practice of the three theories
of child development for each of the four helping systems, we
have reviewed the developmental phases within their approximate
age spans. Although we have repeatedly stressed that a child's
chronological age should not serve as an exacting criterion for
evaluating his behavior, we have, nonetheless, for convenience,
kept our discussion within the limits of "normal" chronology. It
is, however, important for the helper—whoever he or she may be,
whatever his or her particular role, and whatever the specific field
—to remember that individual development is never fully com-

pleted nor completely "normal" at any one point in an individual's life. Few children will develop cognitively in all ways as indicated in the Piagetian phases; few children will successfully resolve *all* affective conflicts at the modal phases described by Eriksonian theory; and few will achieve full satisfaction or tension reduction from *every* goal-directed response according to Searsian findings. As indicated earlier, a helper may find himself dealing with a school-age child whose major difficulty stems from an unresolved aspect of an earlier phase or whose behavioral problem resembles more closely one typical of an earlier phase.

Thus, a helping professional must not only recognize the developmental goals and tasks typical of the phase the child should be undergoing but must also recognize the dominant developmental patterns—emotional, cognitive and behavioral. It is possible that the themes of several developmental phases are manifested in the child, at a given point, as we examine different aspects of his functioning. Therapeutic intervention, then, must take into account the phase typically normal of the child's age range, on the one hand, and on the other, the aspects of other developmental phases that are actually operating in the evolvement of the child's personality.

A clearer understanding of a child's actual level of functioning and the meaning of his life experience can guide the helping professional in assisting the client so that the client will gain more salutary experiences and a belief in his own competence, and will dispel the disquieting fear of not being adequate. Furthermore, in all of child development, and in all facets of the professional helping efforts, it is the *nature* of the interpersonal relationship which is paramount. Every interpersonal relationship holds the beginning of a personal promise of mutual significance. But again, each such personal promise depends upon an overall social atmosphere in which there can be potential trust and hope. The burning questions of our day—the problematic issues of international and intergroup relationships—seem to be directly correlated to the degree of personal satisfaction and meaningfulness each individual can find himself.

Since all of child development and child-rearing practices must be anchored in a deep trust in human beings, we need to aim at achieving in the human community at large the very trust we try to foster in the interpersonal relationships of our children. Above all, our knowledge, skills, and convictions must assure our children and youth that *each has a future of which he is a part, and that his future is a part of his society's developmental past and present.*

Bibliography

1. Ackerman, N., *The psychodynamics of family life*, New York, Basic Books, 1958.
2. Ackerman, N., Social role and total personality, *Amer. J. Orthopsychiat.*, 1951, **21** (6), 1–17.
3. Aebli, H., *The development of intelligence in the child*, Minneapolis, Univer. Minnesota Press, 1950.
4. Albee, G. W., *Mental health manpower trends*, New York, Basic Books, 1959.
5. Anthony, E. J., The significance of Jean Piaget for child psychiatry, *Brit. J. Med. Psychol.*, 1956, **29**, 20–34.
6. Baldwin, A. L., *Behavior development in childhood*, New York, Holt, Rinehart and Winston, 1955.
7. Bartlett, Harriett M., *Analyzing social work practice by fields*, New York, National Association of Social Workers, 1961.
8. Bartlett, Harriett M., *Social work practice in the health field*, New York, National Association of Social Workers, 1961.
9. Bartlett, Harriett M., Toward a clarification and improvement of social work practice, *Social Work*, 1958, 3 (2), 3–9.
10. Bell, J. E., *Family group therapy* (Monogr. no. 64), Washington, D.C., U.S. Public Health Service, 1961.
11. Bijou, S., & D. M. Baer, *Child development: A systematic and empirical theory*, New York, Appleton-Century-Crofts, 1961.
11a. Biestek, F. B., *The casework relationship*, Chicago, Loyola Univer. Press, 1957.
12. Boehm, W. W., The nature of social work, *Social Work*, 1958, 3 (2), 10–18.
13. Boehm, W. W., *The social casework method in social work edu-*

cation; Vol. X: *The social work curriculum study,* New York, Council on Social Work Education, 1959.

13a. Boehm, W. W., Social work: Science and art, *Soc. Serv. Rev.,* 1961, 35 (2), 144–153.

14. Bronfenbrenner, U., Freudian theories of identification and their derivatives, *Child Develpm.,* 1960, 31 (1), 15–40.

14a. Dennis, W., *Current trends in psychology,* Pittsburgh, Univer. Pittsburgh Press, 1947.

15. Dubos, René J., *The Mirage of Health,* New York, Anchor Books, 1961.

16. Duvall, Evelyn M., *Family development,* Chicago, Lippincott, 1957.

17. Dollard, J. *et al., Frustration and aggression,* New Haven, Yale Univer. Press, 1941.

18. Eaton, J. W., A scientific basis for helping, in A. J. Kahn (Ed.), *Issues in American social work,* New York, Columbia Univer. Press, 1959, pp. 270–293.

19. Erikson, E. H., The California Loyalty Oath: An editorial, *Psychiat.,* 1951, 14 (3), 244–245.

20. Erikson, E. H., *Childhood and society,* New York, W. W. Norton, 1950.

21. Erikson, E. H., Childhood and tradition in two American Indian tribes, in O. Fenichel *et al.* (Eds.), *The psychoanalytic study of the child,* New York, International Univers. Press, Vol. 1, 1945, 319–350.

22. Erikson, E. H., Clinical studies in childhood play, in R. C. Barker *et al., Child behavior and development,* New York, McGraw-Hill, 1943, pp. 411–428.

23. Erikson, E. H., *Comments on permissiveness,* paper read at the Staff Training Institute, Univer. Pittsburgh, 1955.

24. Erikson, E. H., Configurations in play: Clinical notes, *Psychoanal. Quart.,* 1937, 6, 139–214.

25. Erikson, E. H., The dream specimen of psychoanalysis, *J. Amer. Psychoanal. Assn.,* 1954, 2 (1), 5–56.

26. Erikson, E. H., Ego development and historical change, in Phillis Greenacre *et al.* (Eds.), *The psychoanalytic study of the child,* New York, International Univer. Press, 1946, Vol. II, 359–396.

27. Erikson, E. H., Ego identity and the psychosocial moratorium, in Helen Witmer & Ruth Kotinsky, *New perspective for research,* Washington, D.C., U.S. Dept. of Health, Education and Welfare, 1956, pp. 1–23.

28. Erikson, E. H., Freud's *The Origin of Psychoanalysis, Int. J. of Psychoœnal.,* 1955, 36 (1), 1–15.

29. Erikson, E. H., Identity and the life cycle; Selected papers, *Psychol. Issues* (Monogr.) 1959, **1** (1).
30. Erikson, E. H., *Juvenile delinquency*, paper read at the Staff Training Institute, Univer. Pittsburgh, 1954.
31. Erikson, E. H., Observations on Sioux education, *J. Psychol.*, 1939, **7**, 101–156.
32. Erikson, E. H., Observations on the Yurok: Childhood and world image, *Amer. Archaelo. Ethnol.*, 1943, **35** (10), 257–301.
33. Erikson, E. H., On the sense of inner identity, in *Conference on health and human relations*, New York, McGraw-Hill, 1953, pp. 124–146.
34. Erikson, E. H., The problem of ego identity, *J. Amer. Psychoanal. Assn.*, 1956, **4** (1), 56–121.
35. Erikson, E. H., Problems of infancy and early childhood, in P. G. Davis (Ed.), *The cyclopedia of medicine*, Vol. 12: *Surgery and specialties*, Philadelphia, F. A. Davis, 1940, pp. 714–730.
36. Erikson, E. H., Psychoanalysis and the future of education, *Psychoanal. Quart.*, 1936, **4**, 50–66.
37. Erikson, E. H., Review: Psychoanalysis for teachers and parents, *Psychoanal. Quart.*, 1936, **5**, 291–293.
38. Erikson, E. H., The roots of virtue, in J. Huxley (Ed.), *The humanist frame*, New York, Harper & Row, 1961, pp. 145–166.
39. Erikson, E. H., Sex differences in the play configurations of preadolescents, *Amer. J. Orthopsychiat.*, 1951, **21** (4), 667–692.
40. Erikson, E. H., Studies in the interpretation of play; Pt. I: Clinical observations of play disruption in young children, *Genet. Psychol. Monogr.*, 1940, **22**, 557–671.
41. Erikson, E. H., Toys and reasons, in Clara Thompson, *An outline of psychoanalysis*, New York, Random House (Modern Library), 1955, pp. 227–247.
42. Erikson, E. H., Traumatische Konfigurationen im Spiel, *Imago*, 1937, **23**, 447–516.
43. Erikson, E. H., Wholeness and totality: A psychiatric contribution, in C. J. Friedrich (Ed.), *Totalitarianism*, Cambridge, Harvard Univer. Press, 1954, pp. 156–171.
44. Erikson, E. H., *Young man Luther: A study in psychoanalysis and history*, New York, W. W. Norton, 1958.
45. Erikson, E. H., Youth and the life cycle, An interview, *Childr.*, 1960, **7** (2), 43–49.
46. Erikson, E. H., Youth: Fidelity and diversity, *Daedalus*, 1962, **19** (1), 5–27.
47. Erikson, E. H., and Joan Erikson, The power of the newborn, *Mademoiselle*, June, 1953, pp. 62, 100–102.

48. Erikson, E. H., and Kai T. Erikson, The confirmation of the delinquent, *Best articles and stories*, 1958, **2** (7), 43–46.
49. Erikson, E. H., in B. Schaffner (Ed.), *Group processes,* New York, Josiah Macy, Jr. Foundation, 1956.
   a. Transactions of the first conference.
   b. Transactions of the second conference.
50. Erikson, E. H., in M. J. E. Senn (Ed.), *Symposium on the healthy personality*, New York, Josiah Macy, Jr. Foundation, 1950, pp. 91–146.
51. Erikson, E. H., in J. M. Tanner and B. Inhelder (Eds.), *Discussions on child development*, New York, International Univers. Press.
   a. Vol. III, 1958, pp. 91–215.
   b. Vol. IV, 1960. pp. 136–154.
52. Flavell, J. H., *The developmental psychology of Jean Piaget,* Princeton, N.J., Van Nostrand, 1963.
53. Follett, Mary P., *Creative experience*, New York, Longmans, 1924.
54. Freud, S., *The ego and the id,* London, Hogarth, 1950.
55. Freud, S., *The problem of anxiety*, New York, W. W. Norton, 1936.
56. Gitelson, M., and E. H. Erikson, Play therapy, *Amer. J. Orthopsychiat.*, 1937, 8 (3), 499–524.
57. Gorman, Joanna F., Some characteristics of consultation, in Lydia Rapoport (Ed.), *Consultation in social work practice*, New York, National Association of Social Workers, 1963, pp. 21–32.
58. Grinker, R. R. (Ed.), *Toward a unified theory of human behavior*, New York, Basic Books, 1956.
59. Grinker, R. R., *et al.*, *Psychiatric social work: A transactional case book*, New York, Basic Books, 1961.
60. Gross, N., *et al.*, *Explorations in role analysis*, New York, Wiley, 1958.
61. Hall, C., & G. Lindzey, *Theories of personality*, New York, Wiley, 1957.
61a. Harris, D. B. (Ed.), *The concept of development*, Minneapolis, Univer. Minnesota Press, 1957.
62. Hartmann, H., *Ego psychology and the problem of adaptation*, New York, International Univers. Press, 1958.
63. Jaco, E. G. (Ed.), *Patients, physicians and illness; A sourcebook in behavioral science and medicine,* New York, Macmillan, 1958.
64. King, C., *Working with people in small communities*, New York, Harper & Row, 1958.

65. Kluckhohn, C., & H. A. Murray, *Personality in nature, society, and culture*, New York, Knopf, 1956.
66. Kluckhohn, Florence, & J. P. Spiegel, *Integration and conflict in family behavior* (Report no. 27), Topeka, Kans., Committee on the Family, Group for the Advancement of Psychiatry, 1954.
67. Konopka, Gisela, *Group work in the institution*, New York, Whiteside, 1954.
68. Konopka, Gisela, *Eduard C. Lindeman and social work philosophy*, Minneapolis, Univer. Minnesota Press, 1958.
69. Levin, H., & R. R. Sears, Identification with parents as a determinant of doll play aggression, *Child Develpm.*, 1956, **27** (2), 135–153.
70. Lindzey, G. (Ed.), Handbook of social psychology, Cambridge, Addison-Wesley, 1954.
    a. Vol. I: Theory and method.
    b. Vol. II: Special field and application.
71. Lippitt, R., *et al.*, *The dynamics of planned change*, New York, Harcourt, Brace & World, 1958.
72. Lohr, Evelyn, *Current biography*, New York, H. W. Wilson, 1952, pp. 522–523.
73. Lynd, H. M., *On shame and the search for identity*, New York, Harcourt, Brace & World, 1958.
74. Maas, H. S., & I. R. E. Engler, Jr., *Children in need of parents*, New York, Columbia Univer. Press, 1959.
75. Mays, W., Jean Piaget: The man and his work, *Hibbert J.*, 1957, **56**, 134–139.
76. Midcentury White House Conference on Children and Youth, *A healthy personality for every child*, Raleigh, N.C., Health Publication Institute, 1951.
77. Miller, Neal E., & J. Dollard, *Social learning and imitation*, New Haven, Yale Univer. Press, 1941.
78. Miller, Neal E., *et al.*, Reformulation of the frustration and aggression theory, *Psychol. Rev.*, 1941, **48**, 337–342.
79. Mowrer, O. H., *Learning theory and personality dynamics*, New York, Ronald, 1950.
80. Munroe, Ruth L., *Schools of psychoanalytic thought*, New York, Holt, Rinehart and Winston, 1955.
81. Murchison, C. (Ed.), *The psychological register*, Worcester, Mass., Clark Univer. Press, 1932, Vol. III.
82. Murphy, G., *Personality: A bio-social approach to origins and structures*, New York, Harper & Row, 1947.

83. Neuman, L. J., & J. W. Hughes, The problem of the concept of role: A resurvey of the literature, *Social Forces*, December, 1931.

84. Odier, C., *Anxiety and magic thinking*, New York, International Univers. Press, 1956.

85. Parsons, T., *Essays in sociological theory, pure and applied*, New York, Macmillan, 1949.

86. Parsons, T., & R. F. Bales, *Family, socialization and interactional process*, New York, Macmillan, 1955.

87. Parsons, T., & E. A. Shils, *Toward a general theory of action*, Cambridge, Harvard Univer. Press, 1951.

88. Perlman, Helen H., *Social casework: A problem-solving process*, Chicago, Univer. Chicago Press, 1957.

89. Piaget, J., Autobiography of Jean Piaget, in H. Langfeld, *et al.* (Eds.), *A history of psychology*, Worcester, Mass., Clark Univer. Press, 1952, Vol. IV, 237–256.

90. Piaget, J., The child and modern physics, *Scientific American*, 1957, **196** (3), 46–57.

91. Piaget, J., *The child's conception of physical causality*, London, Routledge & Kegan Paul, 1930.

92. Piaget, J., *The child's conception of the world*, London, Routledge & Kegan Paul, 1951.

93. Piaget, J., *The construction of reality in the child*, New York, Basic Books, 1954.

94. Piaget, J., How children form mathematical concepts, *Scientific American*, 1953, **189** (20), 74–79.

95. Piaget, J., *The judgment and reason in the child*, New York, Harcourt, Brace & World, 1929.

96. Piaget, J., *The Language and thought of the child*, New York, Harcourt, Brace & World, 1926.

97. Piaget, J., *Logic and psychology*, New York, Basic Books, 1957.

98. Piaget, J., *The moral judgment of the child*, New York, Macmillan, 1955.

99. Piaget, J., *The origin of intelligence in children*, New York, International Univers. Press, 1952.

100. Piaget, J., *Play, dreams and imitation in childhood*, London, Heinemann, 1951.

101. Piaget, J., Principal factors determining intellectual evolution from childhood to adult life, in Harvard Tercentenary Conference, *Factors determining human behavior*, Cambridge, Harvard Univer. Press, 1937, pp. 32–48.

102. Piaget, J., Problem of consciousness and symbolic processes, in H. E. Abramson, *Problems of consciousness*, Transactions of the

Fourth Conference, New York, Josiah Macy, Jr. Foundation, 1954.

103. Piaget, J., Psychologie der Fruehen Kindheit, in D. Katz, *Handbuch der Psychologie* (2nd ed.), Basle, Switzerland, Benno Schwabe, 1959, pp. 275–315.

104. Piaget, J., *The psychology of intelligence*, London, Routledge & Kegan Paul, 1950.

105. Piaget, J., & B. Inhelder, *The growth of logical thinking from childhood to adolescence*, New York, Basic Books, 1958.

106. Piaget, J., in P. S. Osterrieth, *et al.*, *Le problème des stades en psychologie de l'enfant*, Symposium de l'Association de Langue Française, Paris, Presses Universitaires, 1956, pp. 33–105.

107. Piaget, J., in J. Tanner & B. Inhelder (Eds.), *Discussions on child development:*
   a. Vol. I, London, Tavistock, 1956, pp. 31–33; 69–72; 89–94; 104–105.
   b. Vol. II, London, Tavistock, 1956, pp. 58–62, 256–263.
   c. Vol. III, New York, International Univers. Press, 1958, pp. 114, 154–162.
   d. Vol. IV, New York, International Univers. Press, 1960, pp. 3–28, 77–83, 87–135.

108. Pollak, O., Design of a model of healthy family relationships as a basis for evaluative research, *Soc. Serv. Rev.* 1957, **11** (4), 369–376.

109. Rapaport, D., A Historical survey of psychoanalytic ego psychology, in E. H. Erikson, Identity and the Life Cycle, *Psycholo. Issues* (Monogr.), 1959, **1** (1), New York, International Univers. Press, 5–17.

110. Rapaport, D., *Organization and pathology of thought*, New York, Columbia Univer. Press, 1941, pp. 154–192.

111. Rapaport, D., The theory of ego autonomy: A generalization, *Bull. Menninger Clinic*, 1958, **22** (1), 13–35.

111a. Rapoport, Lydia, The concept of prevention in social work, *Social Work*, 1961, **6** (1), 3–12.

111b. Rapoport, Lydia, The state of crisis: Some theoretical considerations, *Soc. Serv. Rev.*, 1962, **36** (2), 211–217.

111c. Redl, F., The art of group composition, in Susanne Schulze, *Creative group living in a children's institution*, New York, Association Press, 1951, pp. 79–96.

112. Schwartz, W., The social worker in the group, in National Conference of Social Welfare, *The social work forum*, New York, Columbia Univer. Press, 1961, pp. 146–177.

113. Sears, R. R., Child psychology, in W. Dennis, *et al.*, *Current trends in psychology*, Pittsburgh, Univer. Pittsburgh Press, 1947, pp. 50–74.

114. Sears, R. R., Dependency (unpublished manuscript), Palo Alto, Calif., Stanford Univer., 1961.

115. Sears, R. R., Effects of frustration and anxiety on fantasy aggression, *Amer. J. Orthopsychiat.*, 1951, **21** (3), 498–505.

116. Sears, R. R., Experimental analysis of psychoanalytic phenomena, in J. M. Hunt (Ed.), *Personality and the behavior disorders*, New York, Ronald, 1944, Vol. I, 306–332.

117. Sears, R. R., Frustration and aggression, in P. L. Harriman, *Encyclopedia of psychology*, New York, Philosophical Library, 1941, pp. 215–218.

118. Sears, R. R., Identification as a form of behavior development, in D. B. Harris, *The concept of development*, Minneapolis, Univer. Minnesota Press, 1957, pp. 149–161.

119. Sears, R. R., Identification, sex typing and guilt (unpublished manuscript), Palo Alto, Calif., Stanford Univer., 1957.

120. Sears, R. R., Influence of methodological factors on doll play performance, *Child Develpm.*, 1947, **18** (4).

121. Sears, R. R., Mark Twain's dependency and despair, paper read at the Conference of the American Psychological Association, New York, September, 1961.

122. Sears, R. R., Personality, *Annu. Rev. Psychol.*, 1950, **1**, 105–118.

123. Sears, R. R., Personality development in contemporary culture, *Proc. Amer. Philos. Soc.*, 1948, **92** (5), 363–370.

124. Sears, R. R., Relation of fantasy aggression to interpersonal aggression, *Child Develpm.*, 1950, **21** (1), 5–6.

125. Sears, R. R., Relationship of early social experiences to aggression in middle childhood, *J. Abnorm. Soc. Psychol.*, 1961, **63** (3), 466–492.

126. Sears, R. R., Social behavior and personality development, in T. Parsons & E. A. Shils, *Toward a general theory of action*, Cambridge, Harvard Univer. Press, 1951, pp. 465–478.

127. Sears, R. R., *Survey of objective studies of psychoanalytic concepts*, New York, Social Science Research Council, 1951.

128. Sears, R. R., & J. W. Whiting, Some child-rearing antecedents of aggression and dependency in young children, *Genet. Psychol. Monogr.*, 1953, **47**, 135–236.

129. Sears, R. R., *et al.*, Effect of father separation on preschool children's doll play aggression, *Child Develpm.*, 1946, **17** (4), 219–243.

130. Sears, R. R., *et al.*, *Patterns of child rearing*, New York, Harper & Row, 1957.

131. Spiegel, J., Resolution of role conflict; Part I: Problem solving in social casework, *Psychiat.*, 1957, **20** (1), 3–53.

132. Stock, Dorothy, & H. A. Thelen, *Emotional dynamics and group culture*, New York, National Training Laboratory, 1958.

133. Thomas, E., *et al.*, The expected behavior of a potentially helpful person, *Human Relations*, 1955, 8 (2), 165–174.

134. Tillich, P., *The spiritual and theological foundation of pastoral care*, paper read at the Conjoint Meeting of the Council for Clinical Training and the Institute of Pastoral Care, Atlantic City, 1956.

134a. Vinter, R. D., *Essential components of social group work practice*, Ann Arbor, Univer. Michigan Press, 1959.

135. White, R. W., Competence of the psychosexual stages of development, in M. Jones (Ed.), *Nebraska symposium on maturation*, Lincoln, Neb., Univer. Nebraska Press, 1960, pp. 97–140.

136. Witmer, Helen L., Delinquency and the adolescent crisis, *Facts and Facets*, No. 11, Washington, D.C., U.S. Dept. of Health, Education and Welfare, 1960.

137. Witmer, Helen L., and Ruth Kotinsky, *Personality in the making*, New York, Harper & Row, 1952.

138. Wolff, P. H., The developmental psychologies of Jean Piaget and psychoanalysis, *Psychol. Issues* (Monogr.), 1960, **2** (1).

139. Wright, B., *Attitude toward emotional involvement and professional development in residential child care*, Unpublished doctoral dissertation, Chicago, Univer. Chicago, 1957.

Further Readings

Allport, F. H., *Theories of perception and the concept of structure*, New York, Wiley, 1955.

Ausubel, D. P., *Theory and problems of child development*, New York, Grune and Stratton, 1958.

Benedict, Ruth, Continuities and discontinuities in cultural conditioning, in C. Kluckhohn, *et al.* (Eds.), *Personality in nature, society, and culture*, New York, Knopf, 1956, pp. 522–531.

Bennis, W. G., *Group observation*, Boston, *Research Reports and Technical Notes*, No. 7, 1958.

Bettelheim, B., *The informed heart: Autonomy in a mass age*, New York, Macmillan, 1960.

Bettelheim, B., *Love is not enough*, New York, Macmillan, 1950.

Blake, R. A., & G. V. Ramsey, *Perception: An approach to personality*, New York, Ronald Press, 1951.

Boehm, W. W., The contribution of psychoanalysis to social work and education, *Social Work*, 1958, *34* (9), 487–494.

Boehm, W. W., The role of values in social work, *The Jewish Soc. Serv. Quart.*, 1950, *26* (4), 429–438.

Bowlby, J., *Maternal care and mental health*, Geneva, Switzerland, World Health Organization, 1952.

Brown, Muriel W., Change is the way of life, *Chldr.*, 1958, *5* (1), 30–33.

Burmeister, Eva, *The professional houseparent*, New York, Columbia Univer. Press, 1959.

Carbonara, Nancy, *Techniques for observing normal child behavior*, Pittsburgh, Western Psychiatric Institute and Clinic, Univer. Pittsburgh, 1961.

Carmichael, L., *Manual of child psychology*, New York, Wiley, 1946.

Cattell, J. (Ed.), *American men of science*, New York, Bowker, Vol. III, 1956.

Chambers, Juanita, Maternal deprivation and the concept of time in children, *Amer. J. Orthopsychiat.*, 1961, *31* (2), 406–419.

Cohen, N. E., *Social work in the American tradition*, New York, Holt, Rinehart and Winston, 1958.

Commager, H. S. (Ed.), *Living ideas in America*, New York, Harper & Row, 1951.

Conzemius, Rosemary, P. Glasser & R. D. Vinter, *Diagnosis in social group work*, paper read at The School of Social Work, Ann Arbor, Univer. Michigan, December, 1960.

Dennis, W., *Current trends in psychology*, Pittsburgh, Univer. Pittsburgh Press, 1947.

Dewey, J., *The school and society*, Chicago, Univer. Chicago Press, 1907.

Dollard, J., & N. E. Miller, *Personality and psychotherapy*, New York, McGraw-Hill, 1950.

Doob, L. W., *Social psychology*, New York, Holt, Rinehart and Winston, 1952.

Dubos, R. J., *The mirage of health*, New York, Harper & Row, 1959.

Eliot, Martha M., Strategy for children, *J. Soc. Work*, 1957, *1* (4), 3–11.

Erikson, Florence H., Play interviews of four-year-old hospitalized children, Purdue, Ind., *Monogr. Soc. for Res. Child Develpm.*, 1958, *23* (3) (Whole No. 69).

Feigl, H., Principles and problems of theory construction in psychology, in W. Dennis (Ed.), *Current trends of psychological theory*, Pittsburgh, Univer. Pittsburgh Press, 1951.

Flanagan, J., The critical incident technique, *Psych. Bull.*, 1954, *51* (4), 327–358.

Frank, L. K., Research for what?, *J. Soc. Issues*, 1957, Suppl. No. 10.

Freud, Anna, *The ego and the mechanisms of defense*, New York, International Univers. Press, 1955.

Freud, Anna, & Dorothy Burlingham, *War and children*, London, Medical War Books, 1943.

Freud, S., *The basic writings of Sigmund Freud*, New York, Random House (Modern Library), 1938.

Freud, S., *Beyond the pleasure principle*, New York, Boni and Liveright, 1935.

Freud, S., *A general introduction to psychoanalysis*, New York, Permabooks, 1956.

Freud, S., *An outline of psychoanalysis*, New York, W. W. Norton, 1949.

Ginzberg, E. (Ed.), *The nation's children,* New York, Columbia Univer. Press.
Vol. I: *The family and social change,* 1960.
Vol. III: *Problems and prospects,* 1960.
Ginzberg, E. (Ed.), *Values and ideas of American youth,* New York, Columbia Univer. Press, 1961.
Greenwood, E., Attributes of a profession, *Social Work,* 1957, *2* (3), 45–55.
Greenwood, E., Social science and social work: A theory of their relationship, *Soc. Serv. Rev.,* 1955, *29* (1), 20–33.
Greenwood, E., Social work research: A decade of reappraisal, *Soc. Serv. Rev.,* 1957, *31* (2), 311–320.
Grossbard, H., *Cottage parents: What they have to be, know and do,* New York, Child Welfare League, 1960.
Havighurst, R. J., *Human development and education,* New York, Longmans, 1953.
Hechler, J., Social controls in institutional treatment, *Social Work,* 1956, *1* (2), 61–67.
Heider, Grace M., What makes a good parent, *Childr.,* 1960, 7 (6), 207–212.
Hilgard, E. R., *Theories of learning,* New York, Appleton-Century-Crofts, 1956.
Jones, H., *Reluctant rebels,* New York, Association Press, 1960.
Jourard, S. M., *Personal adjustment: An approach through the study of healthy personality,* New York, Macmillan, 1958.
Kesson, W., Intellective development in children: A conference on Piaget's contributions in relation to other theories of children's thinking, *Items,* Social Science Research Council, 1960, *14* (3).
Knight, R. P., & C. P. Friedman, *Psychoanalytic psychiatry and psychology,* New York, International Univers. Press, 1954.
Lazarsfeld, P. F., & A. H. Barton, Qualitative measurements in the social sciences: Clarification, typologies and indices, in D. Lerner & H. Laswell, *The policy of sciences,* Stanford Univer. Press, 1951, pp. 155–192.
Leighton, A. H., *et al.,* *Explorations in social psychiatry,* New York, Basic Books, 1957.
Lerner, D., *The human meaning of the social sciences,* New York, Meridian, 1959.
Linton, R., Status and role, in H. D. Stein & R. A. Cloward (Eds.), *Social perspectives on behavior,* New York, Macmillan, 1958, pp. 175–176.
Lippman, H. S., Diagnosis and treatment of children in groups, in National Association of Social Workers, *Use of groups in psy-*

chiatric setting, New York, National Association of Social Workers, 1960, pp. 53–72.

Littner, N., The child's need to repeat his past, *Soc. Serv. Rev.,* 1960, *34* (2), 128–148.

Littner, N., Patterns of child rearing (book review), *Soc. Serv. Rev.,* 1960, *31* (4), 461–463.

Lynn, R., & I. E. Gordon, Maternal attitudes to child socialization: Some social and national differences, *Brit. J. soc. Psychol.,* 1962, *1* (1), 52–55.

Maas, H. S., The place of research in child welfare programs, in Child Welfare League of America, *Six papers on child welfare problems,* New York, Child Welfare League, 1953, pp. 11–18.

Maccoby, Eleanor E., Role-taking in childhood and its consequences for social learning, *Child Develpm.,* 1959, *30* (2), 239–252.

Maccoby, Eleanor E., The taking of adult roles in middle childhood, *J. abnorm. soc. Psychol.,* 1961, *61* (3), 493–503.

McCormick, Mary J., The role of values in the helping process, *Soc. Casewk.,* 1961, *42* (1), 3–9.

McCormick, Mary J., The role of values in social functioning, *Soc. Casewk.,* 1961, *42* (2), 70–78.

Maier, H. W., Child (and youth) care as a method of social work, in Child Welfare League of America, *Training of child-care staff,* New York, Child Welfare League, 1963, pp. 62–81.

Maier, H. W., Children in need of institutional care, in J. S. Roucek (Ed.), *The unusual child,* New York, Philosophical Library, 1962, pp. 161–176.

Maier, H. W., A child's cognitive conquest of space and time, *Ind. J. soc. Res.,* 1961, *2* (2), 31–38.

Maier, H. W., Group living: A unique feature in residential treatment, in National Association of Social Workers, *New Perspective on services to groups: Social work with groups,* New York, National Association of Social Workers, 1961, pp. 124–132.

Mathew, W. M., Successful adjustment: A frame of reference, *Amer. J. Orthopsychiat.,* 1960, *30* (4), 667–675.

Mayer, M. F., *A guide for child care workers,* New York, The Child Welfare League, 1958.

Mayer, M. F., The parental figures in residential treatment, *Soc. Ser. Rev.,* 1960, *34* (3), 273–285.

Medinus, G. R., *An investigation of Piaget's concept of development of moral judgment in six- to twelve-year-old children from the lower socio-economic group,* Unpublished doctoral dissertation, Minneapolis, Univer. Minnesota, 1957.

Meier, Elizabeth C., Social and cultural factors in casework diagnosis, *Social Work*, 1959, *4* (3), 15–26.

Midcentury White House Conference, Pledge to children, in *Proceedings of the Midcentury White House Conference on Children and Youth*, Raleigh, N.C., Health Publications Institute, 1951.

Muller, Lydia, *Recherches sur la compréhension des règles algébriques chez l'enfant*, Neuchâtel, Switzerland, Imprimerie Delachaux aux Niestlé S. A., 1956.

Munn, N. L., *The evolution and growth of human behavior*, Boston, Houghton Mifflin, 1955.

Murphy, Lois B., Effects of child-rearing patterns on mental health, *Childr.*, 1956, *3* (6), 213–218.

Murray, H. A., *et al.*, Dramatic productions test, in *Explorations in personality*, New York, Oxford Univer. Press, 1938, pp. 552–582.

National Association of Social Workers, Identifying fields of practice in social work, *Social Work*, 1962, 7 (2), 7–14.

Nowlis, O., The search for significant concepts in a study of parent-child relationships, *Amer. J. Orthopsychiat.*, 1952, *22* (2), 286–299.

Peller, Lilli E., Libidinal phases, ego development, and play, in *The psychoanalytic study of the child*, New York, International Univers. Press, 1954, Vol. IX, 178–198.

Perlman, Helen H., The role concept and social casework: Some explorations; Part II: What is social diagnosis?, *Soc. Serv. Rev.*, 1962, *36* (1), 17–31.

Popper, K. R., *The logic of scientific discovery*, New York, Basic Books, 1959.

Redl, F., & D. Wineman, *The aggressive child*, New York, Basic Books, 1957.

Robinson, J., *et al.* (Eds.), *Psychiatric in-patient treatment of children*, Washington, D.C., American Psychiatric Association, 1957.

Rogers, C. R., *Characteristics of a helping relationship*, Suppl. No. 27, Ottawa, Department of National Health and Welfare, March, 1962.

Rosenfeld, M., Strangeness between helper and client, *Soc. Serv. Rev.*, 1964, *38* (1), 17–25.

Schulze, Susanne, *Creative group living in a children's institution*, New York, Association Press, 1951.

Siegel, S., *Nonparametric statistics for the behavioral sciences*, New York, McGraw-Hill, 1956.

Smedslund, J., Constancy and conservation: A comparison of the systems of Brunswick and Piaget, in K. E. Hammond (Ed.), *Probabilistic functionalism: Egon Brunswick's psychology*, Denver, Univer. Denver, 1962.

Smith, E. A., *Social welfare principles and concepts*, Seattle, Univer. Washington Press, 1961.

Spergel, I., A multidimensional model for social work practice: The youth worker example, *Soc. Serv. Rev.*, 1962, *31* (1), 62–71.

Spock, B., *Baby and child care*, New York, Pocket Books, 1957.

Spock, B., et al., *A baby's first year*, New York, Pocket Books, 1956.

Stein, H. D., & R. A. Cloward, *Social perspective and behavior*, New York, Macmillan, 1958.

Stock, Dorothy, & H. A. Thelen, *Emotional dynamics and group culture*, New York, National Training Laboratories, 1958.

Strauss, A. L., The development and transformation of monetary meanings in the child, *Amer. Sociol. Rev.*, 1952, *17* (3), 275–286.

Strauss, A., & K. Schuessler, Socialization, logical reasoning and concept development in the child, *Amer. Sociol. Rev.*, 1951, *16* (4), 514–523.

Stuart, H. C., et al., *The healthy child: His physical, psychological, and social development*, Cambridge, Harvard Univer. Press, 1960.

Studt, Eliot, Therapeutic factors in group living, *Child Welf.*, 1956, *35* (1), 1–6.

Towle, Charlotte, *The learner in education for the professions*, Chicago, Univer. Chicago Press, 1954.

White, R. W., Motivation reconsidered: The concept of competence, *Psychol. Rev.*, 1959, *66*, 247–333.

Whiting, J. W., & I. L. Child, *Child training and personality, A cross-culture study*, New Haven, Yale Univer. Press, 1953.

Winnicott, D. W., *The child and the outside world*, New York, Basic Books, 1957.

Witmer, Helen L. (Ed.), *Maternal deprivation*, New York, Child Welfare League, 1962.

Wolff, P. H., The developmental psychologies of Jean Piaget and psychoanalysis, *Psychol. Issues* (Monogr.), 1960, *2* (1), International Univers. Press (Whole No. 5).

Woodward, Mary, Concepts of space in the mentally subnormal studied by Piaget's method, *Brit. J. Soc. Clin. Psychol.*, 1962, *1* (1), 25–37.

Zehrer, F. A., Review of *Patterns of child rearing*, *Amer. J. Orthopsychiat.*, 1958, *28* (2), 430–431.

Appendix

The Complete Works

of the Three Theorists[1]

ERIK H. ERIKSON

Original Writings

1930. Die Zukunft der Aufklärung und die Psychoanalyse, *Zeitschrift der Psychoanalytik Paedagogie*, 1930, *4*, 201–216.

1931a. Psychoanalysis and the future of education, *Psychoanal. Quart.*, 1935, *4*, 50–68.

1931b. Bilderbücher, *Zeitschrift der Psychoanalytik Paedagogie*, 1931, *5*, 13–19.

1936. Psychoanalysis and the future of education, *Psychoanal. Quart.*, 1936, *4*, 50–66.

Review: Psychoanalysis for teachers and parents, *Psychoanal. Quart.*, 1936, *5*, 291–293.

1937a. Configurations in play: Clinical notes, *Psychoanal. Quart.*, 1937, *6*, 139–214.

1937b. Traumatische Konfigurationen im Spiel, *Imago*, 1937, *23*, 447–516.

1939. Observations on Sioux education, *J. Psychol.*, 1939, *7*, 101–156.

[1] Listings are arranged by year of original publication.

1940a. Studies in the Interpretation of play, *Genet. Psychol. Monogr.*, 1940, *22*, 557–671.

1940b. Problems of infancy and early childhood, in P. G. Davis (Ed.), *The cyclopedia of medicine;* Vol. 12: *Surgery and specialties*, Philadelphia, F. A. Davis, 1940, pp. 714–730.

1940c. Studies in the interpretation of play: 1-Clinical observation of play disruption in young children, *Genet. Psychol. Monogr.*, 1940, *22*, 557–671.

1941. Further explanations in play construction, *Psychol. Bull.*, 1941, *38*, 748.

1942. Hitler's imagery and German youth, *Psychiat.*, 1942, *5*, 475–493.

1943a. Observations on the Yurok: Childhood and world image, *Amer. Archaeol. Ethnol.*, 1943, *35* (10), 257–301.

1943b. Clinical studies in childhood play, in R. C. Barker, *et al.*, *Child behavior and development*, New York, McGraw-Hill, 1943, pp. 411–428.

1945a. Childhood and tradition in two American Indian tribes, in O. Fenichel, *et al.* (Eds.), *The psychoanalytic study of the child;* Vol. 1, New York, International Univers. Press, 1945, pp. 319–350.

1945b. Plans for the veteran with symptoms of instability, in Louise Wirth, *Community planning for peacetime living*, Palo Alto, Calif., Stanford Univer. Press, 1945.

1946. Ego development and historical change, in Phillis Greenacre, *et al.* (Eds.), *The psychoanalytic study of the child*, New York, International Univers. Press, 1946, Vol. II, pp. 359–396.

1949. Ruth Benedict, in A. L. Kroeber (Ed.), *Ruth Fulton Benedict: A memorial*, New York, Viking Fund, 1949.

1950a. *Childhood and society*, New York, W. W. Norton, 1950.

1950b. In M. J. E. Senn (Ed.), "Growth and crises of the healthy personality," *Symposium on the healthy personality*, New York, Josiah Macy, Jr. Foundation, 1950, pp. 91–146.

1951a. Sex differences in the play configuration of pre-adolescents, *Amer. J. Orthopsychiat.*, 1951, *21* (4), 667–692.

1951b. Statement to the Committee on Privilege and Tenure of the University of California on the California Loyalty Oath: An editorial, *Psychiat.*, 1951, *14* (3), 244–245.

1952. Remarks, in *Healthy personality development in children as related to programs of the federal government*, New York, Josiah Macy, Jr. Foundation, 1952, pp. 80–95.

1953. On the sense of inner identity, in *Conference on health and human relations*, New York, McGraw-Hill, 1953, pp. 124–146.

1954a. *Juvenile delinquency*, paper read at a teaching seminar, Pittsburgh, Department of Child Psychiatry and Child Development, Univer. Pittsburgh, 1954.

1954b. Wholeness and totality: A psychiatric contribution, in C. J. Friedrich (Ed.), *Totalitarianism*, Cambridge, Harvard Univer. Press, 1954, pp. 156–171.

1954c. The dream specimen of psychoanalysis, *J. Amer. Psychoanal. Assn.*, 1954, *2* (1), 5–56.

1954d. Identity and totality: Psychoanalytic observations on the problems of youth, *Human Develpm. Bull.*, Chicago, The Human Development Student Organization, 1954, pp. 50–82.

1954e. On the sense of inner identity, in R. P. Knight and C. R. Friedman (Eds.), *Psychoanalytic psychiatry and psychology, Clinical and theoretical papers, Austen Riggs Center*, Vol. I. New York, International Univers. Press, 1954, pp. 131–170.

1954f. Problems of infancy and early childhood in G. Murphy & A. J. Bachrach, *Outline of abnormal psychology*, New York, Random House, 1954, pp. 3–36.

1954g. In B. Schaffner (Ed.), *Group processes* (Transactions of the First Conference, 1954), New York, Josiah Macy, Jr. Foundation, 1956.

1955a. In B. Schaffner (Ed.), *Group processes* (Transactions of the Second Conference, 1955), New York, Josiah Macy, Jr. Foundation, 1956.

1955b. Toys and reasons, in Clara Thompson, *An outline of psychoanalysis*, New York, Random House, 1955, pp. 227–247.

1955c. Sex differences in the play configurations of American adolescents, in Margaret Mead & Martha Wolfenstein (Eds.), *Childhood in contemporary cultures*, Chicago, Univer. Chicago Press, 1955, pp. 324–241.

1955d. The origin of psychoanalysis, *Int. J. Psychoanal.*, 1955, *36* (1), 1–15.

1955e. Comments on permissiveness, paper read at Staff Training Institute, Department of Child Psychiatry and Child Development, Univer. Pittsburgh, 1955.

1956a. Comments at a round-table discussion about a consideration of the biological, psychological and cultural approaches to the understanding of human development and behavior, in J. M. Tanner, *Discussions on child development*, New York, International Univers. Press, 1960, Vol. IV, 133–154.

1956b. The problem of ego identity, *J. Amer. Psychoanal. Assn.*, 1956, *4* (1), 56–121.

1956c. Ego identity and the psychosocial moratorium, in Helen Witmer & Ruth Kotansky, *New perspective for research*, Washington, D.C., U.S. Department of Health, Education and Welfare (#356), 1956, pp. 1–23.

1956d. The first psychoanalyst, *Yale Review*, Autumn, 1956, pp. 40–62.

1957. Sigmund Freud's Psychoanalytik Krise and Trieb und Umwelt in der Kindheit, in Frankfurter Beitraege zur Sozialogie, *Freud in der Gegenwart*, Frankfurt, Germany, Europaeische Verlaganstalt, 1957, pp. 10–30; 43–64.

1958a. *Young man Luther: A study in psychoanalysis and history*, New York, W. W. Norton, 1958.

1958b. In J. Tanner & B. Inhelder (Eds.), *Discussions on child development* (comments on a roundtable discussion), New York, International Univers. Press, 1958, Vol. III, 16–18; 91–215.

1958c. The nature of clinical evidence, *Daedalus*, 1958, *87* (4), 65–87.

1959. Identity and the life cycle: Selected papers, *Psychol. Issues* (Monogr.), 1959, *1* (1), New York, International Univers. Press.

1959b. Late adolescence, in D. H. Funkenstein (Ed.), *The student and mental health*, New York, World Federation for Mental Health & The International Association of Universities, 1959.

1960. Youth and the life cycle: An interview, *Childr.*, 1960, 7 (2), 43–49.

1961. The roots of virtue in J. Huxley (Ed.), *The humanist frame*, New York, Harper & Row, 1961, pp. 145–166.

1962a. Youth: Fidelity and diversity, *Daedalus*, 1962, *19* (1), 5–27.

1962b. Reality and actuality, *J. Amer. Psychoanal. Assn.*, 1962, *10* (3), 451–473.

1963a. *Youth: Change and challenge* (Ed.), New York, Basic Books, 1963.

1963b. The Golden Rule and the cycle of life, in R. W. White (Ed.), *The study of lives*, New York, Prentice-Hall, 1963, pp. 412–428.

1964a. Inner and outer space: Reflections on womanhood, *Daedalus*, 1964, *2*, 582–606.

1964b. *Insight and responsibility*, New York, W. W. Norton, 1964.

Collaborative Writings

1937. and M. Gitelson, Play therapy, *Amer. J. Orthopsychiat.*, 1937, *8* (3), 499–524.

1953. and Joan Erikson, The power of the newborn, *Mademoiselle*, June, 1953, pp. 62; 100–102.

1958. and Kai T. Erikson, The confirmation of the delinquent, *Best articles and stories*, 1958, *2* (7), 43–46.

JEAN PIAGET

Original Writings

1924a. *The language and thought of the child*, New York, Harcourt, Brace & World, 1926.

1924b. *The judgment and reason in the child*, New York, Harcourt, Brace & World, 1928.

1926. *The child's conception of the world*, London, Routledge & Kegan Paul, 1951.

1927. *The child's conception of physical causality*, London, Routledge & Kegan Paul, 1930.

1932. *The moral judgment of the child*, New York, Macmillan, 1955.

1934. Children's philosophies, in C. Murchison, *A handbook of child psychology*, Worcester, Mass., Clark Univer. Press, 1934, pp. 534–547.

1936. *The origin of intelligence in children*, New York, International Univers. Press, 1952.

1937a. *The construction of reality in the child*, New York, Basic Books, 1954.

1937b. Principal factors determining intellectual evolution from childhood to adult life, in Harvard Tercentenary Conference, *Factors determining human behavior*, Cambridge, Harvard Univer. Press, 1937, pp. 32–48.

1941. *The child's conception of numbers*, New York, Humanities, 1952.

1945. *Play, dreams and imitation in childhood*, London, Heinemann, 1951.

1947. *The psychology of intelligence*, London, Routledge & Kegan Paul, 1950.

1952a. Autobiography of Jean Piaget, in H. Langfeld, *et al.*, *A history of psychology*, Worcester, Mass., Clark Univer. Press, 1952, Vol. IV, 237–256.

1952b. Psychologie der Fruehen Kindheit, in D. Katz, *Handbuch der psychologie* (2nd ed.), Basle, Switzerland, Benno Schwabe, 1959, pp. 275–315.

1953a. Genetic psychology and epistemology, *Diogenes*, 1953, No. 1, pp. 49–63.

1953b. *Logic and psychology*, New York, Basic Books, 1957.

1953c. How children form mathematical concepts (with biographic sketch), *Scientific American*, 1953, *189* (20), 74–79.

1953d. Roundtable discussions, in J. M. Tanner and B. Inhelder (Eds.), *Discussions on child development*, Vol. I, London, Tavistock, 1953, pp. 31–33; 69–72; 89–94; 104–105.

1954a. Le langage et la pensée du point de vue génétique, *Acta Psychologica*, 1954, *10*, 51–60.

1954b. Problem of consciousness and symbolic processes, in H. E. Abramson, *Problems of consciousness: transactions of the fourth conference* (March 24–31, Princeton, N.J.), New York, Josiah Macy, Jr. Foundation, 1954.

1954c. Roundtable discussions, in J. M. Tanner and B. Inhelder (Eds.), *Discussions on child development*, Vol. II, London, Tavistock, 1954, 58–62, 256–263.

1955a. Roundtable discussions, in J. M. Tanner and B. Inhelder (Eds.), *Discussions on child development*, Vol. III, New York, International Univers. Press, 1955, pp. 114, 154–162.

1955b. The development of time concepts in the child, in P. H. Hoch & J. Fubin, *Psychopathology of childhood*, New York, Grune and Stratton, 1955, pp. 34–44.

1956a. The definition of stages of development, in J. M. Tanner & B. Inhelder (Eds.), *Discussions on child development*, New York, International Univers. Press, 1960, Vol. IV, 116–135.

1956b. Equilibration and the developmental structures, in *ibid.*, 98–115.

1956c. The general problems of the psychobiological development of the child, in *ibid.*, 3–28.

1956d. Reply to comments concerning the part played in the psychobiological development of the child and Introductory Discussion in *ibid.*, 77–83; 87–97.

1956e. In Osterrieth, P. S., *et al.*, *Le problème des stades en psychologie de l'enfant*, Symposium de l'Association de Langue Française, Paris, Presses Universitaires, 1956, pp. 33–105.

1957. The child and modern physics, *Scientific American*, 1957, *196* (3), 46–57.

1959. Peering into the mind of a child, *The UNESCO Courier*, 1959, 12, 4–7.

Collaborative Writings

1948. and B. Inhelder, *The child's conception of space*, New York, Humanities Press, 1956.

1956a. and B. Inhelder, *The growth of logical thinking from childhood to adolescence*, New York, Basic Books, 1958.

1964. and B. Inhelder, *The early growth of logic in the child*, New York, Harper & Row, 1964.

ROBERT R. SEARS

Original Writings

1936a. Experimental studies of projection, *J. Soc. Psychol.*, 1936, 7, 151–163.

1936b. Review of Lewin's *A dynamic theory of personality*, *Psychol. Bull.*, 1936, *33* (7), 548–552.

1941a. Frustration and aggression, in P. L. Harriman, *Encyclopedia of psychology*, New York, Philosophical Library, 1941, pp. 215–218.

1941b. Non-aggressive reactions to frustration, *Psychol. Bull.*, 1941, *48* (4), 343–349.

1942. Success and failure: A study of motility, in Q. A. McNemar & M. A. Merill (Eds.), *Studies in personality*, New York, Mc-Graw-Hill, 1942, pp. 235–258.

1943. *Survey of objective studies of psychoanalytic concepts*, New York, Social Science Research Council, 1951.

1944a. Experimental analysis of psychoanalytic phenomena, in J. M. Hunt (Ed.), *Personality and the behavior disorders*, New York, Ronald Press, 1944, Vol. I, 306–332.

1944b. Personality and motivation, *Rev. Educ. Res.*, 1944, *14* (5), 368–380.

1947a. Child psychology, in W. Dennis *et al.*, *Current trends in psychology*, Pittsburgh, Univer. Pittsburgh Press, 1947, pp. 50–74.

1947b. Influence of methodological factors on doll play performance, *Child Develpm.*, 1947, *18* (4).

1948. Personality development in contemporary culture, *Proc. Amer. Philos. Soc.*, 1948, *92* (5), 363–370.

1950a. Relation of fantasy aggression to interpersonal aggression, *Child Develpm.*, 1950, *21* (1), 5–6.

1950b. Ordinal position in the family as a psychological variable, *Amer. Sociol. Rev.*, 1950, *15* (3), 397–401.

1950c. Personality, *Annu. Rev. Psychol.*, 1950, *1*, 105–118.

1951a. Social behavior and personality development, in T. Parson & E. A. Shills, *Toward a general theory of action*, Cambridge, Harvard Univer. Press, 1951, pp. 465–478.

1951b. Effects of frustration and anxiety on fantasy aggression, *Amer. J. Orthopsychiat.*, 1951, *21* (3), 498–505.

1951c. A theoretical framework for personality and social behavior, *Amer. Psychol.*, 1951, *6* (9), 476–483.

1957. Identification as a form of behavior development, in D. B. Harris, *The concept of development,* Minneapolis, Univer. Minnesota Press, 1957, pp. 149–161.

1960. Transcultural variables and conceptual equivalence, in B. Kaplan (Ed.), *Studying personality cross-culturally,* New York, Harper & Row, 1960, pp. 445–455.

1961a. *Mark Twain's dependency and despair,* paper read at the American Psychological Association, New York, September 1, 1961.

1961b. Relationship of early social experiences to aggression in middle childhood, *J. Abnorm. Soc. Psychol.,* 1961, *63* (3), 466–492.

Collaborative Writings

1940. and C. I. Hovland & W. E. Miller, Minor studies in aggression: Measurement of aggressive behavior, *J. Psychol.,* 1940, *9* (2), 277–281.

1941a. and C. I. Hovland, Experiments on motor conflict, *J. Exp. Psychol.,* 1941, *28,* 280–286.

1941b. and N. E. Miller, *et al.,* Reformulation of frustration and aggression theory, *Psychol. Rev.,* 1941, *48,* 337–342.

1941c. and J. Dollard, *et al., Frustration and aggression,* New Haven, Yale Univer. Press, 1941.

1946. and Margaret Pinter & Pauline S. Sears, Effect of father separation on preschool children's doll play aggression, *Child Develpm.,* 1946, *17* (4), 219–243.

1950. and G. W. Wise, Relationship of cup-feeding in infancy to thumb-sucking and the oral drive, *Amer. J. Orthopsychiat.,* 1950, *20,* 123–138.

1953. and J. W. Whiting, Some child-rearing antecedents of aggression and dependency in young children, *Genet. Psychol. Monogr.,* 1953, *47,* 135–236.

1956. and H. Levin, Identification with parents as a determinant of doll play aggression, *Child Develpm.,* 1956, *27* (2), 135–153.

1957. and Eleanor Maccoby & H. Levin, *Patterns of child rearing,* New York, Harper & Row, 1957.

Index